# From River Banks to Shearing Sheds

## 30 YEARS with FLYING ARTS

The story of one man's dream to give people living in outback Queensland the same opportunity to study fine art as people in the city—helping them overcome the mental isolation of life in the bush.

by

Marilyn England

Publisher: Suzanne Wickenden
www.smartype.com.au



Book Design: Smartype Design Studio
Cover Design: Wayne Minnis
Printed in Brisbane, Australia.
First published 2009.

National Library of Australia
Cataloguing-in-Publication entry:
*From River Banks to Shearing Sheds: Thirty years with Flying Arts.*
Includes index
ISBN 978-0-9805837-1-7

When interviewing personnel connected with Flying Arts every effort has been made to build a correct history of the organisation despite one key figure declining to be interviewed. The source of most of the photographs is unknown but I have acknowledged any individual where possible. Also, as many of the people depicted are unknown I would appreciate it if I could be contacted for a possible future update. Similarly, every effort has been made to trace copyright holders of the material and photographs used in this book. The publishers regret any errors and omissions and would like to hear from anyone who has any information otherwise. We are indebted to Flying Arts students and tutors for the large amount of information which, due to the constraints of the book, we have been unable to publish at this time and apologise to anyone who is disappointed.

Paintings featured on cover:
Jack Wilson *The Bunyas*
Jo Forster *Untitled*
Coralie Busby *Wynnum Night Creatures*



# Acknowledgments

I wish to thank all those students of Flying Arts Inc. who have been so enthusiastic in supplying information on the activities of the school. Of particular assistance have been present and former students : Kathryn Brimblecombe Fox (Dalby), Maree Cameron (Dalby), Robyn Bauer (Dalby), Mabs Blackband (Dalby), Jack Wilson (Dalby), Eva Hekel (Brisbane), Mary Norris (Gladstone), Coralie Busby (Bundaberg), the family of Jean Mesner (Eidsvold), Ellie Neilsen (Biloela), Rita Kershaw (Rockhampton), Auda Maclean (Baralaba), Stephanie Broadhurst (Rolleston), Ruth Francis (Longreach), Vince Bray (Mt. Isa), Chris Elcoate (Mt. Isa), Gladys Cooney (Julia Creek), Jo Forster (Richmond), Anne Lord (now at James Cook University, Townsville), Anneke Silver (Townsville), Josephine McTaggart (Innisfail), Ivy Zappala (Gordonvale), Char Speedy (Quilpie), Beth Tully (Quilpie), Judith Banks (Goondiwindi), Jocelyn Cameron (Goondiwindi), Patricia Garner (Goondiwindi), Kath Leonard (Goondiwindi), friends of Janis Somerville (Glenmorgan), Carol McCormack (Glenmorgan), the family of Betty Turner (Yaraka), Marie Biggins (Emerald), Julie Shepherd (Emerald), Patricia Gee (Hughenden), Sandra Burchill (Malanda), Peggy Uebergang (Inverell).

I particularly wish to thank Mervyn Moriarty for the hospitality extended to me when I travelled to New South Wales to interview him on his years with Flying Arts. His reminiscences have been crucial to this story. Helen Moriarty supplied more information and I have learned much from the following tutors who generously gave their time: Kevin Grealy, Rob. Hinwood, Beverley Budgen, Irene Amos, Bela Ivanyi, Lucja Ray and Pat Hoffie.

I wish to thank Associate Professor Robyn Stewart from the University of Southern Queensland who was President of Flying Arts from 1991 to 1994; Christine Campbell who, as Executive Officer for Flying Arts in Brisbane from 1994 to 2004, allowed me access to their archives and also the current CEO of Flying Arts, Stephen Clark, who has assisted with the launch of this book.

A special debt is owed to my Thesis supervisors: Dr. Geoff Ginn from the University of Queensland, and Glenn Cooke from the Queensland Art Gallery. Glenn's extensive knowledge of Queensland artists was of great assistance. Others who have assisted are Dr. Robin Trotter, Dr. Craig Douglas and Hilda Maclean (who indexed this book) from Griffith University, Dr. Peter Spearrit from the University of Queensland. John Gilfoyle, retired Elders Stock & Station Agent from Roma who encouraged me to publish. Also Bruce Strachan and Glenn Cooke for their help with editing, my daughter, Sue Wickenden, whose expertise in publishing has been invaluable, and Wayne Minnis from Smartype who designed the cover.

This book is dedicated to all those women (and a few men) who formed friendships and shared their dreams at the Flying Arts workshops

# Contents

# Introduction

Flying Arts began in 1971 when Brisbane artist Mervyn Moriarty learned to fly to take his art school to the bush. His workshops were always popular and well-attended. Why did it come to mean so much to everyone? Ruth Francis from Longreach believed the experience was a journey of the soul through the land of the imagination.

She wrote that before he came she'd always wanted to capture the beauty of nature and keep it with her to stop herself from being homesick. But as she lived in the bush there was no-one to teach her how to paint. To travel to the city to meet artists and teachers took time and money which they just didn't have. When her husband was stationed at Blackall she did find a teacher, Jan Shaw, who ran a class for about eight people and thus she began her journey into the exciting world of art. Then they moved to Longreach.

When Mervyn came to Longreach the town had only just formed an art group and friends persuaded her to go with them to his Eastaus workshops. It wasn't easy and there were tears, but for her it was the beginning of a wonderfully exhilarating journey which has lasted all her life.

At the Longreach workshops Ruth met many of Merv's students who had travelled long distances and coped with amazing obstacles to attend. Mervyn was well aware of their thirst for knowledge and commented that they were like blotting paper – soaking up every scrap of information he offered. For the first time they found that their dreams were being taken seriously and it gave them a sense that what they were doing was worthwhile.

Ruth wrote that Mervyn would dissect, encourage and re-direct their work – it left them severely challenged: 'it broadened our cultural knowledge – we read more and listened more to music and poetry. We had long discussions on whether one should paint to please others and sell our work, or just keep growing in unexpected ways. We learned to be honest but kind in any criticism. We learned to understand ourselves and others and it brought with it a wonderful sense of community.'

Ruth's story was repeated by women of all ages (and some men) all over Queensland. Hundreds of people living on lonely station properties and farms in rural Queensland were happy to drive many kilometres over rough bush roads to the creative art workshops.

Part of the answer for his success lies in the structured two-year art course Mervyn Moriarty introduced when he flew to regional Queensland. He was teaching 'modern' art, a more creative art where emphasis is focussed on the subjective sensibility of the artist. He said that students must never copy what they saw. He told them that creative art is experimental art where the artist must use his or her imagination to express their feelings; students have to think about what they are doing, what they want to say, and through their art, go wherever their imagination takes them to impart their feelings to the canvas. He emphasised that an artist's freedom was to be whatever he (or she) wanted to be and to work in whatever way they wanted to work to achieve their goal.

Modern art had been taught in Sydney and Melbourne from the early 1930s, but did not arrive in Queensland until the 1950s.

From the end of the nineteenth century, Australian artists had travelled to France and Europe to experience for themselves the work of contemporary European artists at a time when Impressionism reigned. After returning home they were keen to pass their enthusiasm for 'modern' art on to fellow artists.

When George Bell opened his school of modern art in Melbourne in 1931 many young artists flocked to the school. In the following years a number of his students became top Australian artists. Among them were Russell Drysdale, Sali Herman, Peter Purves-Smith and Fred Williams.

In Sydney, Rah Fizelle and Grace Crowley's school, which began in 1932, paralleled Bell's in Melbourne. In the wake of the success of these artist-operated schools, by the 1940s the New South Wales education department acknowledged the importance of artists fostering creativity in students and began employing contemporary artist/teachers such as Godfrey Miller, Ralph

Balson and John Passmore (artists who were soon revered by their students), at the East Sydney Technical College. Passmore and Balson later taught at the Julian Ashton School of Art in Sydney. John Olsen, whose influence on Mervyn Moriarty's work was noted during his exhibition at the Johnstone Gallery in Brisbane in the 1960s, was taught by Passmore.

Young artists in Brisbane were not so lucky. The official art school, the Central Technical College, was still teaching skills-based traditional art that had originated at the South Kensington School of art in nineteenth century London. Its regulated methods of teaching art stifled creativity.

However, in 1939 Europe was plunged into war and people fled the beleaguered countries being attacked by Germany – some came to Australia. By the late 1940s hundreds of refugees from war-torn Europe were arriving in Australia and a few settled in Brisbane.

In 1955 Newcastle artist Jon Molvig, who received his training from Godfrey Miller at the East Sydney Technical College came to Brisbane to take over an art school at St. Mary's church hall at Kangaroo Point – the only Brisbane school teaching creative art.

It had opened in Ann Street Brisbane in 1951 when English artist, Richard Rivron, began teaching in Brisbane. It attracted a number of students and Rivron soon moved to more suitable premises at Kangaroo Point. Two years later he left Queensland and the school was taken over by Margaret Cilento who had trained in New York. She left for America the following year and passed her classes on to John Rigby. Rigby was already working as a commercial artist so asked fellow artist, Jon Molvig he if could take over the school.

Molvig readily agreed. He had spent three years overseas since leaving the East Sydney Technical College and was now reaching the zenith of his own creativity. His work was eye-catching enough for Rudy Komon, an émigré from Eastern Europe, to travel to Brisbane to recruit him as the first in his stable of artists to exhibit at the new Paddington gallery in Sydney which he opened in 1959.

During the 1950s and '60s newcomers from interstate were also influencing the artistic taste of people in Brisbane. Brian Johnstone, who arrived in Brisbane as *aide-de-camp* to Governor Sir John Lavarack, opened the Johnstone Gallery in 1952 and his Brisbane-born wife Marjorie assisted him in building up a clientele. In 1957 they moved the gallery to their home in Bowen Hills. The Sunday morning opening of works by contemporary Australian artists at the Johnstone Gallery was a social event for Brisbane. In those years artists from Melbourne and Sydney such as Sidney Nolan, Arthur Boyd, John Perceval, Donald Friend, Lawrence Daws and many others exhibited at the Johnstone Gallery.

Charles Blackman, Ray Crooke, Lawrence Daws and Robert Dickerson spent time in Queensland after exhibiting. Robert Hughes, who later became a leading art critic in America, was another frequent visitor at this time. As friends of Molvig, visiting artists met at his studio and mixed with his students. Parties were a frequent occurrence at Molvig's studio and the atmosphere was definitely bohemian. As a student of Molvig, Mervyn Moriarty learnt a great deal about contemporary creative art while listening to the many discussions on art held over a glass of red wine at Molvig's studio.

Among those who influenced Queensland art at this time were two Queensland Art Gallery Directors: Robert Haines from Victoria who brought a number of contemporary European travelling exhibitions to Brisbane in the 1950s; he was followed by Laurie Thomas from Western Australia who exhibited contemporary Australian art at the Queensland Art Gallery in the 1960s.

Dr. Gertrude Langer was another who favoured 'modern' creative art. After fleeing Europe with her architect husband she settled in Brisbane at the beginning of World War II. She was to have a profound influence on Mervyn Moriarty's teaching career and it was through her activities that the dream of a Flying Art School was born.

Drs. Karl and Gertrude Langer had arrived in Brisbane in 1939 after escaping from Vienna following Hitler's invasion of Austria. They were both highly educated. Gertrude had attended the University of Vienna, obtaining her Phd in 1933. She studied History of Art with Professor Josef Strzygowski and during her training spent time at the Sorbonne in Paris, studying with Henri Focillon. Karl graduated as an architect from the master class of Peter Behrens who had also trained famous architects Mies van der Rohe and Le Corbusier.

Soon after settling in Queensland Gertrude Langer began giving lectures on art history and art appreciation at her home on Coronation Drive, Toowong. Her classes quickly became popular and it was not long before Professor MacFarlane from the University of Queensland (which was still on the CTC campus during WWII) arranged for a lecture theatre in his Physiology Department in William Street to be made available for her use.

In 1952 both Karl and Gertrude joined the newly formed Queensland Art Gallery Society. By 1953 Gertrude had become art critic for the *Courier Mail* and in 1961 she became President of the Queensland Division of the Arts Council of Australia.

On becoming President of the Queensland Arts Council, one of her first initiatives was to set up a Vacation School for creative arts at the St. Lucia campus of the University of Queensland.

The art teachers she employed were artists from Eastern Europe – Stanislaus Rapotec and Desiderous Orban. They were contemporary artists and at that time were teaching at the University of New England in Armidale for the New South Wales Adult Education Department.

Dr Gertrude Langer targetted country students in particular, and in the following years her August vacation school became so popular that students had to be turned away. Responding to the demand, by 1967 she was holding annual Arts Council workshops in country towns and one of the teachers she recruited to take creative art to the bush was Mervyn Moriarty.

He was a charismatic teacher and students loved his workshops. Because so many came to him after class seeking further tuition, he felt he had to help them fulfil their dreams. He could see that a number of the people he taught were talented and he knew that without more intensive training they had no chance of developing their talent.

With this in mind he discussed the problem with his wife, Helen. The Flying Doctor, established in 1928 to provide medical services in Queensland's outback, pointed the way for him. He decided that if he learnt to fly he could defeat distance by flying his own art school to the bush.

After making the decision to go ahead with a flying art school, Dr Langer supplied him with the names of Art Council representatives in country towns to get the school started.

Arthur Creedy, an Englishman who had arrived from Kuwait in 1967 to become Director of Cultural activities for the Queensland government was another who gave assistance.

Having taught English Literature at the University of Leeds for twelve years – one of the few universities in England to have creative artists living on campus – Creedy knew the benefits of fostering creativity. Both Langer and Creedy saw Moriarty's school as a wonderful opportunity for people living in regional Queensland to have a cultural grounding previously only available to city dwellers, and they encouraged him in his venture.

Sending art and craft workshops to the country was not a new concept. Teachers had travelled to regional areas to set up art and craft classes before 1971, but they had never been a success. Kevin Grealy, senior potter for Flying Arts from 1978 to 1982, taught at those early craft workshops sponsored by the Queensland Education Department. He described them as being poorly organised, sporadic and of little value. He was critical of the disorganised way individual artists and potters were sent to teach in country towns, and cited the lack of co-ordination when potters covered the same ground, doubling up on the same educational trips. With no on-going tuition to give students a thorough grounding in all aspects of pottery, they wasted the time of the tutor and achieved nothing.

A 1979 paper, prepared by Jeff Shaw from Kelvin Grove College of Advanced Education for a conference set up by teachers involved in Tertiary Art & Design Education, agreed with Kevin's comments. It also described the poor quality of the early adult education workshops: 'which have resembled, with their grandstanding nature, more of a side show alley than an educational initiative. Government funds had for years assisted country towns to bring in tutors from Brisbane, but these unplanned art and craft workshops were a costly failure. A prime example was the sending of three different ceramic artists to one town to supply three similar raku schools, with no attempt being made to advance the local level of skill.'

Moriarty's proposal, a structured two-year art course being taught by contemporary artists who focussed on creativity, gave students an art course previously only available to people living in major cities such as Sydney and Melbourne.

Both Langer and Creedy knew that many country people were desperately seeking something to keep their minds active, something that took them away from the pressures of farm life. They believed the school proposed by Mervyn Moriarty was an ideal solution.

With their blessing, in August 1971 he flew his first 'Eastaus' creative art workshops to towns and centres throughout the State. In the following years he flew artists along the coast north to Thursday Island and the Torres Strait, west to Mt. Isa and Quilpie, and south to Inverell in New South Wales. Four times a year for twelve years he flew to towns and station properties along these routes to conduct his workshops.

For many inland towns the arrival of the small plane piloted by tall and lean Mervyn Moriarty with his flowing red hair and beard was an event; in the early years he was often accompanied by his wife Helen, in later years he brought other artists.

By teaching a structured course of creative art the Eastaus workshops attracted hundreds of students.

To find out why the school was so successful, the story of Flying Arts will begin by looking at the life of Mervyn Moriarty. The following chapters will described the problems faced by Kelvin Grove College of Advanced Education and later the University of Southern Queensland following their takeover of the school. Stories and artworks by Mervyn Moriarty, three early tutors and some of its country students will complete the story of Flying Arts.

## Eastaus workshops in the early 1970s Photos courtesy Leah Cameron

**QUILPIE was a town too far west for structured art tuition until Mervyn Moriarty flew his art school "Eastaus" to the bush**

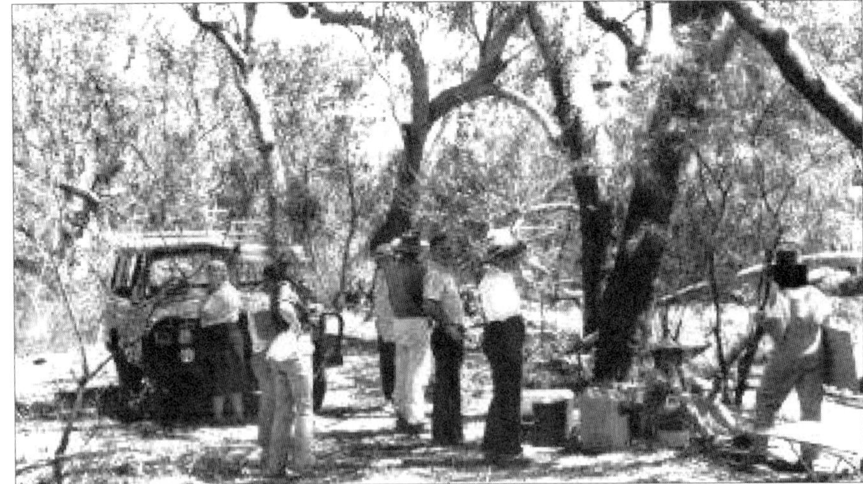

Drawing class down by the Bulloo River at Quilpie c1980

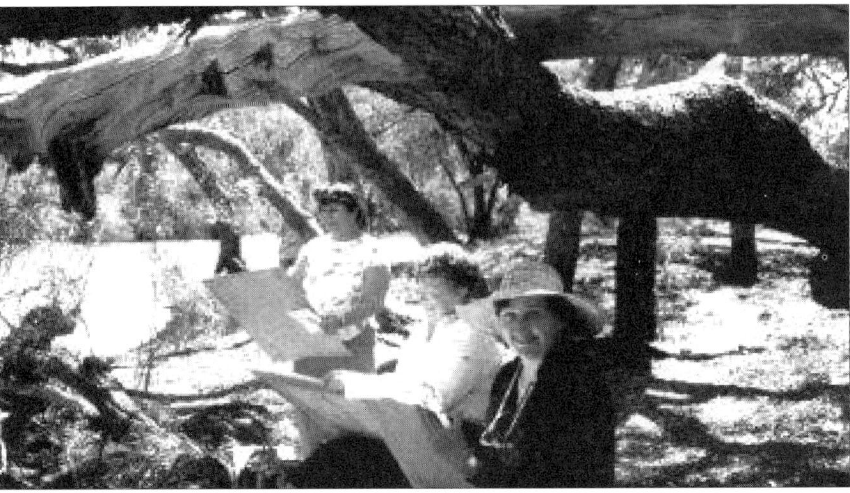

Charcoal drawing lesson on the banks of the Bulloo River, Quilpie

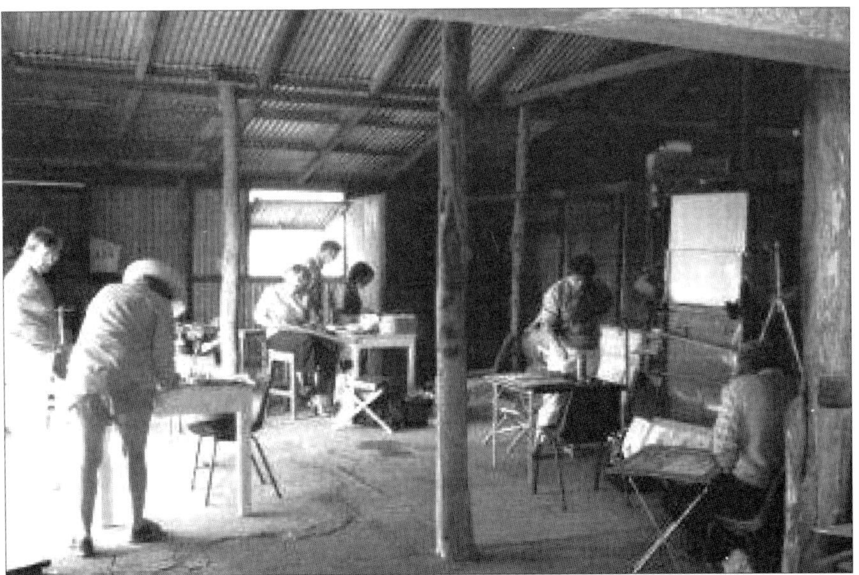

Painting in the Wool Shed on the Boran Property, Quilpie District c 1980

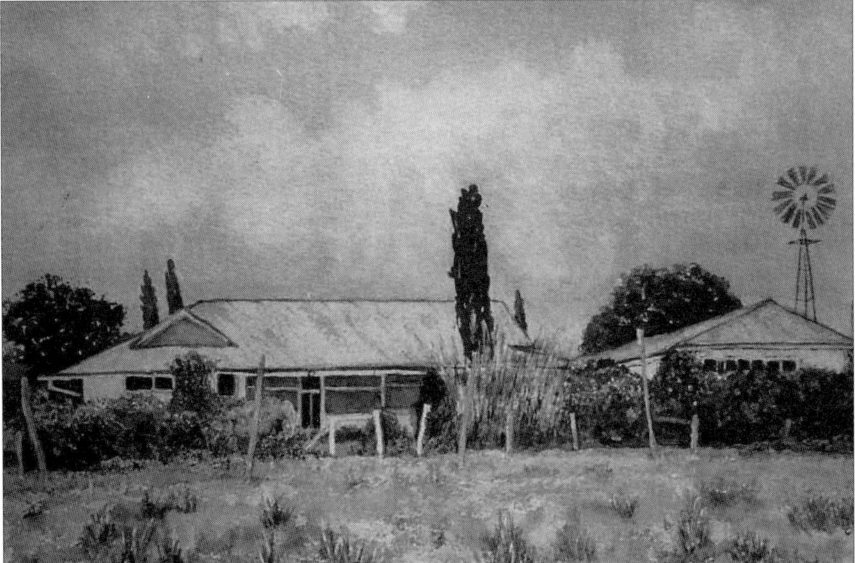

Char Speedy from Quilpie painted "Tallyabra," a station property outside Quilpie

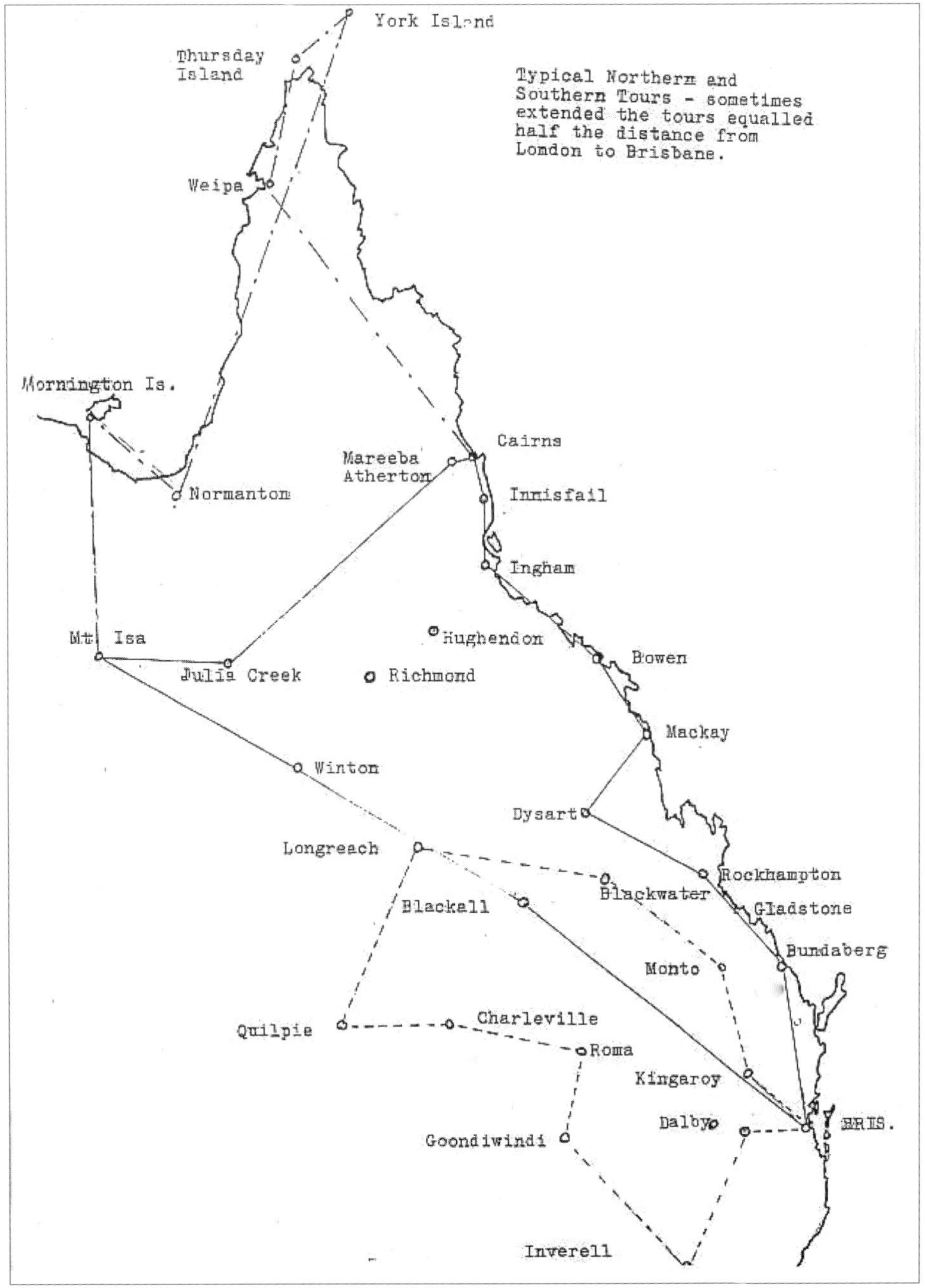

# The Birth of a Dream

Typical Northern and Southern Tours - sometimes extended the tours equalled half the distance from London to Brisbane.

York Island
Thursday Island
Weipa
Mornington Is.
Normanton
Mareeba
Atherton
Cairns
Innisfail
Ingham
Hughendon
Bowen
Mt. Isa
Julia Creek
Richmond
Mackay
Winton
Dysart
Longreach
Rockhampton
Blackwater
Gladstone
Blackall
Bundaberg
Monto
Quilpie
Charleville
Roma
Kingaroy
Dalby
BRIS.
Goondiwindi
Inverell

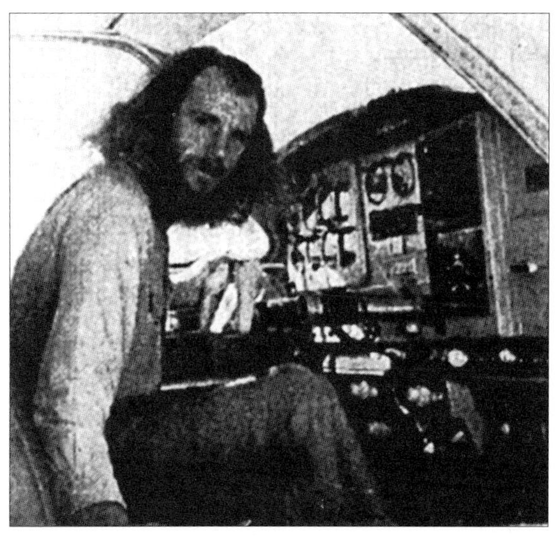

## Routes flown by Mervyn Moriarty 1971-1982

The typed map shows his 1970s flight paths.

# 1971-1982 Mervyn Moriarty – the birth of a dream

Mervyn Moriarty was born in Brisbane in 1937, his family lived in Moorooka. In those days Moorooka was just another small suburb in sleepy Brisbane, the capital of Queensland. Unlike Sydney and Melbourne where people kept up with the latest trends from Europe, Brisbane people were more isolated. The pace of life was slow and trains and trams were the only form of transport for most. In the quiet streets of Brisbane, a few cars mingled with horses pulling carts belonging to the butcher, the baker, the clothes-prop man and other suppliers making their household delivery rounds.

Although Mervyn was the only member of the family to take up art, he came from a creative background. His father was an actor and producer, his aunt was a talented musician who taught piano and a brother and sister were musical.

He could never remember a time when he wasn't drawing or painting, and his parents were always supportive of his efforts. For Christmas and birthdays they gave him paints, brushes, pastels and books on painting.

Then came the war and with it came an influx of outsiders. The population soared with the arrival of the American army. Camps were set up around Brisbane and transport trucks began to rumble through city streets. Soldiers on leave, or passing through on their way north, lounged around hotels in the centre of town or frequented the new milk bars springing up along Queen Street.

Refugees fleeing Hitler's Europe began to trickle into Australia and some, like Drs. Gertrude and Karl Langer, settled in Brisbane. Following the war, European immigration to Australia increased. The newcomers who came to Brisbane brought their culture with them and Queensland's capital city began to lose its small country town image.

By 1952 when Mervyn, at the age of 14, started his art training at the Central Technical College in George Street, many of the old city buildings, with their wooden verandahs, were giving way to four and six storey office blocks.

At the Central Technical College, Mervyn began his training with Melville Haysom. Although Haysom was a traditional artist, he encouraged his young pupil to find his own way. For Mervyn he was always a fine mentor, teaching him the basic techniques of drawing, preparing his canvas, and how to apply and mix colours.

However, being young and enthusiastic, he was looking for something more – as he put it:

'I was trying to find my feet as a young artist. I was full of enthusiasm and confidence and I was searching for a new way of thinking. One day, while walking along Queen Street, I saw a 'modern' (figurative but not representational) painting by local artist Jon Molvig in an art display panel in the *Courier Mail* offices – it blew me away and I wanted to meet the artist.'

Shortly afterwards, while he was attending an art camp at Cunningham's Gap organised by Haysom, a fellow student told him that creative art (after Molvig's style) was being taught by Andrew Sibley in a downstairs room at Richard Tong's shop in Brunswick Street, Fortitude Valley.

It was not long before he caught a tram to Brunswick Street to look for the studio and when he found it he remembered it vividly, fifty years after he walked into the room:

'When I found Sibley's studio I felt as though I was in another world. I remember thinking: is this Bohemia? Is it hell, or is it a dungeon in a back street of New York? The room was fogged with cigarette smoke and the electric light in the room gave it an orangey sort of colour as it lit up the smoke – it made the room into an extraordinary place. I found it exciting and quickly joined Sibley's classes. It was not long before I met Jon Molvig who, as a friend of Sibley, often came to the studio when classes were over.

'When I saw Molvig I spoke to him and introduced myself. We soon got around to the subject of art and I began by arguing with him over certain art practices, I didn't know it was not a good idea to disagree with Molvig. Despite that it was not long before we became friends.'

As Mervyn got to know Molvig he began to hero worship him. 'He was so good to me and helped me in any way he could, he even gave me his old car after he bought himself a new one when his exhibitions with Komon became so successful.' Mervyn was impressed with the emphasis Molvig placed on creativity and individual expression and he began attending Molvig's life classes held at Corroboree House in Hartley Street, Spring Hill. He recalled that 'those life classes provided me with a means of looking at reality other than its physical appearance.'

When Molvig travelled to Sydney to deliver paintings to Rudy Komon he invited Mervyn to accompany him and while there he met Sydney's art community: Russell Drysdale, John Passmore, Charles Doutney, Robert Klippel, Sali Herman, John Olsen, Stanislaus Rapotec, William Rose, Peter Upward and Clement Meadmore, who all had their studios within a few blocks of the well-known McElhone Stairs leading down the cliff face to Wooloomooloo and the docks.

It was in Sydney that he became familiar with abstract art. It influenced his preference for abstraction from the early 1960s right through to his years with Flying Arts.

When Mervyn joined Molvig at Corroboree House in 1958, it was a centre where southern artists mixed with students while visiting Brisbane to exhibit at the Johnstone gallery. The wildly bohemian atmosphere at the frequent parties held at Corroboree House and the relaxed and easy lifestyle of the studio appealed to him. He found that the numerous discussions on art did much to broaden his knowledge of creative art. It influenced him to follow Molvig's methods when, in later years, he took his own art school to the bush.

While attending Molvig's classes Mervyn received his Honours Diploma from the Central Technical College for colour, lettering and display. During the day he worked as a window display artist for Finney Isles & Co, now David Jones, at its department store in Queen Street where he was creating paper sculptures to decorate the shop windows for special occasions. During one Christmas season his designs were so spectacular a journalist from the *Telegraph* interviewed him, photographed him at work, and featured the story in a half page newspaper article. However, wanting to follow his preference for fine art, he left in 1963 to return to the Central Technical College as a part-time teacher.

When his parents died, Mervyn moved in with Andrew Sibley and other artists in a run-down building on Petrie Terrace. In 1962 he won the Johnsonian Club Prize. His win was controversial and he recounted the amusing story attached to it:

'It was a modern painting and Laurie Thomas, the Director of the Queensland Art Gallery, came around to see me one night – I was painting at my studio up on Petrie Terrace; I was painting away and Laurie turned up with his usual two bottles of beer and said: "Merv, I've got some news for you." I said, "oh what". Then he said: "well, you have won the Johnsonian prize, they gave you the prize." Then he added, "I gave you the prize because it was a really good painting, but they didn't want you to have the prize. The Johnsonian Club vetoed it, they wouldn't accept my decision because they didn't think it was acceptable to their club." Laurie then told me that he said to them, "well that's okay, you veto it and I will ring every newspaper in Australia and tell them what sort of a Club you are." This shocked them so much they gave me the prize.

'Nobody in Brisbane wanted modern art then, they had no understanding of abstract art. Laurie did so much for Queensland art, he was a very good evaluator and helped put the Queensland Art Gallery on the map.

'It was at that time that the Picasso, *La Belle Hollondaise*, disappeared from the Queensland Art Gallery. It vanished just as it was about to be sold. They were going to sell it and everyone was trying to find a way of stopping the sale.

'Students were walking up and down the street to draw attention to the sale in the newspapers. None of this had any effect on the proposed sale and then it disappeared. The newspapers made a big fuss and a week later it turned up wrapped in brown paper on the verandah of Lady Rubin's home. As it had been a bequest from Major Rubin, she could not be accused of stealing it.

'The police came out but there were no fingerprints on it. No one ever found out who did it although we students had a fair idea of who the hero was. The important thing was that the Picasso remained in Queensland.'

When this happened Mervyn was following the trend towards abstraction in painting which became popular in the 1960's. However he soon found he needed more freedom to follow his own ideas for teaching its more imaginative concepts and in September 1966 he left his teaching job at the college and opened a school at 'The Studio' – a room under St. Mary's Church hall at Kangaroo Point where both Molvig and Roy Churcher had previously taught. (Roy Churcher, who later become a teacher with Flying Arts, was an English artist who emigrated to Australia following his marriage to Brisbane girl, Betty Cameron.)

Although he placed emphasis on creativity, technical skills were not neglected, and students had 'homework' to improve their drawing skills and colour mixing ability. He described what happened next:

'My teaching career was placed on hold in 1967 when, through my association with Molvig, Komon asked me to join his 'stable' of artists. He wanted me to paint enough canvases for three solo exhibitions at his Sydney Gallery over the following three years.

'To fulfil his request I had to close my school at Kangaroo Point to concentrate on painting. Komon paid me a retainer, but I also taught fine art part time at the Department of Architecture, University of Queensland to help out.'

By this time Mervyn was married to Barbara. She already had two boys of her own when Mervyn's son Andrew came along, but she helped Mervyn to establish a full-time career as an artist.

In the 1960s Mervyn was regarded as a young upcoming contemporary artist. In 1962 he won a number of other local art prizes besides the Johnsonian Club Prize, and exhibited with 'Fourteen Queensland Painters' at the Johnstone Gallery. In 1963 he exhibited in a solo exhibition at the Bonython Gallery in Adelaide, and in group exhibitions in Hobart, Melbourne, Sydney, Brisbane and nearby country towns.

In the same year he won the Royal National Association Prize for 'Industrial Modern' at the Brisbane exhibition which was judged by Laurie Thomas. In 1964 he again exhibited at Gallery F in the Johnstone gallery.

Over the next few years his exhibitions were favourably reviewed by Dr. Langer in her capacity as *Courier Mail* art critic. In 1968 she invited him to teach at the Queensland Arts Council vacation schools she conducted at the University of Queensland.

By now her classes had become so popular that, along with the annual vacation workshops at St. Lucia which were held in August, she was promoting 'demand' workshops through Arts Council representatives in country towns where, once a year, small art groups could apply for an artist/teacher to hold a creative art workshop in their area. Besides teaching at St. Lucia, Mervyn now began taking workshops at Blackall, Barcaldine, Mary Kathleen, Townsville and Charleville.

It was at a workshop in Charleville in 1970 that a student, Dr. Dorothy Herbert from the local hospital, introduced him to flying. She used her own aircraft to visit patients in outlying districts and invited him to accompany her on a short flight. While in the air she allowed him to handle the controls and get a feel for the plane.

Mervyn recalled the experience: 'I loved the thrill of flying and found it inspiring. I knew the vacation schools were inadequate and afterwards I began to think that it was one way I could take my art school to the bush.

'I could see that people were coming to those workshops annually and more often than not they had a different teacher on each occasion.

'Between workshops students had no contact at all, they were coming in from country towns and they would have no contact with anyone between one visit and another so they were never really able to build on something from one position or one stage of the evolution of their understanding of art and art activity to the next. Nor were they able to add to it at the next workshop, because it would not be held until twelve months later. I saw that this would always be a problem.'

Mervyn's marriage with Barbara had not survived the strain of his full-time art career and when he thought about flying his school to the bush he spoke to his new wife, Helen. They decided that, by using the experience he had gained from the Arts Council vacation workshops, he could re-open his Brisbane school and extend its services to regional Queensland. With Helen as a partner he registered the school under the name of 'Eastaus' (for eastern Australia) early in 1971, and began taking flying lessons. They were not as difficult as he envisaged – he loved flying, and fortuitously his prizemoney for winning the 1970 Cook Bicentenary Art Award with his painting *Another Place* came at the right time to pay for his lessons.

In April 1971 he opened his Eastaus Flying Art School at 207 Adelaide Street Brisbane, and by the middle of 1971 he was ready to receive his pilot's licence.

Unfortunately he received a setback which delayed taking his workshops to the bush. Arthur Creedy, the Queensland Director for Cultural Activities, was so enthusiastic about his venture he phoned the Department of Civil Aviation in an endeavour to get the licence through quickly. However the DCA officers objected to being pushed by someone they saw as a government bureaucrat and delayed the issue of Mervyn's licence. When he finally

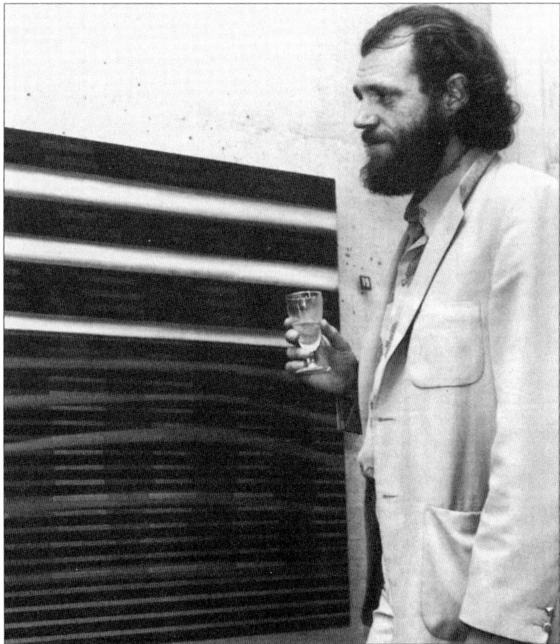

Merv's winning entry for the 1970 Cook Bicentenary Art Award *Another Place*
Courtesy *Courier Mail*

received it on a Wednesday in October, he flew to his first workshop the following Friday.

While waiting for the licence, both Dr. Langer and Arthur Creedy assisted him in setting up the school. Using information they supplied he was able to make contact with local Arts Council representatives in a number of country towns. He printed and distributed brochures outlining the ambitions of the school and placed advertisements in regional newspapers. During this time, with the assistance of former pupils Sheelah Mee and Paul Griffiths, he taught at the school he had set up in Brisbane in conjunction with his country school and travelled by car to teach at Ipswich, Toowoomba and Dalby.

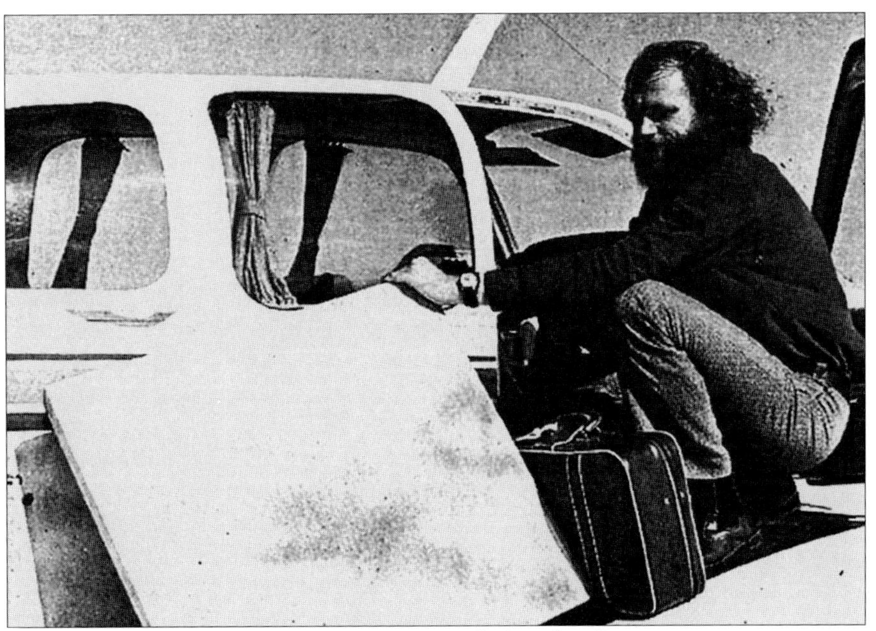

Getting ready for takeoff

The first brochure printed to advertise the school contained a foreword signed by Arthur Creedy describing the aims of the 'Eastaus' School of Art:

*A brilliant idea which harmonises with the basic plans to develop culture in Queensland country areas, with stress on activity in its purest and most original form of creativity.*

*It is analogous to the Flying Doctor Service, Flying Cabinet Service, a rider and outrider to the Queensland Art Gallery's Art Train, which is being resuscitated.*

*Future developments of the school, which include the other creative arts and the performing arts, will help to develop at least 50 to 60 cultural centres which are developing outside the metropolis in Queensland. This will at last pump the blood into the frozen fingertips of Northern and Western Queensland.*

The brochure listed Roma, Charleville, Blackall, Barcaldine, Emerald, Rockhampton, Gladstone, Bundaberg, Biloela and Maryborough as the first towns to be visited. A flight to northern Queensland – Cairns, Tully, Atherton, Mackay, Townsville, Richmond, Mount Isa and Cloncurry – was planned for the latter part of the year. Visits to centres in NSW were planned for the future.

Word of mouth, newspaper advertising and the brochures brought a number of interested enquiries and in the following twelve months the school was asked to fly to more than twenty country towns.

In November 1971 the *North West Star* at Mt. Isa announced that the Flying Art School was 'Off to a Flying Start' with fifteen students from Mt. Isa.

The undated map at the beginning of this chapter, thought to have been produced in a newsletter around 1973, shows the first towns he visited.

The more extensive northern tour took in twelve towns: Bundaberg, Gladstone, Rockhampton, Mackay, Bowen, Ingham, Innisfail, Cairns, Mareeba, Julia Creek, Mt. Isa and Winton.

In north-western Queensland he held classes at Mt. Isa, Julia Creek and sometimes at Richmond.

The workshops were so popular students travelled by car to workshops at Julia Creek after they finished at Mt. Isa. Others drove from Julia Creek to Jo Forster's property, 'Trivaltore,' near Richmond for a second workshop.

The same map also showed the southern route. It began at Dalby. From there he flew to Inverell, Goondiwindi, Roma, Charleville, Quilpie, Longreach, Blackwater, Monto and Kingaroy.

In coastal towns his students were generally townspeople, although people from rural properties within a radius of 300 kms. travelled to town to attend the Eastaus workshops.

In western towns the majority of students came from station properties in those early days. There is no real explanation for this but Mervyn often landed on their airfields to teach in their woolsheds and the network of students from outlying properties may have inhibited outsiders from joining.

Student stories at the end of this book graphically describe the lack of any cultural activities available to people living in rural Queensland when Mervyn first flew out of Brisbane in 1971.

### When creative art workshops arrived at the sugar town of Bundaberg

Coralie Busby from Bundaberg was the first country student to enrol in the Eastaus flying art school. Mervyn and Helen put her enrolment on the wall of the studio at their home in Mt. Nebo as a memento.

Coralie recalled that there were no cultural activities in Bundaberg in the 1960s – there were no art classes or art galleries, not even a library. If the townspeople wanted books they travelled to the library at Gin Gin as the Bundaberg Council believed that with the advent of TV people would stop reading.

Coralie began painting in the late 1960s when she joined a newly formed local art group. Although most were beginners they were enthusiastic, and in 1970 the Bundaberg Art Society held its first annual exhibition for members to exhibit their work.

Brisbane artist Roy Churcher was invited to judge and he quickly realised they needed professional tuition. Soon after Roy Churcher's visit Mervyn contacted them and made arrangements for their first workshop.

Like many other students Coralie praised the quality of his teaching: 'we learnt so much from him and people travelled for miles to take advantage of the wonderful tuition he provided.'

Although the course was meant to finish in two years Coralie remained with the school for twelve years. She claimed that Flying Arts changed her life, she was the first representative for the area, enthusiastically extolling the benefits of the school to everyone, and classes quickly grew. She boarded Mervyn and Helen when they came to Bundaberg; her garage was the venue for early workshops; and in 1970 she opened the first art gallery in Bundaberg (Allamanda Gallery) in the front section of her home for students to exhibit and sell their work.

Workshops were only part of the services the school supplied. Coralie spoke of the books Mervyn used to complement his teaching. For the two-year course he provided a series of twenty-three books for use by students between visits. They contained ongoing exercises to improve drawing skills, and a colour wheel for students to learn to mix colours. She remembered how invaluable the books were to her as a beginner: 'While he was teaching Mervyn was writing art books for us. There were twenty-three books as the course was meant to be finished in two years and he wrote the lessons just one step ahead of us all the time but they were great books, they taught us so much and we all stayed with the school for a lot longer than two years.'

### Dalby – a grain growing centre on the Darling Downs

Unlike Bundaberg, in 1971 Dalby had a well established art group which met once a week. The Dalby Art Group began in 1958 when the Adult Education Department sent them their first tutor, Don Featherston, a watercolourist from Toowoomba who conducted field days and workshops. In 1962 he was replaced by Ron Murray, also from Toowoomba, who taught both oil and watercolour painting. Over the years other traditional artists from Toowoomba came to teach their local art group.

Jack Wilson, a leading figure with the Dalby Art Group from its beginning, recounted his feelings about Mervyn's classes and what they meant to him. He wrote in glowing terms of the arrival of Eastaus in the early 1970s and the way creative art, and talks given by guest artists such as Clifton Pugh, stimulated their group: 'When Mervyn arrived he opened our eyes to contemporary art and a new and exciting way of looking at reality. He freed us from the narrowness of traditional painting as we knew it and we were now free to use our imaginations. Mervyn came as a breath of fresh air and dragged us into the 20th century.' Today Jack's colourful watercolours can be seen in the Dalby collection and at the Ipswich Regional Gallery.

Other Dalby artists wrote enthusiastically about the arrival of Flying Arts to their town and the difference it made to their lives. Joan Gill wrote of how she continued her art training at the Freemantle Technical College when her husband was transferred to Western Australia. Others, like Mabs Blackband, loved the creative art classes but were content to remain hobby artists. An undated newspaper cutting she supplied (which appears to have been written around 1975) described Mervyn's students as being made up of housewives, high school students and three men . . . 'through the Eastaus workshops Dalby was considered the most gifted country group in Queensland and Dalby paintings were being exhibited in Brisbane, Canberra and Sydney.' Mabs Blackband's work was amongst the paintings Eastaus sent south in the mid 1970s.

Although she was only twelve when Mervyn first came to Dalby, Kathryn Brimblecombe-Fox spoke enthusiastically about the workshops:

'We would bring our paintings to the class and Mervyn or the artist he had with him would then discuss the work, so three-quarters of the first day would be spent talking about each other's work. This was great because it provided an opportunity for self-reflection and getting really good feedback. In the classes we were experimenting rather than producing a work. It was a cultural experience and the best were the discussions on art. Art education at primary school was really fairly poor and the books put out by the Flying Arts School were great groundwork towards my success as an artist. I learnt a fair bit, there was a lot of [technical] information about the type of paints and about how to glaze and what oils to use and how to mix them.

Eastaus wasn't about how to do things, it was more about looking. Once you see it, how can you change it. Mervyn was very careful not to influence the student with his own work.'

In 1977, at age seventeen, Kathryn, backed by her training and experiences with Flying Arts and five years of art at secondary school, won the open section of the state-wide Queen's Golden Jubilee Art Competition and was awarded her prize by the Queen when she toured Australia.

### In the far west shearing sheds at Surat and Dagworth became art studios

From Dalby Mervyn flew to Surat and a 1975 workshop was described by Lenore Nicklin, journalist for the *Sydney Morning Herald* who wrote: 'Coming in to land at Surat Mervyn says: "Would you lean forward please – this is a very short strip." Sometimes when he lands on station strips the owner comes out and flashes a mirror and makes a fire to show the wind direction. Often station strips are quite close to each other and it has been known for the Flying Arts plane to land on the wrong strip. At Surat Bob Nason greets us and drives us to his property 'Telgalzie', a 40,000 acre sheep and cattle station.

With the class, who have already driven up and made themselves at home, we will stay in the shearers' quarters. The quarters are very comfortable and the emus, sprinting past the back are decidedly picturesque although the "watch out for the snakes" warning given by Mrs. Joan Schwennesen made us more wary. Jill Cameron pulls in, apologising for being late but she has just driven 90 miles and has had two flat tyres on the unmade road.

Pieces of butcher's paper four feet wide are handed around and out comes the pencils and charcoal. Mervyn says the stimulus of the school has brought out the creative potential in the one-time gumtree-in-the-paddock painters, "now there is as much genuinely creative work developing in the country as there is anywhere else."

The next morning a couple of the class went for a swim in the nearby dam. Bob Nason lit the wood stove and one of the early risers has put the sausages on. The Flying Arts workshops meant a great deal to Bob who enthusiastically recounted his feelings for the Eastaus workshops: "The great thing has been a visual awareness of the rhythm of nature: the relationship of land to sky, to water, to trees, to everything in the natural environment."'

Dagworth Station was another early stopping off place. Sheelah Mee travelled with Mervyn as a guest artist and she remembers it as a wonderful centre: 'Carol Curr, whose husband Robert had Dagworth, wanted Merv there for a couple of days, so she had to get enough people to make it worthwhile. The local policeman and his wife joined, and all the farm hands on their property. Everyone she knew had to join to make up the numbers and come along to the classes. I remember she won a prize for her art at the Winton Show, and Robert won I don't know how many ribbons for his horses and his cattle, but he was so excited because "she's won a prize for art"'.

### At Rockhampton – the beef capital of Australia

Of the towns on the northern trip, Rockhampton had the school's largest classes, often numbering 30-40 students, with many travelling from as far away as Gladstone and Emerald. The town had a well established art group before Flying Arts arrived, it was a branch of the Brisbane-based Royal Queensland Art Society (RQAS) which began in Rockhampton in 1950.

Art was taught as part of Adult Education at the Rockhampton Technical College and Rockhampton boasted a regional gallery. Opened in 1968, it was one of only two regional galleries in Queensland in 1971.

Rita Kershaw, later to become a prominent Rockhampton artist, was the first local Flying Arts representative. When writing of her experiences she described the inadequacies of the Rockhampton adult education classes:

'I started painting by going to adult education classes which eventually became TAFE, then I joined the local RQAS, but it was Mervyn who really started all of us painting in Rockhampton.

I was a student at his first class in 1971. Mervyn said he wanted us to paint the way we wanted to paint, he didn't try to force any particular style onto us, I went abstract straight off. I had had a little bit of training in technique from the adult education tutors but they weren't as good. They were not professional artists, but people who had done some painting before teaching, there really wasn't very much in Rockhampton in the early days as regards art.

We had students coming in from Comet, Emerald, Baralaba, Yeppoon and Gladstone and people would phone in to ask when the plane was due before they began their drive to

Rockhampton. Flying Arts and the group gave us the support we needed to continue as artists.

The art culture has changed since then. In those days no-one understood our creative art and we did not sell our work, people only bought representational art. Many of us are now professional artists and all give praise to Mervyn and Eastaus school for giving us something that so enriched our lives.'

### Julia Creek and the Mitchell grass country of the north west

In Julia Creek, Glad Cooney and Jo Forster wanted to start art classes for local children. Glad had trained as an art teacher at the Teachers' Training College, Kelvin Grove, but knew her training was inadequate.

She was the north-western correspondent for ABC Radio when she first met Mervyn at a Townsville Arts Council workshop and he told her of his flying art school. To bring the school to the north-west she announced it over the ABC at Longreach, and asked all those wanting art lessons to get in touch with either Jo at Richmond, or herself at Julia Creek, in order to set up local workshops.

Glad loved the workshops Mervyn provided and found they taught her to look more deeply at her surroundings: 'I felt that he brought culture to the region. Before he came we would look at this great, broad country of ours that we thought was featureless, there were so few trees, but he made us see the seasons. In the wet season the grass would be so beautiful and green but as winter came the green would disappear, yet as the grass turned to other colours we found they were just as beautiful as they danced in the mirages.

'At the Training College we had only learned to paint watercolours but Mervyn taught us so much more. He would often play Indian music while we worked and I remember looking at some old Noogoora burr and, as I looked, the colours seemed to come to life and I thought "this is a painting"; I became so absorbed in it as I began painting it – I wasn't copying it, there was something more.'

Anne Lord, another student from the north-west, is now a professional artist teaching art at James Cook University in Townsville. She grew up on a property outside Julia Creek and first met Mervyn at an early workshop. She described him as 'a dynamic person brimming with enthusiasm and creative energy.' He influenced her decision to develop her interest in painting by encouraging her to go to art school in Sydney (it is notable that he did not suggest Brisbane). 'It was he who told me that I should continue with my work and suggested I apply to the National Art School, so I followed his advice and attended that school during the subsequent changes it went through over the next few years. His faith in my ability was important to me and it probably kept me going to art school when I was extremely homesick. Following his visits Mervyn always left me eager to progress with my work and follow my dream to become an artist.'

Mervyn spoke of the reciprocal effect when a student expressed her deepest feelings through her painting: 'On one occasion I arrived in Julia Creek extremely tired; the constant flying and teaching over the last week had taken its toll and I was struggling to keep going. When I walked into the room where the workshop was to be held and saw a painting by Myra Beach the effect was instantaneous. It was such a strong picture I knew she had put enormous hours of intense work into it. It was an expression of her horror at a weed taking over the land she loved so much, those plains, and there was this weed that had been introduced from South Africa taking over the land. It was a shrub, a small tree that was turning the grass plains into forest. Her picture was about those weeds, and she had put so much passionate love into the picture that it just instantly put vitality back into me and I was able to go off for the rest of the day as though I had just had a charge. But the charge was in the picture and the commitment, someone's passionate feeling was expressing itself through their art.'

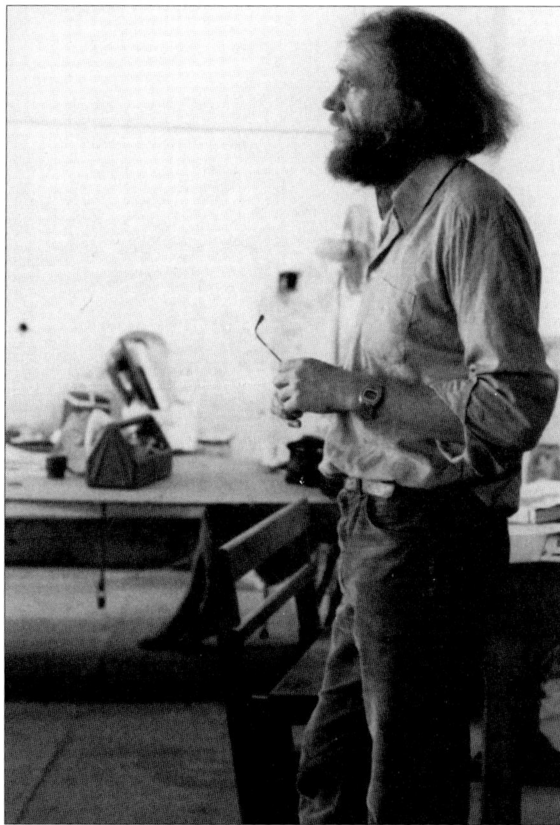

Mervyn teaching at Rockhampton 1970s

### The rise of Mervyn's dream

For his venture to be successful money was essential – it was always a problem which confronted him. By 1973 student numbers in the school were steadily growing, but fees were not covering costs, and the expense of hiring and fuelling a small aircraft was taking its toll. All his resources had gone into the school along with $3000 from Helen. Over the previous two years, while establishing the school, they saved on expenses by taking only $30 a week for living expenses, relying on home-grown vegetables and eggs from their rented property at Mt. Nebo to supplement their needs. Another saving was made by using volunteer help from Mervyn's sister Jenny and his Brisbane students to type and duplicate the books supplied to country students. However, despite their efforts, by late 1973 their resources were exhausted and they could no longer finance the school.

The Queensland Branch of the Arts Council of Australia had given the school whatever help it could through Dr. Langer, but was unable to make a financial contribution. Arthur Creedy from Cultural Activities supported Flying Arts with small grants, i.e. in 1972 he gave $1500, early in 1973 he allocated another $1000, but it was not enough. With over 240 country students dotted throughout eighteen centres the school needed substantial funding. Mervyn wrote to the Arts Council of Australia requesting financial assistance; the Council replied saying that, as the school had no precedent, it was unable to support it.

But 1973 was a time of dramatic political change in Australia. In December 1972 the Labor party won office, and the new prime minister, Gough Whitlam, educated at Sydney University - completing an arts degree before studying law - was known for his fondness for the arts.

In desperation Mervyn wrote directly to Whitlam and, surprisingly, he received a reply. Whitlam stated that he thought the school was a great idea and he had a friend whom he would ask to come to Queensland to tour with the school to assess what Eastaus was achieving.

When the 'friend' arrived Mervyn found that he was well-known Australian artist, Clifton Pugh, who had won the Archibald Prize in 1972 with his portrait of Whitlam. Pugh came at his own expense and Mervyn spoke enthusiastically of his visit: 'We got on extraordinarily well and he contributed enormously. He came back from that trip absolutely exhausted, because it really was a tough trip and he wasn't well, but he wrote to the Australia Council recommending it very highly and the Council gave the school a grant of a few thousand dollars, that was enough to keep us going until we could organise ourselves into a non-profit organisation and form a Board and be registered as a non-profit organisation. When we did that they gave us a sizeable grant, a grant which was sufficient to keep the school operating.'

So, following Pugh's visit, Mervyn received his money, but before they would get a larger grant a Board had to be set up to manage school expenditure.

Creedy again came to their aid. He appointed retired politician, Sir Vernon Christie, who had been the Speaker of the House in the Victorian Bolte government, as president. Other members of the Board were: Monica Crouch – Secretary; Harold Munro – Treasurer; John Marshall; Wing Commander Gordon Olive; and Russell Cuppaidge.

With the establishment of a Board the school needed a more suitable name and early in 1974 the name 'Eastaus' was changed to 'The Australian Flying Arts School'.

Mervyn understood that grants from the Arts Council of Australia would continue and he expanded the activities of the school.

In April 1974 under the heading, 'Wanted: Artist with Wings', the Sydney *Sun Herald* advertised for a pilot/artist to assist with the bush tours, applicants to be screened by Pugh. The successful applicant was Bela Ivanyi, a young refugee who had fled from the Communist invasion of Hungary. On arrival in Australia Ivanyi completed an art course at the National Art School in Sydney. After finishing the course he taught in Sydney before moving to Cairns in northern Queensland. Flying Arts paid for Bela to be taught to fly and he became the second pilot/artist with Flying Arts. He flew the northern route when Mervyn flew west.

Although, with his gruelling workload, he desperately needed help from a second artist, Mervyn also believed that, to produce their best work, students needed a different viewpoint. He could now implement this philosophy and taught at three of the four annual country workshops in western towns while Bela taught at the northern centres. For the fourth workshop they changed over. The changeover for one of the four yearly workshops supplied variation for his students. As Vince Bray from Mt. Isa remarked: 'Mervyn sowed the seed, Bela let it grow.'

Mervyn also believed that guest tutors Clifton Pugh, Keith Looby and other Australian artists who flew with him to the workshops, were important for the growth of students. As he explained it: 'I knew that guest tutors often held an entirely different position to my way of thinking and working, but the difference is necessary for the development of the student. Along with the variation I also believe that continuity is essential. The dominant tutor is responsible for building student confidence – if you take away the continuity, the tutor that students can relate to over a period of time, you take out a link between tutor and student that I believe has been tremendously important historically. A fairly long-term relationship enables the learning process to be as much coming from the student as from the tutor. It is that relationship between student and tutor that supplies them with continuity and security.'

With funding in place and the worry of how to pay for the school over at last, Mervyn was eager to seek new outlets and other avenues were explored. Flying Arts workshops were always available wherever they were requested, and he was teaching a class of Europeans and Torres Strait Islanders on Thursday Island when he was invited by a visitor from Yorke Island to bring the school to his village. He found it to be a wonderful experience. When he went to Yorke Island he was impressed with the beauty of the island, the neatness of the houses, and the happy lifestyle of the islanders. Classes were held during the day. In the evening everyone sat around and sang. He thought the singing was similar to a Gregorian chant as people shifted from hymns to traditional native sounds. He found the people of Yorke Island extremely hospitable and friendly: 'On Yorke Island, I learned immensely more than I taught. They were the happiest, most beautiful people I have ever been amongst, I taught the kids and later I taught the adults. The adult class couldn't start until the tide was right because they were all out fishing, so when the tide was right – when it was the wrong time to fish, right time to do something else – they would all come in. When I asked how many people would be coming to the class my friend said 'everyone'. And everyone did come. It was chaos of course but they didn't care, no-one cared. They wanted to learn about mixing colours so they could paint their houses in these new and exciting colours.'

When Clifton Pugh travelled to Yorke Island with Mervyn he was also impressed; he described the houses as 'freshly painted in bright colours – neatly side by side in rows like a paint manufacturer's colour chart.' He noted the natural creativity of the islanders who 'had a sense of design and colour and a freedom which could, with encouragement, develop into something else.' But the workshops on Yorke Island did not continue. Materials to paint or draw were not available to the islanders and their only tradition of the visual arts was small sculptures in pumicestone. Mervyn said that he believed singing and dancing was the creative outlet for these people.

The next stop made by Mervyn and Clifton Pugh on that flight was Mornington Island. Mervyn wanted to explore whether the workshops could benefit Aboriginal people. The visit was not a success. In a series of articles with sketches for the Melbourne *Age*, Pugh described their stay on Yorke Island and recounted the flight to Mornington Island. They found that four visits a year were not enough for the people on Mornington Island, a resident artist was needed. Different tribes had been herded together on the island and Pugh saw it as a tragedy: 'there is an air of despondency. A feeling of disquiet too, for among Mornington's 700 islanders are three major tribal groups and they are not compatible; they never were.'

Despite the failure to establish workshops for indigenous people, Pugh wrote enthusiastically about the work the school was doing in a series of articles for the Melbourne *Age*. He believed that Mervyn was filling a cultural void in Queensland.

In the first article he likened him to a prophet in a non-profit enterprise: 'the pleasures of his life are not success or failure but trying to do something that needs to be done.' During the flight he visited other Eastaus workshops with Mervyn and enlivened his stories for the *Age* with anecdotes.

In his story of Normanton he drew on his own creativity to describe the scene when coming in to land: 'looking down on Normanton, marooned in tidal clay flats through which the waterways coil, you can see why the Aborigines tell of the rainbow serpent who made the rivers.'

When he wrote of the school's achievements on Thursday Island he coloured it with an exotic background story of a solitary white man staying at the local hotel: 'he is straight out of Somerset Maugham – a figure surely planted there to convince the romantic tourist that the tales they read and the films they saw about the decaying gentility of the long gone Empire were true.'

Finally, he wrote of the vast distances the school covered in the far west and described the enthusiasm of people living in the remote Mitchell grass country of Julia Creek and Richmond who travelled so far to attend the workshops:

'Out beyond the Black Stump in north central Queensland is the Mitchell Grass country – 900 miles from north to south, 400 miles from east to west. The flat, flat plains seem endless, unbroken. The trees have long since abandoned the struggle for existence. There is only the red-brown earth and the bleached white grass. The occasional station or tiny township, baking under corrugated iron. The temperature when we arrived was a searing 45° celsius, but it did not dispel the enthusiasm of the art class. There were 15 or so, some had travelled 100 miles or more. In their paintings you can see their dreams. There is green on the canvas – the only green in all that dry land.'

Not only did Clifton Pugh's enthusiasm obtain funding for the school, by writing his entertaining and highly descriptive articles, he gained Australia-wide recognition for the school and what it was doing in regional Queensland.

Following the tour and the receipt of Australia Council funding, the Queensland government also provided funds. In 1974 the school received $10,000 from the state government through Arthur Creedy, and $20,000 from the federal government through the Arts Council.

With the extra funding, in June 1975 Flying Arts moved from Adelaide Street to larger premises at 72-76 Eagle Street. The Education Minister, Val Bird, opened its new offices which not only contained teaching areas for Mervyn's Brisbane school, but also a spacious art gallery to exhibit student work.

The first exhibition opened on 19 June 1975 and people from all over Queensland had the thrill of seeing their work on view at a public space in Brisbane. At the opening the Minister announced that the artworks being exhibited would go on tour to Sydney and Melbourne.

Following official recognition of the school, the Queensland Art Gallery loaned small artworks from its collection to give Mervyn's bush students the opportunity of viewing good quality original artworks.

Student numbers tripled from 240 in 1973, to more than 700 by 1975 and, in 1977, numbers were closer to 900. Added to this, the school was teaching creative art to over sixty students in Brisbane. Funding, so essential for the continuation of the school, was made up of 50% from the Commonwealth government through the Australia Council, 25% from the State government through Arthur Creedy's Cultural Activities and 25% from student fees.

At the new Eagle Street premises a small printing press, operated by Ric McCracken who had previously given his time to Flying Arts on a volunteer basis, was installed to print newsletters, catalogues and art instruction books. Mervyn was pleased with the progress of the school: 'We were taking education out into the country and it was, in a real sense, the first really innovative approach to distance education that had happened for a long time. Correspondence courses existed, although they were nowhere near as good as the art education we gave to students living in isolated parts of the country through our workshops.'

With adequate funding workshops were expanded, and following enquiries from country people for pottery workshops, classes were held in conjunction with the creative art classes.

The first potter to travel with the school was Rex Coleman, a well-known Brisbane potter who trained with Harry Memmott in Brisbane before working with Merv Feeney. Later he studied in Japan, India and the United States. Rex found teaching with Flying Arts was 'total pioneering; really a matter of picking up a lump of clay and putting it on a bare table. There was absolutely nothing to work with and no-one knew anything.'

Other benefits were introduced: While touring, Mervyn followed the precedent set up by the early Arts Council vacation schools; he conducted evening seminars on art history and philosophy during overnight stays at two-day workshops.

To improve the quality of the seminars he purchased a camera and hired a movie projector; he acquired film from Japanese and French Embassies in Brisbane to show students the work being done by overseas artists, and obtained film of interviews with prominent Australian artists.

With the new camera Helen took colour slides showing work produced by groups in Queensland. The slide presentations were accompanied by discussions on the technical and philosophical issues involved in their production.

At the evening seminars students supplied supper and brought their families along. Mervyn found, when talking to husbands, that most were pleased with the school; it gave their wives an interest, making them happier and more content with the hardships of life in the bush.

In contrast a few men were not so pleased; their womenfolk were now more assertive. The workshops had built up the confidence of many women and it appeared that some men in the bush objected to social equity. One man even went so far as to say that, if he could have got away with it, he would have shot the plane out of the sky. On another occasion while he was teaching in a country town, the local aircraft engineer came to the class and asked Mervyn to come with him to look at the plane. While servicing the plane he had noticed broken pieces of metal in the bottom of the drum used to catch oil draining from the engine, among them were two small ball bearings which did not belong to the plane. They could have found their way in by accident when refilling the oil, but his first comment was: 'Merv do you have any enemies.'

## Trouble in Brisbane

Despite its success in regional Queensland there were problems in Brisbane. The administration of the school was not running smoothly, and while Mervyn was on tour, there was an attempt to overturn his Board and instal another Board. There is no evidence to say who was responsible or why it happened – did someone want to take the school away from Mervyn? Was it the manager Audrey Robertson? No-one knows.

To account for the actions, Mervyn was accused of carrying drugs on the plane. The accusation was defeated when Sir Vernon Christie asked for evidence. When told that the Busbys of Bundaberg had made a complaint, Christie visited Bundaberg to verify the story. They were horrified and quickly refuted the suggestion.

Mervyn justified his own denial: 'in his position as chief pilot and artist for the school he would never have been that stupid as to risk his licence.' He admitted that some of the visiting artists may have used drugs, but they had been told drugs were not to be brought onto the plane.

It is significant that, when interviewed, Coralie Busby praised Mervyn for his work and made no mention of drugs. No student or tutor made any allegations of drug use during the years Mervyn worked with them, and if drugs were aboard the plane while on tour, they risked being found while the plane was being serviced by local engineers.

The takeover failed and Sir Vernon Christie's Board was retained, but before changes could be made to the Brisbane administration, federal politics intervened.

In November 1975 the Whitlam government was dismissed and the Fraser government took power in Canberra. Much of the money allocated to the arts via the Australia Council was discontinued. One of the victims was Flying Arts.

Following the loss of Commonwealth funding the State government also cut its funding. Creedy's Cultural Diary noted that Flying Arts received a grant of only $5000 in 1977.

Without government support the school was once again grounded. Faced with the catastrophe, the Board announced that all workshops were cancelled due to economic factors beyond their control – it appeared the school would have to close.

But everyone wanted the school to continue, and in August 1977 the *Courier Mail* noted that Dr. Dorothy Herbert of Charleville suggested approaching mining companies working in Queensland for assistance.

John Walters, President of the Flying Arts Students' Association, sympathised with the 895 students who would suffer. He wrote to students explaining that as the school had received only $30,000 in the last twelve months, it could not carry on.

With the closure of the school threatening, John Walters asked students to lobby their local politicians and Flying Arts students throughout Queensland rallied around. Country people sent letters to Ministers in Brisbane and contacted their local members.

By September 1977 students had written hundreds of letters in support of the school. The outcry caused the Bjelke-Petersen National Party government to make a decision to fund the school and keep it open and $18,000 was immediately allocated to assist the school until the end of the year. It now cost around $120,000 a year to operate and, with help from student fees, the Queensland Education Department would provide for its future funding. However, a condition of the funding was that the school amalgamate with an existing college.

Kelvin Grove College of Advanced Education, (KGCAE) had recently entered the field of community arts education through its new Principal, Dr. Peter Botsman and shortly after receiving the letter Mervyn was visited by Jeff Shaw, Head of the School of the Arts at Kelvin Grove. Although he would no longer be a Director of his school, he understood he would receive a senior lecturer's salary, being employed by KGCAE when not touring. For eight years Flying Arts had been his life and, rather than lose it, he agreed to the proposal and accepted the offer. In March 1978 the school was taken over by KGCAE.

In her reminiscences Sheelah Mee remembered the time well: 'So life went on at the Flying Art School until eventually the money ran out. It stopped us flying, we could not get planes because it was getting harder to pay bills. As Merv had already been paid for the course, when the money ran out he could not ask for more. Of course it wasn't an economical project and was never going to pay for itself, so that's when Kelvin Grove came along. I begged Mervyn not to take up the Kelvin Grove offer. I said to him: "Come on Merv, you are not going to get on with them at Kelvin Grove, you are going to hate it." But he said "I have to go, I can't abandon my students" then I said to him "you'll be the one who is abandoned" and he was.'

When Flying Arts began its operations from Kelvin Grove the key aspects of its formative years were retained. Mervyn and Bela flew with the KGCAE potters to country centres to conduct workshops; Mervyn's books remained in use and the school relied on his structure of personal initiative. The significant change was the support system of experienced personnel working from Kelvin Grove who restructured the management and supervised the day-to-day operations of the school. Flying Arts now appeared to have the other two essentials needed for success – adequate financial backing and sound administration.

However, in 1979 problems surfaced. Bela left the school. The Civil Aviation Department felt he had endangered other aircraft and revoked his pilot's licence following an unscheduled landing at the wrong destination.

With the school's reliance on small planes, an AVGAS shortage from May to October forced a decision to use cars to visit towns in the south-west of the state.

The result was that extremely poor roads made distant towns like Quilpie uneconomical and far inland towns were dropped from the tours. People living in the south west became anxious they would now be abandoned, and Bill Glasson, a western politician, echoed their concern when he drove over 200 kms on bad roads to get to a workshop. On arrival his first words were: 'For goodness sake, don't let the school collapse, we need it out here. It's the best thing after cactoblastis.' It was not long before flights to the far west were re-instated.

In June the following year the school came close to a major disaster when Mervyn had to make a forced landing near Toogoolawah. It was only his skill as a pilot that saved pottery tutor Kevin Grealy and himself from what could have been their last flight.

The *Courier Mail* featured the story under the heading 'Artist's Plane Goes Down in Paddock' and wrote that the plane owned by Sunland Aviation had engine failure at 6000 feet due to a blown piston. Mervyn stated afterwards that he sent a Mayday call to Brisbane control saying he was heading for Redcliffe but may have to make a forced landing.

When the plane started to shake violently he feared an engine fire. He shut the fuel off and was preparing to ditch the plane in Somerset Dam when he saw a paddock that appeared smooth enough to land. While Kevin propped the door open for a quick evacuation he was able, after lifting the plane over a wooden fence and missing trees and rocks, to land in the paddock, coming to a stop among a group of very startled cows. The near miss proved his ability as a pilot. During twelve years flying to the outback it was his only mishap.

Robyn Bauer from Dalby was one student who praised Mervyn's flying ability. She was only ten when she first attended the Eastaus workshops. In later years, after receiving her degree at the University of Queensland, she was employed by the Queensland Art Gallery and found herself in charge of an exhibition of Queensland paintings sent to tour with Flying Arts – she remembered the flight: 'I always thought of Mervyn as this bohemian, red wine drinking person larger than life because he was so big and I had always thought he was a bit scary. But when I actually saw him flying the plane I was absolutely amazed at how meticulous he was, how careful he was. When he was in the air he concentrated only on his flying and he had a reputation of being a really good pilot.'

However, relationships between Jeff Shaw and Mervyn were sometimes strained and, in December 1982, Mervyn left the school following a disagreement with the Flying Arts management committee at Kelvin Grove. His departure was not amicable. The details of his going were never made clear, but the *North Queensland Register* printed the story of his sacking/resignation under the heading 'Flying Artist grounded – art gone from the west': 'Mervyn Moriarty, the man who brought art to thousands of outback Queenslanders through the Australian Flying Art School (AFAS), is without a job. Moriarty and the flying art school were synonymous. The wild-haired, 'flying artist' was responsible for bringing art to the outback. Mr. Moriarty claimed his employer, the Board of the AFAS, sacked him. The Board says the artist resigned.'

Jeff Shaw, as president of the board, declined to be interviewed, instead he sent a press statement to the newspaper stating: 'Flying Arts employed him for only twelve weeks of the year and he left because he wanted a substantial increase in salary which the school was unable to meet.'

Following his departure, the committee did acknowledge the contribution he had made to art education in Queensland with: 'The highest standard of students' work is reflected in the exhibitions and competitions throughout the State and it can be suggested that Mervyn Moriarty, more than any other single teacher, has had state-wide significance in the development of the arts.'

Sir Vernon Christie's reply, also printed by the *North Queensland Register*, read in part: 'the salary received by the artist for being a teacher as well as a pilot was 'laughable' at only $5000 per year.'

Christie stated that he had tried to persuade Mervyn not to take up the KGCAE offer in the first place, as he always doubted the move would be a satisfactory one for him.

The story was featured on *Nationwide* on the ABC, and the *Gold Coast Bulletin* wrote:

'The great tragedy was that the matter under the spotlight, the parting of the ways of the legendary Mervyn Moriarty and his brainchild, the unique Australian Flying Art School, should never have been allowed to get to this stage. Viewers saw an exasperated Moriarty thinly disguising his distress at the apparent loss of his 12-year association with an organization which has undoubtedly made the most valuable contribution, on the widest possible scale, to Queensland's art education.'

The reporter also wrote that Mervyn had no say in the school he founded, as the Constitution drawn up by Shaw kept paid tutors off the Board.

His sacking/resignation was widely publicised in regional Queensland, and his loss was deeply felt by many students. After having taught them for so many years they were not pleased to lose their charismatic mentor. Carol Curr from Winton, an original student with the school, wrote to the *North Queensland Register*. It read in part: 'He made possible the high standard of art and crafts being taught in the north, west and south today. . .The creativity he helped us discover in ourselves, and the hinging together of people in the bush and towns with the same interests, gave us new horizons to reach for and added 'colour' to our lives.'

At Bundaberg a meeting of students called for a review of the situation; they wanted his reinstatement. Students felt there should be a committee of enquiry into the affair, with equal representation being given to board members and students. There was no response from the management committee of Flying Arts.

Money was certainly behind his leaving. With a second wife as well as a child from his previous marriage to support, Mervyn found his income inadequate and the pressure was affecting his marriage with Helen. He asked the committee for an increase in salary, but the request was rejected. He was paid for each teaching trip at the same level as other tutors – it was not the senior lectureship he was promised, despite being the school's founder and pilot. With his country trips interfering with his Kelvin Grove duties, he was unable to augment his Flying Arts income by teaching at the college.

He tried to go back to his Brisbane art school as a part time tutor, but again his country trips made it impracticable. When he resigned from the school in 1978 it was kept open by his former tutors and, although it was a struggle, the Brisbane school survived as a private art training institution. Today it is still operating under the name of the Brisbane Institute of Art (BIA).

When things were at their worst, Mervyn remembered a conversation he had had with Professor Leon Cantrell from the Darling Downs Institute of Advanced Education (DDIAE) – now known as the University of Southern Queensland.

Toowoomba based DDIAE supplied distance education to rural Queensland and he was given to understand the college would welcome the school as part of their programme. A satisfactory salary was part of the package. He contacted DDIAE and they were keen to negotiate. However, Mervyn recalled that after the management committee at KGCAE heard of it, there was a huge row which involved both the Flying Arts management and the Queensland Education Department, and he was given to understand that his services were no longer required.

When Mervyn left Kelvin Grove he tried to open a new flying art school. He flew to Mackay and Rockhampton – towns which, following his departure, were no longer being served by Flying Arts. He bought art supplies and art books to sell on the trip, but with no financial support, the venture failed.

In 1983 he opened a new art school at Paddington in Brisbane. However, stress from losing Flying Arts caused it to close and his marriage to fail. Helen, who had worked so hard to help him launch Flying Arts, had had enough.

Shattered by his experiences, he left Queensland in 1984 to start a new life as 'Artist in Residence' at East Gippsland with the Arts Council of Victoria.

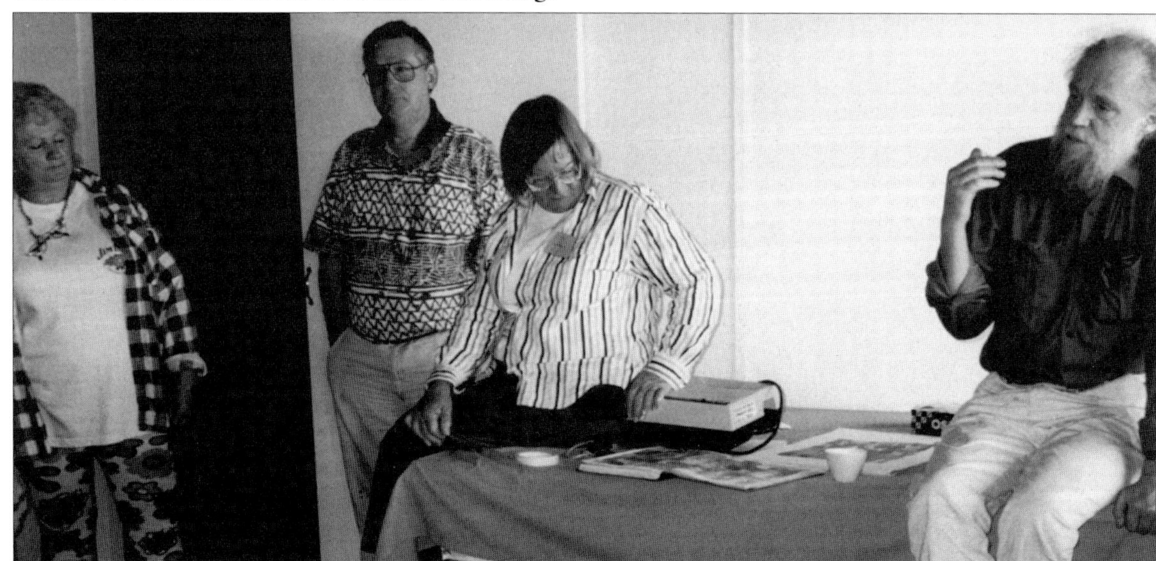

Mervyn taking a class at Emu Park Courtesy Flying Arts archives

## The Glenmorgan Art Group at Myall Park c1972 – photos courtesy Carol McCormack

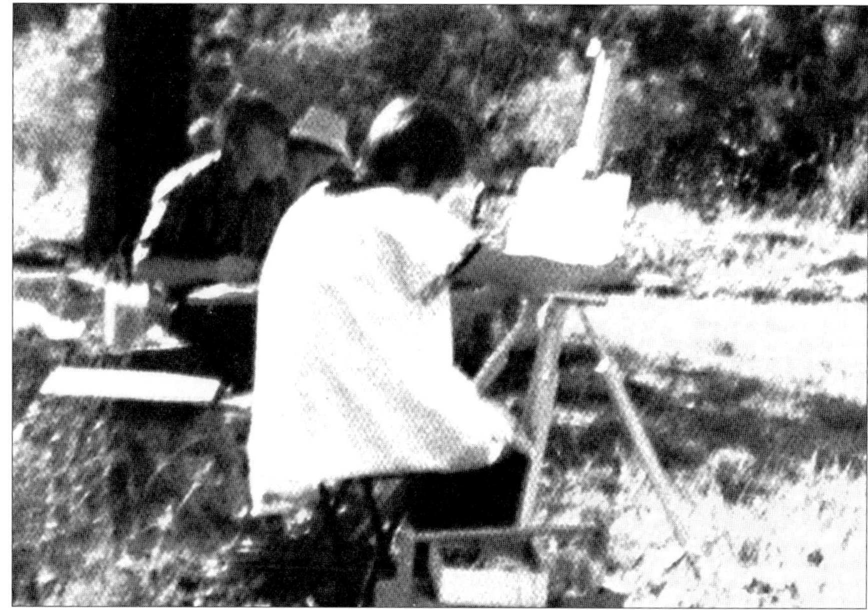

Bob Nason, Liz Jackson at Glenmorgan Art Group seminar at Myall Park

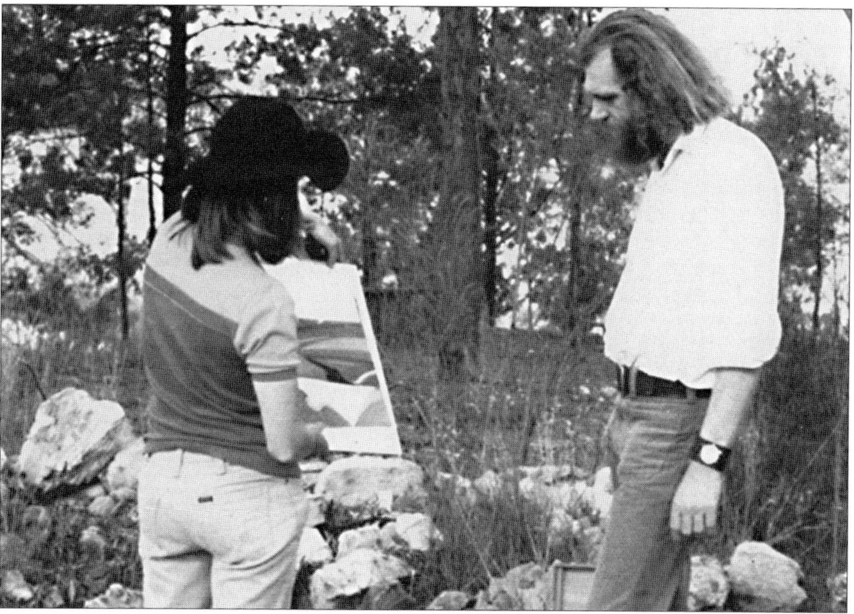

Carol McCormack and Mervyn at Myall Park

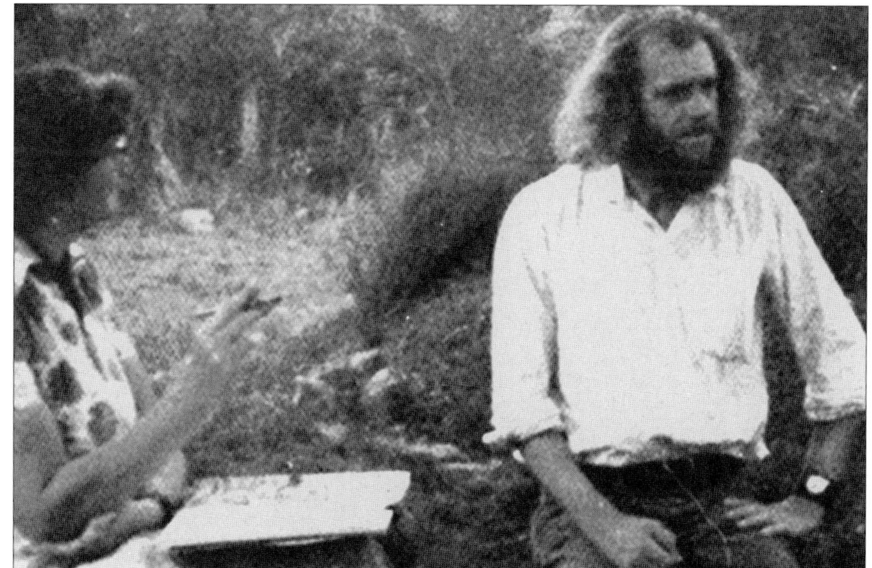

Dorothy Gordon and Mervyn at Myall Park

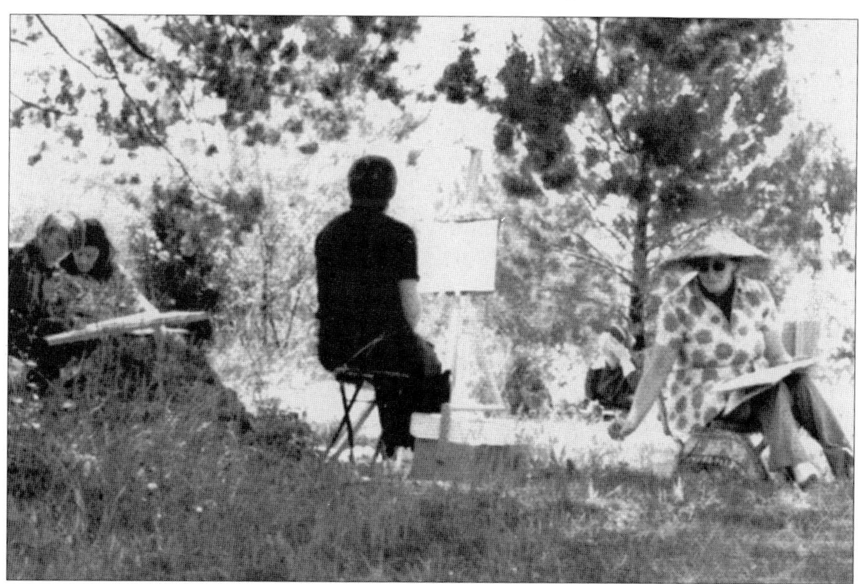

Bob Nason, Joan Schwennesen, Liz Jackson and Dorothy Gordon at Myall Park

## Workshops in the early 1980s **Photos courtesy Beverley Budgen**

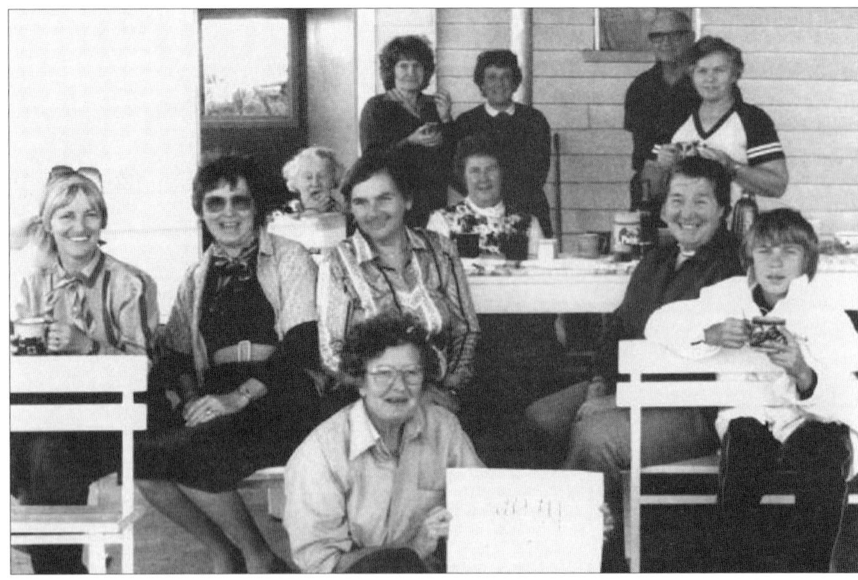

Blackall 1983: Betty Turner holding card. Next row: Jan Gall, Jan Parkinson, Corrie Muir, Joy Arden, Greg is the boy holding a cup. Behind Joy is Rose Dudley, Scott McLymont and Sylvia Wheeler standing at the end

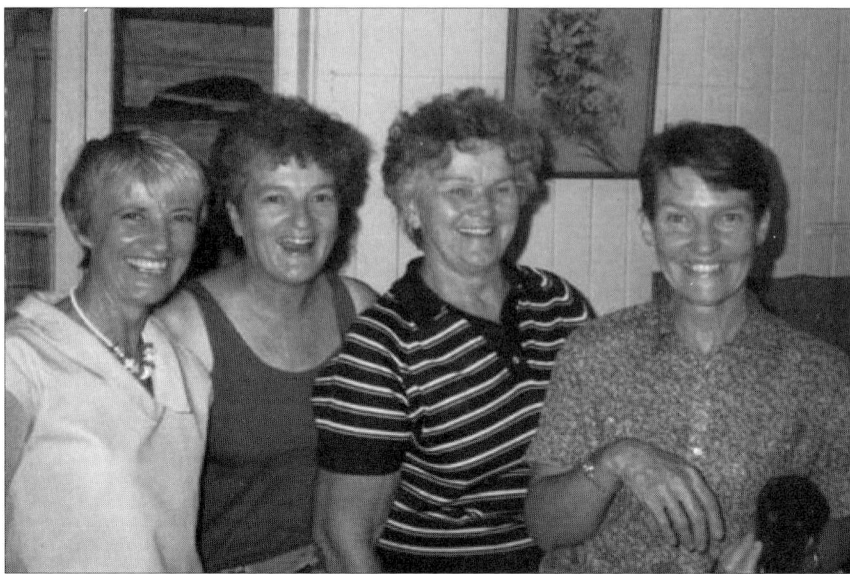

At a Blackall workshop in 1985. Jan Gall, Beverley Budgen, Rose Dudley, and Lyn Fraser of Barcaldine is at the far right

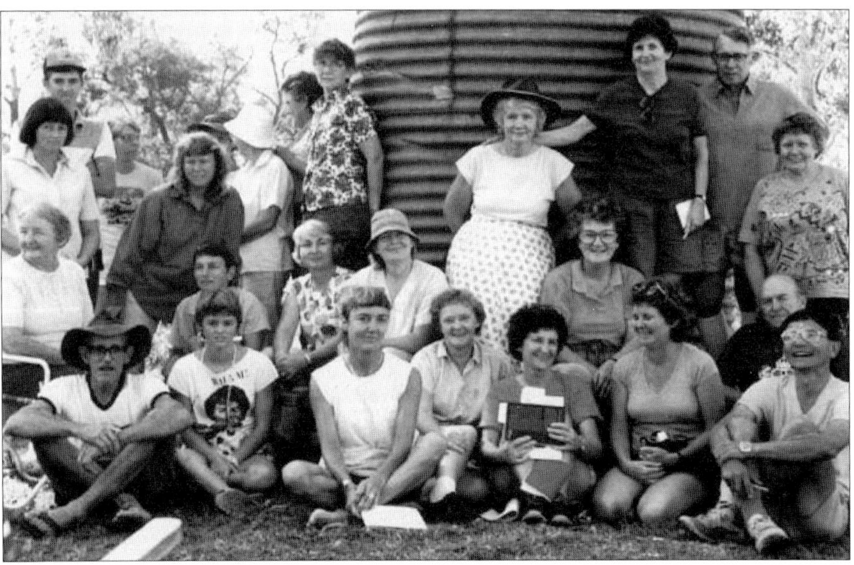

At a workshop in Central Queensland

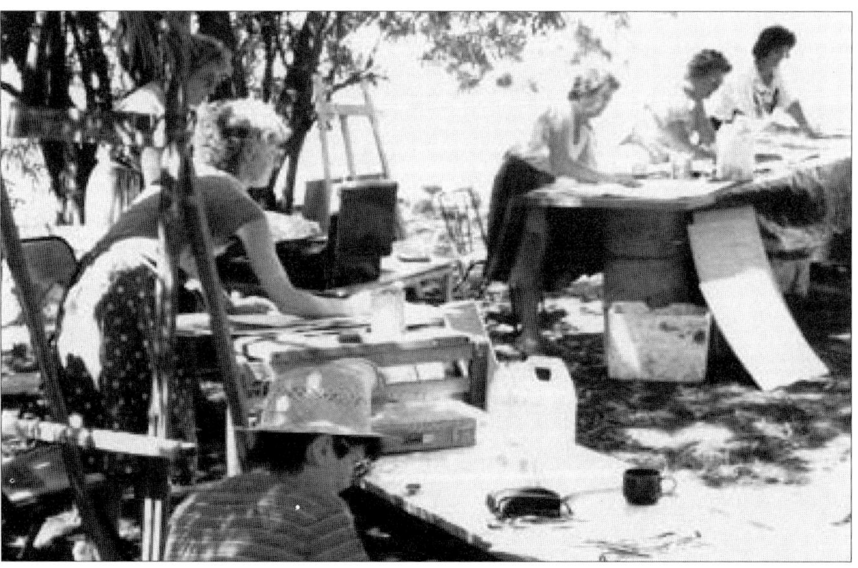

At a workshop on Jo Forster's property Trivaltore

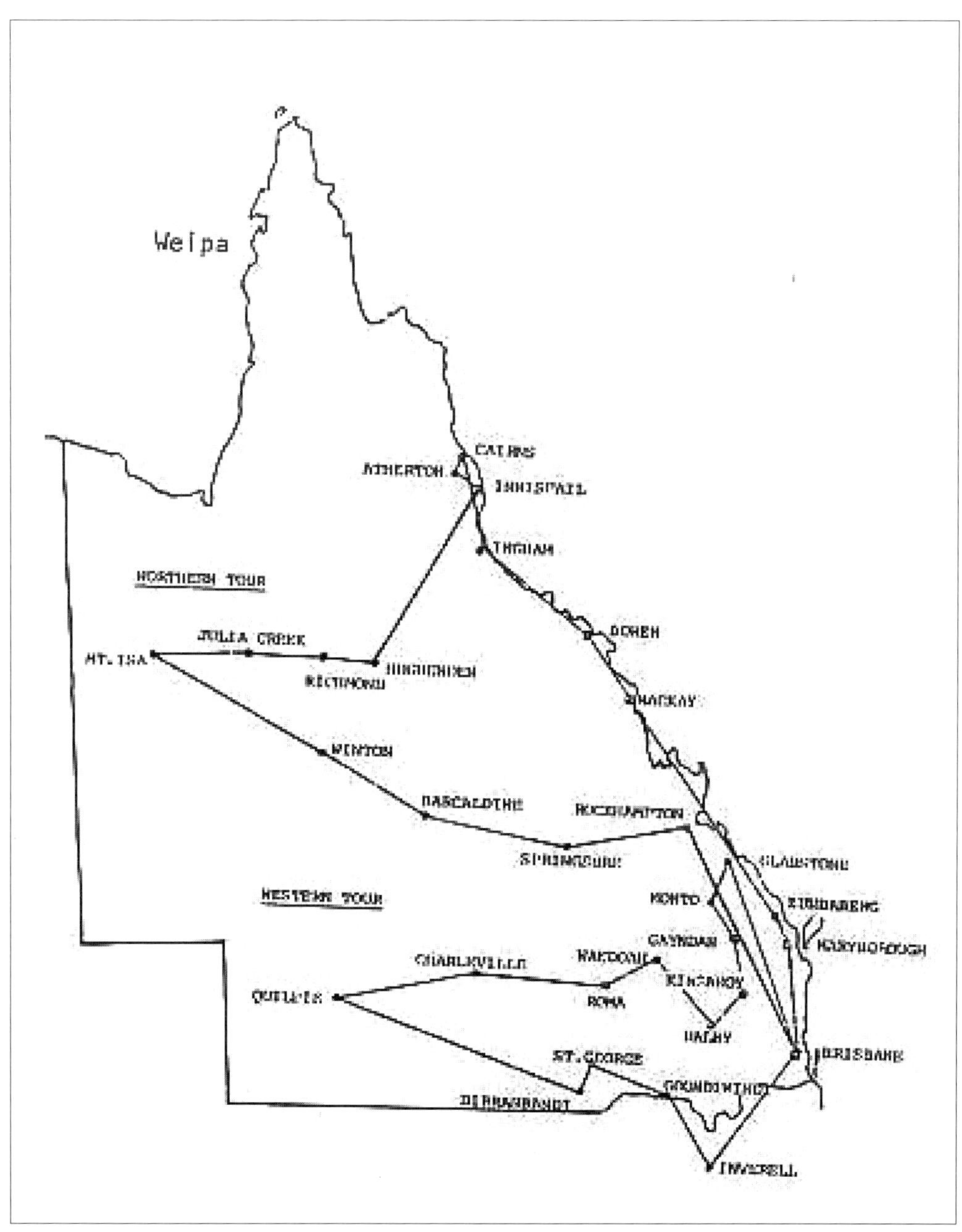


# Flying Arts at Kelvin Grove

## 1978 – 1990

The map shows the early Kelvin Grove Flight paths

# 1978-1990 The Kelvin Grove years

When Flying Arts moved to Kelvin Grove it was moulded into an efficient distance education school through the management committee set up by Jeff Shaw. While remaining autonomous it reaped the benefits of trained management from the college, and drew on the resources of its host to gain maximum advantages from government funding. The years at Kelvin Grove gave the school stability through the efficiency of its government trained bureaucracy and Flying Arts benefited from having an association with other government institutions.

Jeff Shaw's first act as Head of the Arts at KGCAE, was to appoint a new Flying Arts management committee of which he was president. He retained that office until 1990 when the school was transferred to the University College of Southern Queensland.

Under the control of the committee largely recruited from the college, the school at KGCAE began trialing more craft workshops. The difference between 'Art' taught by Mervyn Moriarty and 'Craft' as preferred by Jeff Shaw is explained in *Techniques of Modern Artists* as: 'The difference between the artist and the artisan is the difference between the everyday world and that of the intellect and the senses – we expect the artist, whose aims are more ambitious and complicated, to be more experimental in terms of technique.'

When Mervyn left Flying Arts in 1982 the romance of a pioneering adventure went with him; however, in the twelve years since he opened the school, it had expanded into every corner of regional Queensland and was now an essential part of too many lives to be lost.

The years at Kelvin Grove reinforced the success of Mervyn's original creative art classes when, at the end of the 1980s they remained popular while, following a drop in demand, a number of pottery workshops were discontinued.

A brief look at the history of The Kelvin Grove College of Advanced Education shows that it began its life at Kelvin Grove in 1942 when it was transferred from George Street to its present site. At Kelvin Grove, along with drama, music and physical education, art was part of the curriculum for training Queensland primary school teachers.

By the mid 1970s, although it was still seen as a highly conservative institution, the college had also been training high school teachers for a number of years. However, there is no record of the art department making any changes to its curriculum until 1976 following the arrival of Dr. Peter Botsman as its new principal.

Botsman began to initiate a number of changes. One of these was the appointment of artists as teachers in the Arts Department. He wanted to promote community training in the arts and no longer would the art department be purely for teacher training.

An Associate Diploma geared for personal development was introduced using professional artists who were not 'teacher-trained' to foster creativity in art students. Course content was constantly revised and Botsman encouraged college personnel to expand their contact with the wider community. The college began conducting country workshops and in-service seminars for Queensland teachers.

For four years Jeff Shaw also served on the Craft Board of the Australia Council. He was an astute and ambitious administrator who preferred skills and technique to creativity. His credo was: 'It is good to have expression – but not if it is at the expense of techniques and materials.'

Although he set out to build up craft as an important part of the Flying Arts curriculum, the creative art classes conducted by Mervyn and Bela were retained, and continued to draw large numbers. When Bela left the school the following year he was sorely missed by his students. Rita Kershaw from Rockhampton expressed the regret when she wrote: 'He and Mervyn were opposites with the same feeling for art and we loved both of them, some used to say there were Bela centres and Mervyn centres.'

As president of the management committee, Jeff Shaw's immediate priority was the appointment of experienced personnel as administrators. The first was Bruce Scriven, Head of the Department of In-service and

Continuing Education at KGCAE. Scriven had considerable experience in the provision of distance education and his knowledge was invaluable for the successful operation of country services.

Representatives from major arts and education groups based in Brisbane were invited to participate in the operation of the school, either as members of the committee or as consultants.

By mid 1978 Jeff Shaw's team of consultants included Dr. Peter Botsman (who was also Chairman of the Community Arts Board of the Australia Council); and representatives from the Department of Cultural Activities, the Department of Education, and the Queensland Potters' Association. Key people from community groups, political groups, education agencies and the student body were also invited to contribute to the development of the school.

David Spann from KGCAE was executive secretary, setting up the office and systems needed for day to day operations. Although the founder of the school, Mervyn Moriarty, went to the first meeting as a consultant, he was not given a place on the committee, the Constitution drawn up by Shaw excluded paid tutors. He was retained only as a pilot and art teacher.

Shaw's management committee in Brisbane was impressive, with people from the College of Art at Seven Hills, Queensland Arts Council, the Central Western Queensland Cultural Activities Association at Blackall, the Queensland Day Committee, and the Education Department as members. KGCAE supplied the president, vice-president, and secretary/treasurer. College lecturers in music and art were also on the committee (not being employed by Flying Arts the Constitution did not exclude them). By 1981 the new Executive Secretary, Mrs. Beryl Angus, had an assistant to help with the day-to-day administration of the school.

Through its committee, the school received assistance from all major art education agencies in Brisbane, and it resulted in growth in funding and services at a time when many arts organizations throughout Australia suffered from funding cuts.

With the management committee in place, the school planned to produce four newsletters a year. The first *Gazette* was published in August 1979, the second in December 1979, and Flying Arts began a drive for increased membership.

A competition was set up among students to design a new logo with a prize of $50 for the winner. An annual membership fee of $5 gave members voting rights at Annual or General Meetings, with each group membership carrying an entitlement to three votes.

Tour itineraries were woven around public holidays, local festivals, show days, school holidays, local art competitions and harvest dates, any of which could significantly lower the possible attendance in each centre. For the school to 'pay its way', two-day seminars required a regular attendance of fourteen pupils.

During the years at Kelvin Grove the annual exhibition of student work was held on campus – it became the highlight of those years.

To increase pottery and craft workshops Shaw turned to the Craft Association for assistance. He planned new workshops in ceramics, spinning and weaving, batik and other crafts.

From 1978 pottery workshops were a major part of the school curriculum and Kevin Grealy – Principal Lecturer in ceramics; Rob Hinwood and Rex Coleman (all from KGCAE) were its first tutors.

Kevin Grealy's initial training had been with the Central Technical College, but he had attended Molvig's creative art classes before working and studying in Canada. When he became a tutor with Flying Arts he wrote a three-year pottery course as an adjunct to Mervyn's painting manuals.

In the following years he flew extensively throughout Queensland to conduct pottery workshops alongside Mervyn's painting workshops. They were both charismatic teachers and their joint classes were always well attended.

Through their close association, Kevin developed a strong rapport with the school's founder. When Mervyn left the school at the end of 1982 Kevin, believing that his touring partner had been treated badly, tendered his resignation.

### Pottery classes in country towns

The new pottery workshops were welcomed by a number of towns including the Gladstone Area Potters' Group which had been formed in March 1973. It managed 'The Potters Place,' a community craft centre opposite the Gladstone State High School.

In an article on its achievements, the *Gladstone Observer* noted that Gladstone 'had a cultural asset which other centres may well envy and the cost to the community has been comparatively minor because of the dedication, determination and sheer hard work of a small group of people.'

When Mervyn brought Flying Arts to Gladstone in 1976 the first professional potter who came to teach was Ivan Englund. Englund, head teacher of Art at the Meadowbank National Art School and Technical College, was a highly qualified teacher who had taught in Canberra, Melbourne and Wollongong. He was followed by Jean Jacques Vaschalde. However, in her 1977 annual report the retiring president of the Gladstone Potters expressed her dissatisfaction with Flying Arts through cancelled workshops. She hoped 'for better liaison and co-ordination with the school in future.'

Her hopes were realised after the school transferred to Kelvin Grove. In 1978 Kevin Grealy supervised his first Gladstone workshop. Mary Norris, a leading Gladstone potter, supplied a description of those early workshops: 'There was nowhere here to buy anything for pottery until we set up our own shop. When Kevin came there was always hilarity in the group and there would be a function at night when he would play his guitar and sing. He always stayed with one of the student families. We did our first salt firing with Kevin with a funny little antiquated kiln. We now have a really large one which we fire with diesel and wood.'

A second pottery workshop at Gladstone in that year was conducted by Rob Hinwood. The Gladstone Potters wrote to express their satisfaction with the new start at Kelvin Grove and were looking forward to a further workshop in August.

The Flying Arts Gladstone pottery workshops remained popular over the next two years and Ian Currie's workshop was featured in the *Gladstone Observer* where 'local potters were working hard for their *Easter Festival of Pots* to be set up on the waterfront.' In July 1980 the newspaper photographed Rex Coleman giving some helpful tips to the group. At the same time the *Bundaberg News Mail* carried a photograph of Rob Hinwood teaching the Bundaberg Pottery Club.

Mackay was another town to welcome the Flying Arts potters and Peg Horsnell from Mackay Pottery (which began in 1975) wrote that they needed the continuing assistance provided by Flying Arts. When Rex Coleman came with Mervyn in 1976 his visit drew a large attendance. Many of the students attending the Mackay workshops drove in from surrounding towns: Marian, Gargett, Netherdale, Finch Hatton and the mining town of Dysart approximately 200 kms away.

Maryborough Potters also wrote of the success of their first workshop held by Kevin Grealy in 1978 at the Maryborough TAFE College.

Kevin set up another first with a three-day workshop for the Weipa Potters. It was attended by twenty enthusiasts who used the local red clay to decorate their pots.

St. George, Monto and Cairns were other pottery groups that wrote of their appreciation of Flying Arts. When St. George organised an Exhibition in the Balonne Creative Arts Group's room, it was an outstanding success with all pots being sold.

Monto Potters now had a membership of twenty. Their group began in 1976 with only six members; Flying Arts played a major part in the group's development, and members praised the training they received through the school.

Cairns Pottery also wrote thanking the school for recent workshops held in Cairns.

Favourable comments from so many towns showed a similar enthusiasm for Flying Arts' pottery classes as Mervyn's creative painting workshops in the early 1970s; a significant number of country women were attending the pottery workshops for social interaction and support from others with similar interests.

Mary Norris spoke of the disappointment when the Flying Arts workshops to coastal towns were discontinued in 1982: 'When Flying Arts pottery

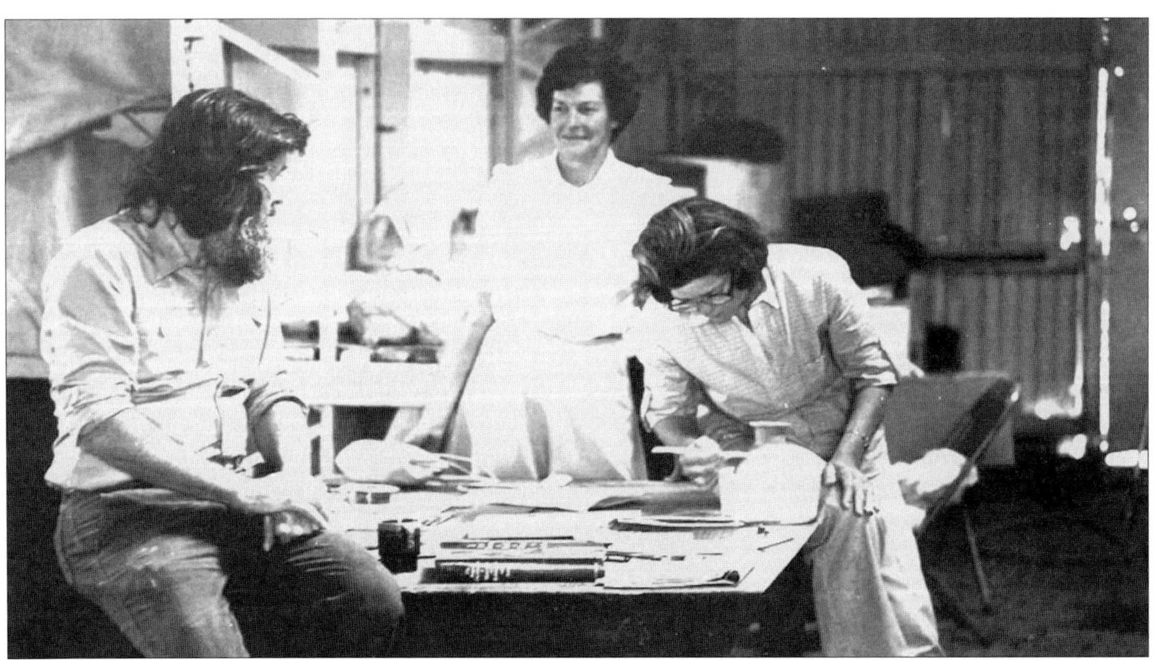

Kevin Grealy taking a Pottery class Courtesy Flying Arts archives

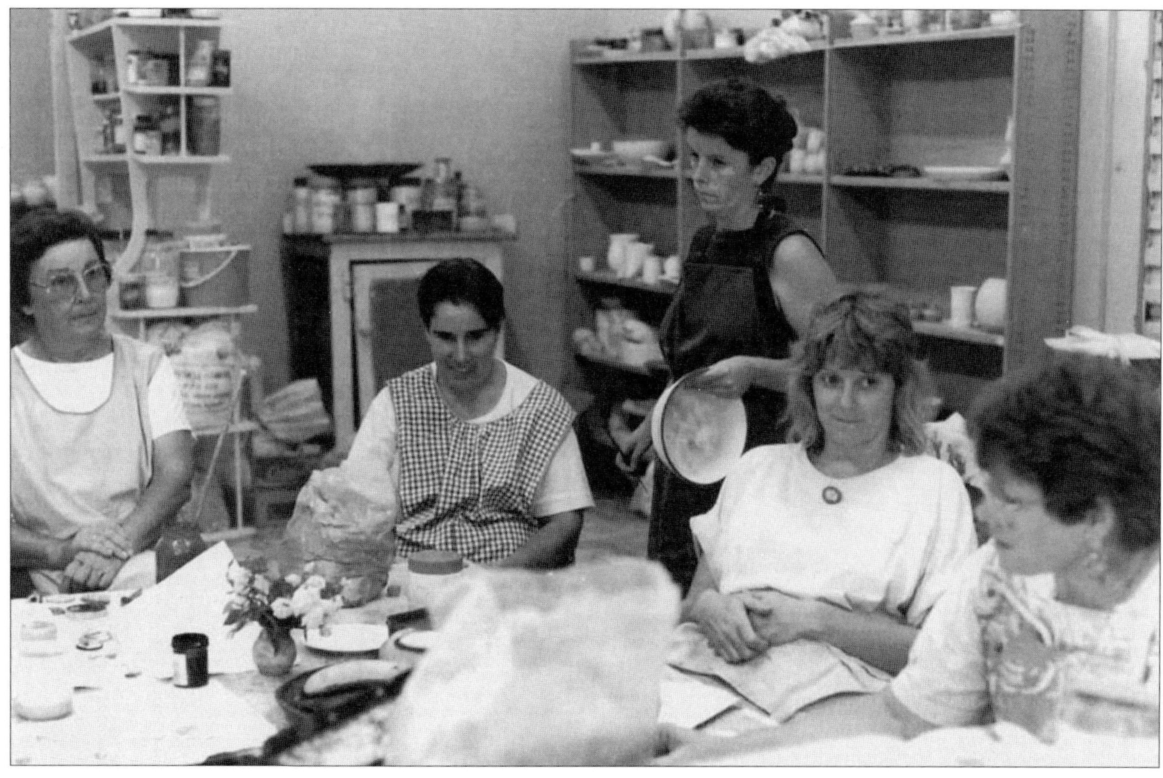

A pottery group working at Longreach Photo courtesy Flying Arts archives

tutors stopped coming to Gladstone, and Gladstone Pottery came under the auspices of the Rockhampton TAFE College, we sorely missed our Flying Arts tutors.'

Other craft workshops tried by Kelvin Grove were fabric printing and dyeing workshops planned for a Central Western Textiles Tour.

The first of these was held in 1979, when Jim Aitkenhead from KGCAE organised a tour to Muttaburra, Longreach, Blackall and Augathella, using the Kelvin Grove College mini bus to take two College staff, an Art Department Lecturer, and the Departmental Assistant (who acted as driver and administrator).

Seven students from the Diploma of Teaching Secondary Art, and Associate Diploma in Visual Arts Courses also accompanied the tour. They covered 3,600 kms. The fees of $525 were paid by the Central Western Division of the Country Women's Association.

A total of eighty-five students attended the second Textiles Tour workshops in 1980 at Augathella, Blackall, Longreach and Muttaburra; again it was led by Jim Aitkenhead who brought a group of Art Major and Associate Diploma students from Kelvin Grove.

A third Textiles Tour was held the following year with forty students, a significant drop from 85, attending workshops in basic screen and block printing and creative embroidery at Augathella, Charleville, Longreach, Muttaburra and Blackall.

In 1980 Flying Arts also tried a Theatre-in-Education tour which tutored schools at Morven, Quilpie, Jundah and Windorah when Greg Rudd, KGCAE lecturer, and eleven drama students provided the children with an opportunity for involvement in drama activities.

The following year a more advanced Theatre-in-Education class, once again co-ordinated by Greg Rudd, went to Cunnamulla State High School, Dirranbandi State School, Surat State School, Mitchell State High School and Injune State School.

Alan Place, a lecturer in graphics at KGCAE and his wife, Rosetta, a professional photographer, conducted photographic silk-screen printing workshops at Longreach and Blackall.

The Flying Arts Management Committee tried to create further interest by having the Crafts Council Resource Centre supply Craft Resource Kits for people living in remote areas. Each kit contained information on ceramics, jewellery, spinning, weaving, machine embroidery, fibre, fabric printing, glass, wood, leather and metalwork.

However, despite the efforts to expand craft workshops, only painting and pottery generated enough interest to remain viable. There is no record that any of the other early craft workshops were continued.

During these trials creative painting remained popular and two-day seminars in advanced painting techniques were held in Cairns, Mackay, Rockhampton and Roma. Guest artist Ian Smith was the tutor and his workshops attracted seventy-six people – twenty-one from Rockhampton.

Smith spoke to the Rockhampton group extolling the benefits that only Flying Arts could supply: 'Budding artists often face a lack of information about new ideas in creativity and styles and the advantage of the Flying Arts is that its members can get together to exchange views and co-operate much more fully.'

In September 1980 Jeff Shaw was a speaker at the National Conference for 'Teaching Crafts in Geographically Isolated Areas' held in Canberra and once again the work of Flying Arts was brought to the attention of the rest of Australia.

Prior to the conference, at Shaw's request, Tim Moorhead, Education Officer for the Crafts Council of Australia, flew with Mervyn and Rex Coleman to assess the work of the school. His report on the activities of Flying Arts was highly favourable: 'Both Merv and Rex are to be congratulated. Your program, in addition to those painting and pottery groups, helps to promote a different kind of education which I like to refer to as 'consumer' education. When talking about consumers we must keep in mind that this does not pertain merely to purchasers. 'Things' are consumed in many ways and it takes a greater number of consumers to support relatively few producers. The special workshop sessions, lectures, demonstrations, exhibitions, etc. all feed these consumers. Your structured courses also help raise the standard and the Australian Flying Arts School is to be congratulated for its efforts.'

By now Flying Arts was becoming recognised as a major supplier of quality art education in regional Queensland and Mrs. Len Davenport, the Queensland Arts Council representative on the AFAS committee, arranged for Flying Arts' tutors Kev Grealy and Roy Oorloff to join Arts Council artists Warren Langley and Barbara Huxham in conducting 'The Seaforth Experiment'.

It was an experiment where thirty-six Australian painters and potters lived and worked for a week at a National Fitness Camp within sight of the Great Barrier Reef. In a delightful setting, the camp showcased the quality of art teaching available in Queensland.

In 1981, once again Flying Arts expanded into New South Wales after a grant was secured by the management committee from the New South Wales Arts Council for Flying Arts to extend its services to the north-western area of the state. The NSW grant was accompanied by an increase in funding levels from the Queensland Department of Cultural Activities.

The school was growing and, by the beginning of 1982, it was operating on a budget of $123,594 to serve 1600 students over a distance of 12,500 kms. Self-generated income through student fees and other sources accounted for almost 40% of the total annual budget.

Although the figures were impressive, Flying Arts had been conducting workshops for ten years, and growth in student numbers in Queensland was beginning to slow as older centres dropped out.

Numbers in some pottery groups remained high, but Gladstone, despite its enthusiasm for Flying Arts tutors, had been taken over by Rockhampton TAFE.

However the ever-popular creative art classes remained loyal to Flying Arts. Working with creative artists kept students returning to workshops long after completing their course and advanced painting students were re-enrolling for the stimulation of working with professional artists from Brisbane.

**Accreditation - an insurmountable hurdle**

Bureaucratic efficiency at Kelvin Grove could not solve every problem. Following a query by Biloela student, Beverley Johnstone, the management committee investigated her proposal for the provision of an academically recognised course, possibly with a diploma, to enable her to move away from 'hobby status' and gain recognition as a qualified artist.

In response, a certificate was designed with an embossed seal of the school. It was numbered and signed by a Flying Arts officer with the student's name, subject, and years of study, with the information being recorded in a bound register. Flying Arts Certificate No. 0001 was issued to Phyllis Roberts of Charleville - a foundation member of Mervyn's original school still attending his creative art classes.

The certificates were popular with some students and during the year a total of twenty-four people requested and received their certificates. However, because they were not woven around an accredited course they were not what Johnstone wanted – they were not recognised by other art institutions or the art industry.

Flying Arts classes were fun, they supplied quality art education in strange places, from local showgrounds to a club hall, an old picture theatre or a disused shearers' quarters, but without recognised accreditation, they could not give students a professional standing. Training people to be mentally active through creative activities remained Flying Arts' strength.

As late as 1988, Jeff Shaw complained about the lack of accreditation: 'It has been a matter of continuing concern to members of the School that the high levels of achievement and study evidenced by many AFAS students cannot yet be recognised by an accredited award. Such awards as are available to city students can facilitate employment and also provide the key to further and more advanced studies and qualifications. It is imperative that external awards should be available to our isolated students, whether in Cape York or Burringbar West, but so far, despite an apparent sympathy, educational sectors and institutions have found themselves unable to provide this much needed service.'

In a bid to know whether it was the lack of accreditation behind the drop in student numbers, Flying Arts conducted a survey to find reasons for the decline. Results showed that enthusiasm was still there, but with people travelling long distances, students wanted a return to a two-day seminar.

In its efforts to stay within budget, Kelvin Grove often supplied only one-day seminars, and the evening talks Mervyn had conducted were no longer taking place.

Students also wanted continuity with one tutor and visits by guest tutors whenever possible. They wanted a return to the type of workshops Mervyn and Bela had given them in the 1970s.

Josephine McTaggart from Innisfail described the dissatisfaction: 'From the students' point of view, I can't stress it strongly enough that a tutor for the whole year (after all it's only 4 or 8 days a year) far outweighs the continual chopping and changing that goes on. A yearly based tuition would be very beneficial to the students; progress will be made so much faster by the students because they can expect the same one back and therefore do the homework; a good teacher/student relationship builds up the confidence in their own ability of those more shaky students – the whole work program will be one of consistency. One has to remember that out here in the country, the majority of students get nothing whatever other than the Flying Arts School, so what chance have they got with four different teachers in a year, telling them four different things.'

### Cooee Bay

The Cooee Bay Art Camp was an outcome of student desire for extended workshops with one tutor. When the Rockhampton group decided to extend its art activities into a 10-day camp Flying Arts was asked to assist. When its Kelvin Grove management declined Bela Ivanyi helped them set up an annual ten-day workshop in creative art. It was open to all, both Flying Arts students and other artists.

In an effort to include students throughout Queensland, the first workshop was held at Tinaroo in northern Queensland and thirty-six Flying Arts students attended. As people from southern Queensland thought Tinaroo too far, the next year they tried Toowoomba, but it was not popular with north Queensland students. Cooee Bay, near Yeppoon, was the next choice and this time, it suited all. The response from students was high, and over the years the Cooee Bay creative art workshops remained popular. In 1982 the group sold all its work at an exhibition held in the foyer of Her Majesty's Theatre in Brisbane.

Bela praised the work achieved at the art camp. He described how the best artists in Australia came to teach the forty or fifty students who came from Cairns, Cooktown, Mackay, Mt. Isa, Rockhampton, Toowoomba, Goondiwindi and Brisbane. A number of guest artists, including Colin Lanceley and Kevin Connor, came from Sydney. Cooee Bay never needed to advertise, 'word-of-mouth' always kept numbers up.

### Correspondence Courses

In an effort to increase its student intake, an entirely new programme of correspondence courses was initiated by the AFAS management committee. A survey was conducted by Flying Arts which found that popular correspondence courses were sculpture, printmaking/graphics and 'fabrics and fibres' (screenprinting, batik, spinning and weaving.); there was also an interest in art history and design.

The new courses began with Ian Currie from KGCAE writing a ceramics course in stoneware glazes for tutor Betty Crombie.

Allin Dwyer supervised a beginners course in Sculpture I; Screen Printing I was set up and supervised by Don Braben, a lecturer in art at Mt. Gravatt CAE, who had taught in Britain, Canada, Zambia and Nigeria; pottery was supervised by Ian Currie from KGCAE; the batik supervisor was Thel Merry who had trained at the East Sydney Technical College. Funding came through special grants from the Crafts Board.

Initially the courses were successful, winning recognition and acclaim throughout Australia among other groups and in specialist publications. It cost $95 to complete a course and by 1984 there were 88 students taking five correspondence courses with the school.

Following a grant from the Utah Foundation of $3375 for the development of a further correspondence course to begin in mid 1984, and as Mervyn's books were no longer being used, Flying Arts tutor Pat Hoffie developed a course in 'Painting and Drawing'.

### Other avenues were explored

In an effort to defray costs the school looked for sponsors – sponsorship could take the form of a guest tutor programme; a catalogue of the school's audio-visual resource material; or assistance in purchasing a car or even an aircraft. In return, Flying Arts offered sponsors a vast publicity network reaching students, not only in Queensland and New South Wales, but also those from Western Australia,

Northern Territory, Victoria, New Zealand and New Guinea, who were enrolling into the new correspondence courses being set up at Kevin Grove.

Despite the efforts of the management committee, sponsorship was slow in coming. It would be several years before Flying Arts gained a major sponsor.

Flying Arts also looked at aboriginal communities. Using a grant from the Aboriginal Arts & Craft Board, Jeff Shaw and aboriginal artist Ron Hurley tutored at a nine-day exploratory tour which flew to Weipa and three aboriginal communities on Cape York – Aurukun, Edward River and Kowanyama. It was hoped the school could develop regular workshops in crafts for the people of Cape York.

The tours created interest, and depending on funding, future workshops were planned. Unfortunately the necessary funds never eventuated.

From the evidence, it can be seen that Jeff Shaw tried hard to promote a number of craft workshops in conjunction with the creative art classes initiated by Mervyn, using experienced teachers from his own and other colleges as tutors; however, results show that, although other courses were tried, only the Flying Arts core workshops in creative art, pottery and the new correspondence courses had the numbers to proceed.

### Guest Tutors

KGCAE was in a position to supply guest tutors and this proved to be a popular move. In 1982, Brisbane hosted the Commonwealth Games and celebrations in conjunction with the Games made it a festival year for the city. Among overseas visitors coming to Brisbane for the Games was a number of experienced craftworkers.

In keeping with its brief to give its students the best possible tuition, Flying Arts employed some of these visitors as guest tutors. Dot Callender, a visiting weaver from Edinburgh with the Victorian Tapestry workshop, accompanied Roy Churcher on the northern tour (Roy Churcher replaced Bela Ivanyi when he left in 1979, however he was not a pilot and the school had to pay for a pilot to ferry artists to northern Queensland).

Alison Whiteford, a freelance drama teacher from Scotland, also flew with Roy Churcher to work with special schools from Cairns to Bowen; Evelyn Roth, a Canadian fibre artist, and English trained Australian potter Gwynn Piggott, also toured – she was a new potter-in-residence on the Kelvin Grove campus with an outstanding record, being represented in galleries and museums in the UK, France, Holland, Canada, Japan and the USA.

Wilma Hollist, spinner, weaver and dyer from the UK, was sponsored by the Craft Council of Queensland to accompany Mervyn on what would be his last south-western tour.

With guest tutors, student numbers increased. In that year Flying Arts visited thirty-six painting centres and thirty pottery centres throughout Queensland. By December, there were 2092 students on the school mailing list; of these 1253 were financial. New (and returning) centres opened at Mareeba, Baralaba, Chinchilla, Mitchell, Glenmorgan, Moree, Tweed Heads, Walgett, Tenterfield, Emerald and Rolleston, with most centres conducting both painting and pottery classes.

The Committee noted that 1982 was a year of quiet but hard-earned growth with surplus funds.

### Women become tutors with Flying Arts

When Mervyn left the school following his confrontation with the Flying Arts management committee Flying Arts had already employed its first female tutor, Pat Hoffie, who toured with the school while still teaching at the Brisbane College of Art.

Hoffie praised her country students when exhibiting her own work at Galerie Baguette in Ascot. She told her interviewer of the essential service supplied by Flying Arts: 'The network of women artists out there who are doing good work is incredible, they are not painting because they think it is fashionable: they are doing it because it comes from a real need. The artwork as a result often ends up being very strong. . . . They have a lot of dedication to the life they lead in the country, and that comes into their painting.'

By 1984 women predominated in Flying Arts, not only as students, but also as tutors. Pottery tutor Lyndal Moor was another early tutor to tour. Her work was featured in *Women's Day* in 1988 after the Queensland Art Gallery bought a number of her pieces. When interviewed by *Women's Day*, she also spoke of the important service the school provided: 'There is a definite need for the school in a place like Queensland. The distances are so great and all the main cities are on the coast. It costs far too much for people to have to travel to the main centres. Many people still have to travel hundreds of kilometres from isolated properties to the country towns to consult with artists.'

Although the tutors who followed Mervyn found that working with Flying Arts was stimulating, they also found it extremely demanding. There was a high turnover of tutors during the 1980s. Some have described the problems they encountered. Their anecdotes highlight the dedication of those who flew with the school.

Lyndal Moor described the unique difficulties of tutors when touring in an article for *Craft Australia:* 'As weight has to be kept to a minimum [when flying], the tutors have to be selective about the teaching equipment they take. Most centres can arrange to have video recorders and slide projectors available to show any films or slides the tutors have chosen.

Tutors are selected first of all for their ability as practising artists, secondly as teachers, and finally for their ability to get along with others and to cope with the unexpected. Tours do not always go as smoothly as planned and disasters can occur along the way, including flood and drought, cyclones and aircraft breakdowns. The climate can vary from the extreme heat of summer in Quilpie to the cold winter nights of Glen Innes.'

Lyndal also described problems arising from different stages of student experience: 'Each class has different needs and, within each group, students are at many levels of expertise and enthusiasm, so the tutors have to cope with this during the course of the teaching day. Each day is exhausting and also exhilarating because of the feedback of dedicated students who are determined to make the most of their day with the Flying Arts School.'

However, flying time also had its rewards: 'The flying time in the morning, ranging from 30 minutes to several hours, is a time the tutors, all visually aware, find most inspiring, and many have used the inspiration from these early morning flights in their own artwork.

Similarly, travellers with the Flying Arts School (and there have been many guests over the years) come to realise just how enormous Queensland is and how varied the terrain. The country changes dramatically at different times of the day, and in different seasons and weather conditions.' Lyndal's story highlights Mervyn Moriarty's dedication to teaching during his twelve years with Flying Arts as both pilot and teacher.

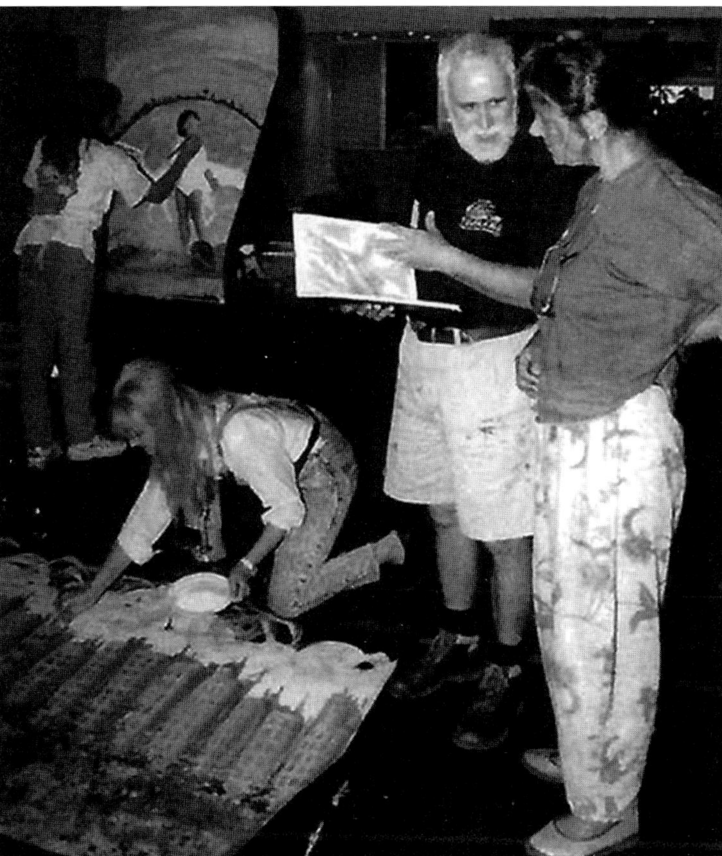

Bonney Bombach with Henry Breikers and students at Hervey Bay
Photo courtesy *The Fraser Coast Chronicle*, Flying Arts *Gazette* July 2001

Beverley Budgen (painting) was another popular early tutor, as was Irene Amos. Following her first country trip in 1985, Irene found the long hours and the constant travelling and teaching was stressful for tutors. A complaint to Kelvin Grove made by some of the tutors read: 'The one area of concern was that an eighteen day work load with twelve days prefaced by early rising to permit periods of flying to arrive at centres and then begin a full day's teaching, allowed for only half day scheduled rest (the first half of that day being spent flying): 'It is inconsiderate to all concerned to program twelve consecutive days without a break for any creative tutor, even understanding the unusual nature of the circumstances prevailing on this occasion.'

Kev Grealy described the disappointments tutors sometimes experienced when flying: 'it's a terrible feeling when you are ten minutes away from a place like Cairns after flying [through the outback] for three weeks and are forced to turn back because of bad weather.'

On northern flights the weather was unpredictable. Mervyn told the story of his plane being diverted from Mackay because bad weather would not allow a small plane to land safely. Traffic controllers had to direct him to Rolleston, west of Rockhampton, where a hole in the high cloud bank would allow him to land.

Flying under these conditions disrupted workshops and must have worried some tutors. Yet, unless it was impossible to fly, tutors always tried to keep to schedules.

However, the difficulties highlight what was possibly the reason for the high turnover of painting and pottery tutors while Flying Arts was at Kelvin Grove. Over 70 touring artists were employed for short periods during the years at Kelvin Grove (more than half of these were women) and although they were enthusiastic, responding generously to the needs of their students, many stayed for only one or two tours. Others stayed for one to two years, some

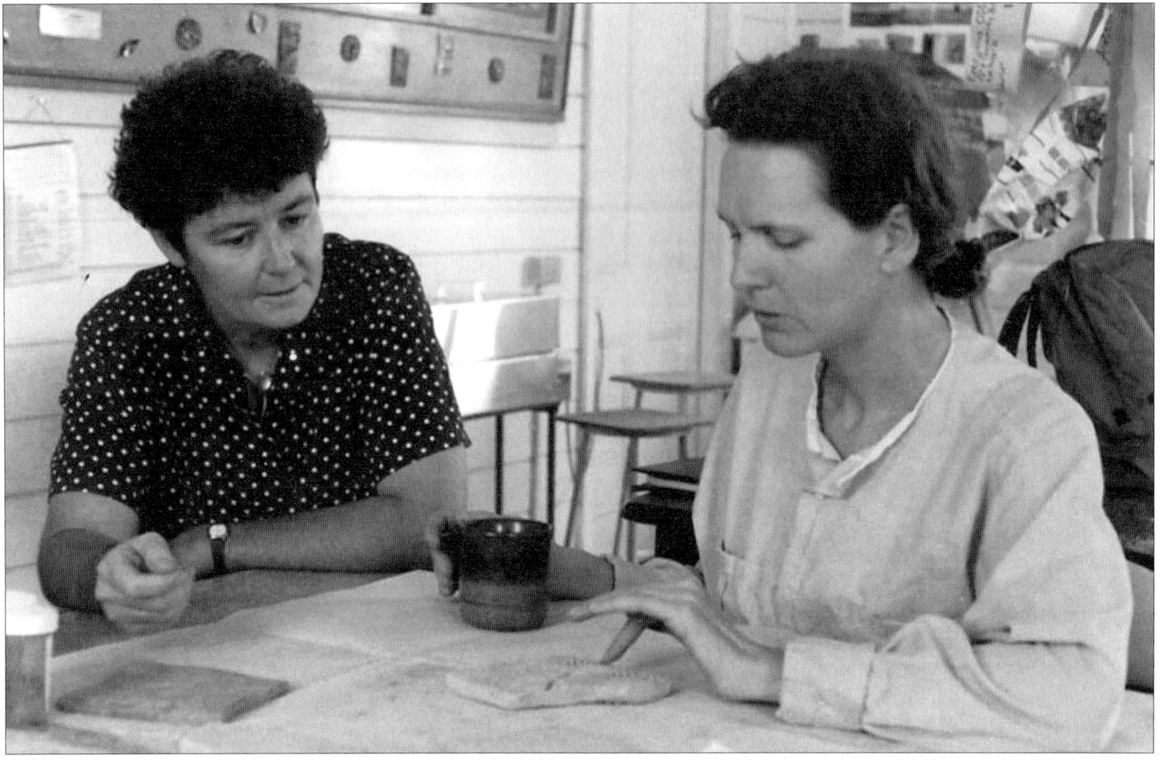

Edith-Ann Murray explaining finer points to Kate Cullity at Barcaldine Pottery Courtesy Flying Arts archives

for three. Only two tutors travelled longer with the school – its founder Mervyn Moriarty, who was with the school for twelve years, and Roy Churcher, who stayed for five.

Roy Churcher is an outstanding example of the dedication of tutors. Although he was living in Melbourne, he continually flew to Brisbane to travel with Flying Arts because he believed in what the school was doing.

In an interview for the Melbourne *Age*, he stated that the people he taught were mainly women involved with the land – nurses, teachers and librarians. He said that one of the aims of the school was to provide as much current information as possible, but he also emphasized other needs: 'A lot of the people in the bush have never seen what we'd call a decent picture. We're trying to build up quality judgement about painting generally and about their own painting. The real crunch out there is what happens when you look at a gum tree. Their conscious life is spent in a natural environment and it's the one they undervalue most. I'm teaching them the qualities of the place where they actually are.'

### Demand Workshops

Following the loss of Mervyn Moriarty in 1983, Kelvin Grove management altered its format and a decision was made to concentrate on the remote and isolated centres of Queensland and Northern New South Wales.

As a measure of austerity, the coastal tours were dropped. Without consulting students, the new tour itineraries for 1983 announced that all tours to coastal towns would cease, the school would only serve western towns. Despite their large classes, Maryborough, Bundaberg, Gladstone, Rockhampton, Mackay, Bowen, Ingham, Innisfail and Cairns would no longer receive visits from Flying Arts.

Instead of regular tours, coastal centres were asked to book a year's programme of four workshops with one tutor for a set price. Workshops were to be for higher level students only and centres could set their own student charges. The new workshops would be self-supporting on demand to complement local TAFE classes. Any groups that wanted to supplement a tour programme at beginner level could also apply for 'demand' workshops.

TAFE was now well established in coastal towns and it was possible that a decision was made by the Education Department for TAFE to supply elementary art education in regional Queensland. However, the response from Flying Arts students was forthright. Rene Macdonald (representative for Bowen Painting Group) wrote of her group's dissatisfaction with 'demand' workshops. She stated that their town was not large enough to pay for the expense of bringing in a tutor four times a year. Other towns expressed the same opinion and the demand workshops were not a success.

In the first year only three demand workshops were requested: Gwynn Piggott gave a seminar to Mackay Potters; Betty Grulke a seminar at

Longreach Spinners and Weavers; and Roy Oorloff took a painting class at Rockhampton. Due to the poor response to demand workshops, in 1984 the committee reinstated the Flying Arts coastal tours.

With a continuing reluctance by centres to apply for demand workshops, Flying Arts made it clear that these workshops were not instead of existing painting or pottery tours, but complemented them. Special workshops were available for groups wanting to further their knowledge in screen printing, photography, paper making, sculpture, stained glass, oil painting, water colour, pottery, weaving and/or spinning, leathercraft, drawing and sketching, and batik. Under these conditions, demand workshops were accepted by students.

Beth Tully from Quilpie described her first demand workshop, writing that artists from Blackall, Yaraka and Quilpie banded together for a five-day watercolour school at the Clarendon Woolshed near Blackall.

Fourteen students lived in shearers' quarters at Clarendon to paint subjects around the property and along the Barcoo River. They worked a 12 hour day, starting at 8 a.m. with tutor Allin Dwyer, and finishing at 8 p.m: 'With Joy Wehl, Char Speedy and Judith Kent we left Quilpie in a four-wheel drive packed to the roof with bedding and painting gear.

The shortest route to Blackall was 316 kms. through Adavale, and despite the bulldust and much dodging of kangaroos, we arrived at Clarendon shed to a warm welcome with much laughter and talk. Most days we went in cars to different spots to sketch and paint, but the 'studio' in the shearing shed produced many varied paintings on site.'

## Memphis in May

Despite the cutback of workshops, KGCAE management assisted students in other ways. With members of a number of government institutions on its committee, in 1984 the Flying Arts Exhibition *For the Love of it* was taken by Mrs. Len Davenport, Queensland Arts Council committee member, to the United States as part of the 1985 'Memphis in May' Festival in Tennessee. It brought international publicity and prestige to the school when all paintings were sold. As Executive Officer, Catherine Hand reported: 'Neither the Flying Arts School nor the Arts Council were prepared for the reception these works received.

'Not only were all the works sold within days of being exhibited but most were sold before they arrived when slides of the exhibition were viewed by the exhibition organisers. Naturally, this was the most tremendous compliment to our students, who rarely have the opportunity of exhibiting their work.'

The American viewers responded warmly. As one American critic wrote 'an intimate and sensitive portrayal of their land and culture . . . offering an enjoyable and quick trip to the Australian outback through the eyes of those who truly know and love it.'

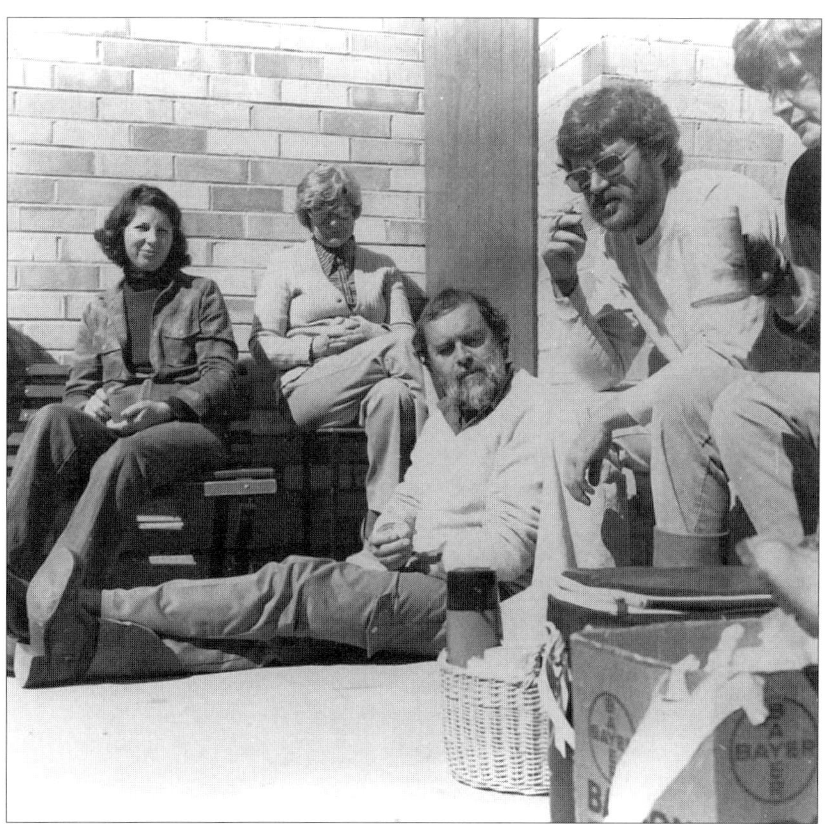


Roy Churcher (second from right) talking to students

Photo courtesy Flying Arts archives

The American organiser, after seeing slides of his work, wanted to buy Peter Heading's outstanding entry *Birds on a Swamp*, but his painting was sold before it left Australia. Peter, at seventeen, was one of Flying Arts younger students. He worked on his parent's property outside Monto and, since leaving school after Grade 10, the only art tuition available to him was Flying Arts. His big regret was that his time for painting depended on the seasons – when it was planting time he had little time to paint. The workshops meant a great deal to him , it was an example of the way the school assisted young people unable to leave the family farm.

'Memphis in May' brought other advantages. The Queensland Art Gallery and Caroline Launitz-Schurer, Assistant Director; Susan Abasa, Senior Education Officer; and Deborah Hart, Education Officer from QAG travelled with Flying Arts to regional centres to meet students and introduce them to some of the QAG artworks. Dr. Stuart Collins, who had taken over from Jeff Shaw as principal lecturer in the School of the Arts BCAE, also flew with the school to meet students.

Two dance tutors, Sue Street and Sharon Boughen, accompanied Flying Arts on a coastal tour to teach dance classes. With renewed interest from regional areas, a ten-day Winter Residential School for students was set up at Kelvin Grove, with Roy Churcher teaching painting and Johanna de Maine teaching pottery.

Following the American success, the Queensland Arts Council toured two Flying Arts exhibitions throughout Queensland in 1986: *Kangulu Caves* featuring artists from Baralaba was one, the other was the school's annual exhibition, *Miniatures*.

Although the year had not started well, with the first coastal tour leaving Brisbane amid power strikes and threatening cyclones, the re-instated coastal centres with their two-day workshops were booming.

In contrast to the success in coastal towns, there was still concern with low attendance figures at smaller inland centres. In an endeavour to supply these centres with workshops, community groups were asked if, in the event they could not gather together a minimum attendance, they would accept a higher base fee.

The response from students was supportive and most centres agreed to the fee, making future tours easier to plan. Myra Beach from Julia Creek, who began painting with Mervyn in 1971, summed up the general feeling with her comment: 'please keep the school flying – you've brought us a wealth of knowledge and awareness of art and I find an unquenchable thirst for more'.

Jeff Shaw's influence with the Craft Board of the Australia Council brought further benefits. In 1986, potters living in Dubbo and Narromine attended a unique pottery workshop when Japanese artist Mitsuo Shoji (trained in Osaka, Japan), travelled to western New South Wales with the school. He held other workshops in Brisbane, Narrabri, Coonamble, Barraba (NSW) and Dalby. When not tutoring with Flying Arts, Mitsuo lectured at the Sydney School of Arts where his students made pots, plates and tableware for exhibition and sale. The visit by an eminent overseas trained tutor revived interest in ceramics in many towns.

Textiles could also foster creativity and they were becoming increasingly popular. Janet de Boer introduced spinning and weaving workshops following requests from coastal spinners and weavers wishing to augment their correspondence courses.

Although she found flying up the coast in a small plane and teaching wherever they touched down was tiring, the enthusiasm of her students brought her a great deal of satisfaction. She found there was a 'real thoughtfulness about standards in the bush, and a sense of pride in what was being achieved – it gave a sense of local identity.'

Among the workshops she conducted was one for a new Fibre Arts Association launched in Mackay. In the next few years the demand for workshops in textiles overtook that for ceramics.

### Found Materials

Found materials were another new avenue emphasising creative experimentation. Modern trends in art practice encouraged the use of 'found materials' and Flying Arts tutors showed students how to use their local materials. Painters experimented with collage, and local clay was used by potters to give their work local identity. As potter Gillian Grigg explained: 'Because so many groups are reforming with new members, there needs to be a 'Back to Basics' approach, with fresh input of information on raw materials and an early field trip to bring this aspect to life. The use of found materials will be incorporated into projects wherever possible to explore the characteristics of the great range of clays, 'openers', pigments and glaze formers to make effective use of them. Advanced students will be encouraged to work in depth on some aspect of a local resource which seems to them worthwhile, and to produce both a report and a body of work utilising results. . . . The active enthusiasm of country groups for discovering and utilising their local resources was great to see. This includes the visual environment as well as potential ceramic materials and fuels.'

Guest tutor, creative artist Cheo Chai-Hiang, from Singapore also recommended 'found materials' and he instructed students on how to use them creatively: 'Lateral thinking is a way of solving problems by rejecting traditional methods and employing unorthodox and apparently illogical means. Find a man-made object, do something to it (dismantle, tear, break, bend, join, squeeze, fold, crumble, stretch, deface, repair, cut etc.) and do something to it again until you can't go any further. Record and describe visually each stage of change in as many ways as you can think of.'

With found materials encouraging people to be creative, the workshops were popular; it seemed that students loved interacting with overseas trained artists to create a unique local product.

However, despite the brief resurgence, with no follow-up guest artists, interest in ceramics continued to decline – only those classes which focussed heavily on creativity, such as painting and textiles, flourished.

### Kelvin Grove loses Flying Arts

By the end of the decade Jeff Shaw reported that the administration was operating smoothly, with touring programmes being supported by correspondence courses attracting both national and international enrolments.

Flying Arts was working with the Visual Arts & Crafts Board of the Australia Council and the Board of Advanced Education Queensland to co-ordinate Pat Hoffie's special Exhibition Research Project – the Decentralised Delivery of Higher Education in the Visual Arts. The school was now serving 1500 students at approximately fifty centres in Queensland and New South Wales - flying and driving over 50,000 kms.

However, the optimism of Jeff's report was premature. Problems began in 1989 when the Arts Council of NSW cut its funding and notified Flying Arts it would no longer finance tours into NSW.

Jeff Shaw was devastated - the NSW funding had been his initiative. He complained bitterly that, after years of beneficial service, NSW removed all support without prior warning. He offered to resign as president to tutor the three 1990 tours already planned for NSW using his own vehicle, taking a living allowance at considerably reduced tutoring fees.

He considered, as did other members of the committee, that to completely cut field contact with NSW students would be damaging to both individuals and the organization.

Flying Arts personnel believed that neither TAFE nor any other educational systems could adequately supply the needs of rural students in Queensland and New South Wales.

NSW centres agreed. They were willing to pay extra to keep Flying Arts coming to their towns and it was agreed that tutor Ron Hurley would tour NSW.

Interestingly, the 1990 itinerary shows that for the most part, students were only requesting the more creative art and textile workshops. Flying Arts planned thirteen tours that year: three western, three coastal, four in south-east Queensland and three into New South Wales. Although all tours would hold painting seminars, due to the steady decline in requests for ceramics workshops over the past few years, these would not be offered on the south east Queensland and coastal tours. A textile artist, yet to be appointed, would replace the ceramics tutor on some tours. Despite this there were still a few pottery centres with good attendances such as Goondiwindi Painting and Ceramics which was included on the NSW tours, and Chinchilla, Kingaroy, Rockhampton and Bundaberg ceramics which became part of the western tour.

Unfortunately, with massive flooding in the west in 1990, many of the planned workshops had to be cancelled that year.

With attendances at ceramics workshops in decline, Jeff Shaw, with the assistance of Pat Hoffie, produced a set of four videos for any groups still requiring tuition in ceramics.

Called the 'Ceramics Video Program'; its Co-ordinator was Edith-Ann Murray. It featured four well-known ceramics artists - Dianne Peach, Warren Palmer, Edith-Ann Murray, and Marc Sauvage, the videos were accompanied by relevant teaching notes. Cost was $180 for Flying Arts members and $220 for non-members. There is no record of sales, it was reported that many students felt they were too costly.

The school was more optimistic about its future when it received an infusion of Commonwealth Tertiary Education Commission funds for the delivery of distance education programs through TSN11 and Pat Hoffie.

However, in October 1990, Flying Arts was hit by crippling fuel cost increases as a result of the Kuwait crisis. Without support from the NSW Arts Council, all future tours to northern NSW were cancelled.

Even bigger changes were to come when the BCAE at Kelvin Grove became part of the Queensland University of Technology (QUT) following the Dawkins Report, which recommended the forced mergers of universities and colleges of advanced education.

When QUT acquired the BCAE Kelvin Grove campus it would no longer host Flying Arts. It was a devastating blow to Jeff Shaw when, on 10 December 1990, the school was transferred to the University College of Southern Queensland (UCSQ).

## Flying Arts workshop photos from 1990s Courtesy Chris Elcoate

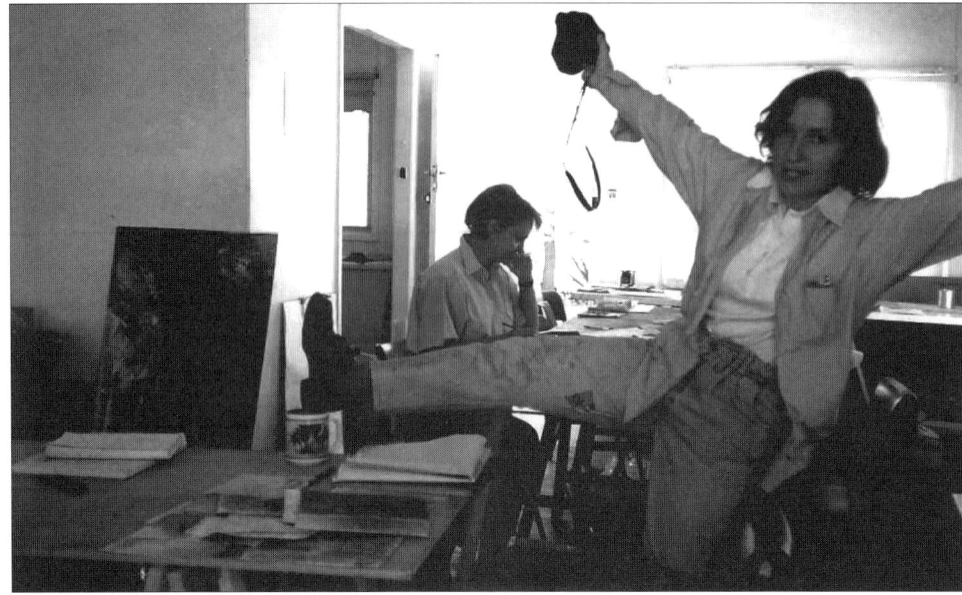

Janet Fountain dancing at Anneke Silver's weekend workshop "Four Seasons" in the Mt. Isa Showgrounds Hall

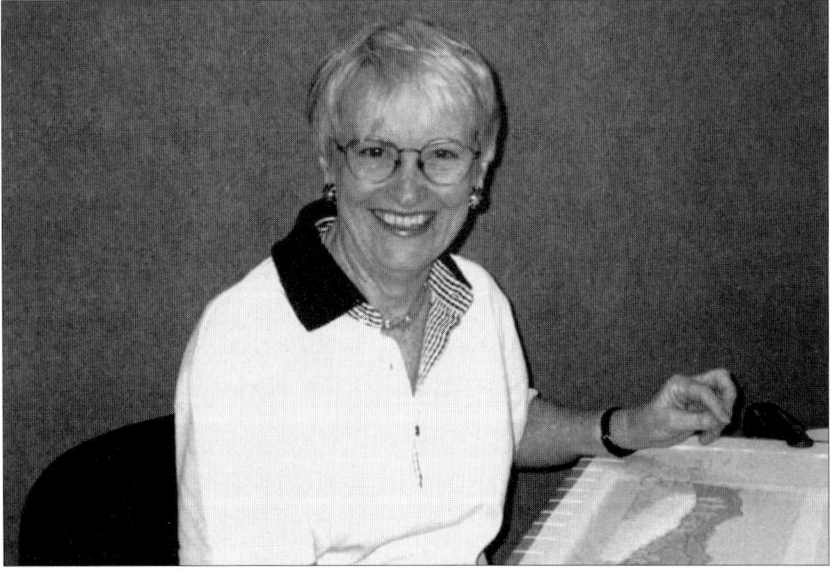

Jan Gall from Blackall at an embroidery class

Photo courtesy Jan Gall

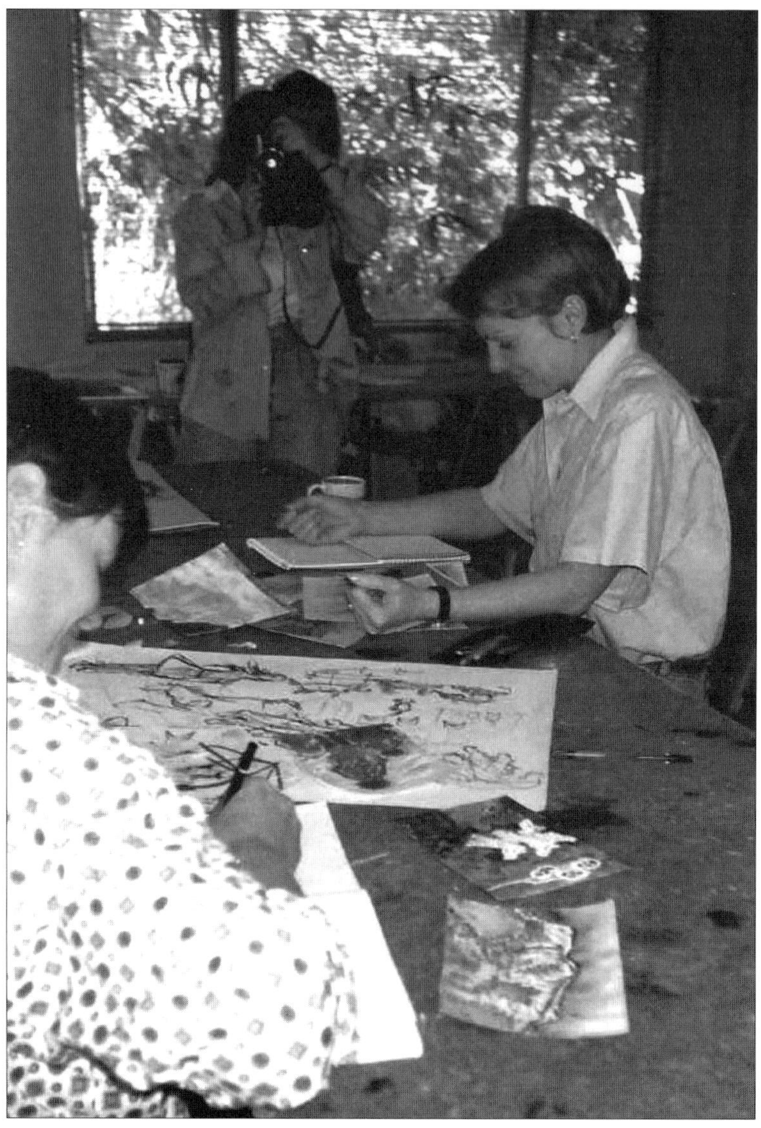

Patti Thompson in foreground
Anneke Silver's weekend workshop
"Four Seasons"

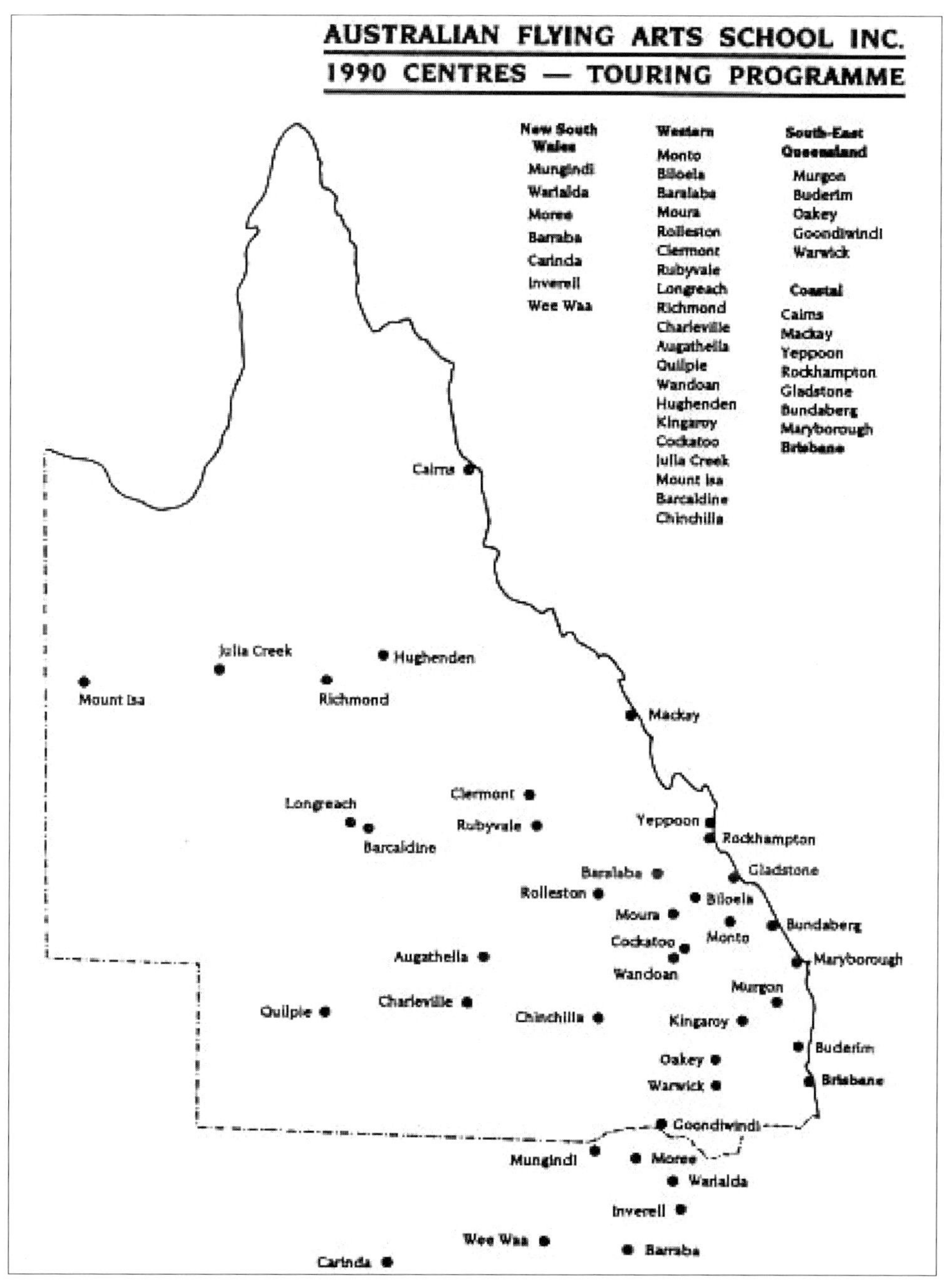


# The Changing Years

## University of Southern Queensland

## 1991 – 2001

Map from the University of Southern Queensland showing towns visited

# 1991-2001 The first ten years with The University of Southern Queensland

In the early 1990s, both State and Federal governments came to recognise the value to Australia of fostering creativity.

The state government began the shift with a report *Queensland: a State for the Arts*, published in 1991; two years later the Federal government followed with *Creative Nation*.

When the Goss Labor government won office in Queensland in December 1989 it demanded more professionalism from those receiving arts funding. Generous grants were available, but they came with conditions. Because accreditation was still unresolved, the traditional Flying Arts student base – country women between the ages of 25 and 55 – were classed as hobby artists and were outside new Arts Queensland funding guidelines.

It came when Flying Arts was relocating to the University College of Southern Queensland (UCSQ) and the school now faced a huge challenge. Over the next ten years significant changes had to be made to meet the new government criteria.

When Professor Leon Cantrell from UCSQ was approached by Mervyn Moriarty in 1982 to take over the school, they lost out to KGCAE, but with the acquisition of Flying Arts by UCSQ in 1991, Professor Cantrell was now able to integrate it with the distance education program of the Darling Downs university.

Although some ceramic workshops were retained, because of their continued popularity, creative painting, drawing and printmaking workshops once again became the staple of Flying Arts activities.

As at KGCAE, Flying Arts remained autonomous; with its offices in Brisbane it was in control of its own destiny, the new relationship allowed it to benefit from services provided by its host.

Initially there were few changes to personnel. Jeff Shaw stepped aside to welcome the new president, Associate Professor Robyn Stewart from UCSQ, and a legal representative, Peter Pagliarino, joined the committee.

Life Membership was given to Jeff Shaw in recognition of his efforts on behalf of the school. Mervyn Moriarty, the founder of the school, was also awarded life membership.

Financially, at the end of 1990 there was a deficit of $12,713.00; however, the Arts Division of the Premier's Department in Brisbane granted the school an extra $30,000, bringing its annual allocation to $164,000.

Expenses had been steadily increasing every year, but to the additional government funding, the Shell Company added sponsorship of $20,000 (up from $5000). $10,000 came from membership fees; $14,000 from workshops; $4300 through residential workshops; and contributions of $1250 came through collaboration with other agencies. It was believed that by December 1992 the deficit could be reduced to $7000.

This carry-forward deficit was due to essential expenditure for increased pilot salary and living allowance; increased plane expenses; and the establishment of a new office.

Two new staff positions were proposed – Program Co-ordinator and Tour Manager/Publicity Officer. To offset the added expense, membership fees were increased slightly and new centres were encouraged to join.

Student interaction continued to flow through the four newsletters published each year by Flying Arts.

The Shell Company, who were now on the Board of Flying Arts, increased its contribution to $20,000 to allow for work by students to be exhibited annually and the subsequent tour of the exhibition throughout Queensland.

The annual exhibition was an important event for students, it gave them an opportunity to showcase and sell their work outside their own towns. To encourage students to show their best work, the following year Shell extended its sponsorship to include a Shell Art Award of $2000 for the winning entry.

An urgent priority was the purchase of a car for the SEQ and NSW tours. With its own car the school could continue holding workshops in north-western NSW, despite the collapse of funding from the New South Wales Arts Council. To cover costs, NSW centres were happy to pay 'Demand Workshop' rates of $200 for a two-day workshop for three tours per year, which would be: ceramics only, painting only, and a tour combining both.

Added to the cost of the car, other expenses had to be underwritten. For example, following a recommendation by the committee's new legal representative, salary increases were implemented for the school's pilot and its correspondence course markers. At KGCAE, markers had been paid an amount well below institutional rates, and the pilot's salary was below the award. The increases justified Mervyn's complaint in the early 1980s that, as a pilot/tutor, he was being underpaid.

The correspondence courses established at Kelvin Grove were having mixed results and needed to be restructured. Although spinning and weaving remained popular, other courses were experiencing difficulties, with many students having problems interpreting course requirements.

Thel Merry reported that batik was no longer being requested and Gillian Grigg reported a dwindling completion rate of assignments in stoneware glazes. And there was little demand for screen printing. Correspondence courses were no longer viable, and in 1994 they were discontinued at Flying Arts, being taken over by the Open Learning Network (OLN).

When OLN acquired its correspondence courses, Flying Arts became part of the proposed new development of a written program in three stages for the OLN network. The first stage, a *Foundation Visual Arts* course was a joint effort between Glenda Nalder from Flying Arts and Arts Educator Karen Warnock. The second stage incorporated *Colour and Design*. The third stage, *Specialised Courses*, was textiles and stoneware glazes – incorporating two of the six Flying Arts correspondence courses.

After talking with students, UCSQ found there was dissatisfaction among long-term members of Flying Arts; they complained of falling standards in recent years. One spoke of 'high school art tuition', insufficient time devoted to worthwhile critique of work, and the lack of promotion of Flying Arts and its activities. The criticism pointed to a loss of enthusiasm by the KGCAE management in the late 1980s, possibly caused by a declining student interest in pottery, coinciding with a cut back in government grants for craft.

To revitalise the school, in 1991 a publicity broadsheet was distributed throughout Queensland by the Flying Arts School - *The First Twenty Years: Australian Flying Arts School.* It contained anecdotes from the school and photographs showing tutors and students and drew attention to the important role played by the school in the lives of people living in rural Queensland . . .

*'It [the school] has been marvellous for the women of the outback. They have no cultural and artistic stimulation other than what they find through the AFAS... the cities are not the only places where talent blossoms. While isolation can be a curse in terms of stimulation and critical feedback, it can also contribute to a strong sense of identity, even intensity... Artists in remote areas are relatively unaffected by short-term fashion dictates of the art market, preferring to be guided by their own convictions and experience... it takes tremendous dedication and courage to pursue an artistic pastime in the outback and for many artists, the Flying Arts School is vital in bolstering that courage... they tend therefore, towards a naïve approach that is very realistic at the same time. They look very closely at what they are painting and they are, of course, very familiar with it. This is why the work's emotional impact comes through so well... it is this huge indifference towards art, this total lack of any conception of its magnitude and its potential to enrich barren lonely lives that set Mervyn Moriarty on his curious crusade twenty years ago... '*

UCSQ encountered an even greater challenge when, in 1991, a State government report was released which was to have a huge impact on Flying Arts.

In *Queensland: A State for the Arts*, with its emphasis on professionalism, funding was available for young people and older people, the disadvantaged and professional artists, but not for middle-aged amateur hobby artists – the category to which the majority of Flying Arts students belonged. Under the new rules, the school was not eligible for government funding.

Adding to the consternation, Arts Queensland's interpretation stated: 'in the interests of social justice, the assessment of applications for people who were not professional artists would be primarily for people of non-English speaking backgrounds, e.g. people whose first language is other than English; young people up to 25 years of age; older people over 55 years of age; and people with disabilities – incapacitated physically, mentally or intellectually by injury or disease, either permanent or impermanent.' Very few of these people were part of the Flying Arts student base.

Following the report, Flying Arts was further disadvantaged after Arts Queensland held forums in all major towns in Queensland to discuss future arts planning decisions for regional communities.

The outcome was that all cultural activities would be planned by local councils, who then applied for funding through the Regional Arts Development Fund (RADF). As well as offering funds on a matching basis, RADF provided opportunities for regionally based artists and interested community representatives to participate in the formulation of a local arts and cultural policy through the assessment of grant applications.

The people not included in any of these guidelines were country men and women living on isolated properties or in towns throughout regional Queensland between the ages of 25 and 55 who wanted to remain hobby artists.

Arts Queensland added to the difficulties when they notified the school that they would not fund education, only professional development. If Flying Arts wanted funding, it could not be identified as a school. ('The Australian Flying Arts School' was its name at that time).

It appeared that government policy was for beginners to attend TAFE colleges for any elementary training in art. RADF would fund other art activities.

To continue to receive funding Flying Arts had to concentrate on the professional development of regional artists and widen its activities to include Aboriginal and Islander peoples, despite the fact that these avenues had already been investigated and had failed. In its report, the government gave no consideration to the important social aspect of the Flying Arts workshops for isolated communities.

Students were devastated by the proposals. As many of Flying Arts students were hobby artists they fell outside the guidelines and they believed that Arts Queensland was being highly discriminatory.

Robin Bassingthwaite from Charters Towers wrote an angry letter, stating that students were geographically and artistically isolated people; although they were amateurs, they were still taxpayers. . . 'What constitutes risk to a student in a city college who is surrounded by supportive peers, and has access to galleries and art literature and criticism, is very different from what constitutes risk to an isolated country person who has no support groups and limited access. Who is going to judge what constitutes risk to us – the Arts Division, the Flying Art School or us?. . . .we want and need AFAS, and I think in the name of true equity, we deserve it.'

As a professional artist and teacher, Flying Arts tutor Kim Mahood voiced her own reservations about the new Arts Queensland policy. She agreed with the concerns of the large proportion of students wanting to remain hobby artists. The Flying Arts workshops were a way of life for these people. She wrote that the mental stimulation of working with creative artists, and the friendships they formed, gave them the support they needed to face the daily pressures of life on the land, stating: 'Support for professional artists, on the other hand, will only ever apply to a small number of people producing art in remote and regional areas; and a proportion of those to whom it does apply will eventually go to the city. City and region are different countries, different cultures and provide different resources'. . .

She also emphasised the injustice of the policy: 'The group which is missing from this spectrum, and which from my observation as a tutor on the NW tour last year and the Southern tour this year comprises the major part of the AFAS membership, is the group for whom art is an essential part, but only a part, of their lives. Most of these people have no desire to become professional. Their lives are tied up with many things, raising children, overseeing their education and running properties. They are frequently very active members of their communities. . . .Most of them are looking for something that challenges them beyond the point they have reached. . . .To disenfranchise this group is to put 'artist' into the category of a product, a commodity which has no value until it has reached a certain level of professionalism.'

She argued that although RADF was an admirable and highly desirable scheme enabling communities to identify their own needs as artists by funding workshops and projects to fulfil those needs, there was no guarantee that future funding through RADF would be for creative art classes:

'All community groups must compete for a limited amount of money from councils, which may be unsympathetic, broke, or both. The prevailing tastes in regional/rural art are conservative and traditional and when a council is putting up a significant amount of money it expects results of identifiable benefit to the community.'

Her argument emphasised that the mental stimulation of creative and imaginative work could easily be lost to a form of painting which merely copied pleasant local scenery. When councils were encouraged to fund their own tutors, merely painting gum trees could once again become the dominant art form.

One angry student, Therese Stuart, agreed with her. In a letter to the *Gazette* she wrote: 'Where does this [Arts policy] leave us? In a cultural time warp? Fossilised? If we are to successfully market our culture will we have to concentrate on works which remind the purchaser of a 'particular place, event or emotion'. This is limiting us in a way which seems directly opposed to the previous guidelines for creative art and to all serious art philosophy.'

Already the new Arts Queensland policies were causing significant changes to regional art groups. Some had quickly 'bitten the professional bullet' to become eligible for public funding. Contemporary art groups in some towns, many of whom were Flying Arts students, were setting up their own local groups in response to the changing conditions. Among these were the Umbrella Studio group in Townsville, Kick Arts in Cairns, Stack Arts Collective in Mt. Isa and Jump-

Up Arts in Goondiwindi. The network previously known as 'The Central Western Queensland Cultural Activities Association', changed its name to 'Arts West'. Other groups were deserting Flying Arts to take up offers of joint support from the RADF through local Councils and Arts Queensland.

'Cultural Tourism' was another policy capable of harming the Flying Arts creative art workshops. Pretty paintings for tourists could soon over-ride creative work in country areas.

Kim Mahood made cutting remarks about the part money played in the production of art for tourism: 'As lifestyles become more and more difficult to maintain through traditional means, a strange phenomenon is taking place all over the world. This is the emergence of the zoo culture, in which endangered groups are subsidized and kept alive by tourism. Once culture becomes a form of entertainment its survival is assured, and it is to this end that artists and arts organizations (a species high on the endangered list) are being encouraged to explore the entertainment potential of what they do . . . and for the regional community with its art political wits about it, rodeo could be examined as a site for post-colonial theoretical discourse. (Rodeo was an example of American culture colonizing the already colonized landscape of the interior). This would be a way of attracting the government funding which may soon be withdrawn from organizations offering obsolete skills-based services.'

Her arguments sounded a warning. RADF presented a very real danger that local councils would allow tourism to dominate the production of local art. By favouring the emotionally pleasing depictions of 'gum trees, kangaroos and local waterholes' for tourists, the role of experimental creative art in stimulating mental development could easily be lost.

The new guidelines were a challenge and to survive, Flying Arts had to change. With Arts Queensland reluctant to fund 'education', particular care had to be taken with nomenclature. If the organization was no longer a school, careful wording of any description of activities was needed, e.g. words like 'students' would have to be replaced by 'members'; words like 'course', 'tutor', 'one lesson', etc. replaced by 'seminar', 'artist on tour', 'workshop', or 'visual arts experiences'.

More emphasis had to be placed on providing opportunities at the higher end of the membership scale in terms of ability, and Flying Arts had to find alternative sources of money for teaching its 'hobby' students.

Professional artists as tour guests could be funded by the Visual Arts Council Board, or the newly formed Arts Industry Training Council.

If Flying Arts wanted to continue workshops for those who, from experience, they knew to be the most in need, changes had to be made.

An early priority would need to be a name change from 'The Australian Flying Arts School' to a name more in keeping with 'professional development' rather than 'education'.

In view of the major changes involved, Flying Arts asked its students to consider their position carefully in relation to the tuition they were receiving, as all future classes would have to have a professional bias following the Arts Queensland Advisory Notice.

Students were asked to fill out a questionnaire to find out whether they wanted to remain with Flying Arts, or felt that the new RADF scheme could meet their needs.

From the hundreds of students who responded the result was overwhelmingly in support of Flying Arts: 74% felt that over the years the school had given them the highest level of support; 87% felt that there was no overlap with any other services available to them; 89% felt that their past tutors had been of the highest quality; 93% felt that without Flying Arts their work would either go backwards or would not progress; 78% felt that the organization was unique in the quality of its teaching by comparison with any other regional art education; 67% felt that, through USQ, the school was supplying them with what they wanted. The support gave Flying Arts the 'green light' to seek ways of circumventing government guidelines.

### Flying Arts uses RADF

Flying Arts' first project under the new guidelines used RADF funding when workshops were planned for indigenous groups. Following the importance placed on 'Cultural Tourism' by the Queensland Minister for Tourism, who made particular mention of Aboriginal and Torres Strait Island culture, the first workshop was a special request for Flying Arts at the Boulia State Primary School on its next north-west tour.

It was a huge success. The school community was largely Aboriginal, and guest artists – Aboriginal artist Judy Watson and Fiona Fell – spent the day with 63 children; they worked with clay and paint on themes relating to the children's heritage and environment. The workshop was the first stage in a planned RADF assisted project in Boulia involving the creation of two murals.

Following the success, Flying Arts asked Judy Watson to conduct its future north-western tours and it was planned for Aboriginal communities in Cairns and Doomagie to be included in its itinerary.

To stay within Arts Queensland guidelines, Flying Arts' coastal tours were changed to residential workshops and Flying Arts targeted the 18-25 year group using accreditation as the key. With accreditation towards academic qualifications as part of its curriculum, Flying Arts could not be regarded as only teaching hobby students.

In conjunction with USQ, a funding submission was drawn up to develop an external module for a Bachelor of Creative Arts in Visual Arts to give country students a recognised qualification through the Open Learning Network. The BA course, with between-tour exercises for beginners through to more advanced members, was to begin early in 1992. Unfortunately the funding did not eventuate and the course was unable to proceed.

Residential workshops now took the place of regular flying workshops in Cairns, Townsville, Mackay, Rockhampton, Gladstone, Maryborough and Bundaberg. Flying Arts was no longer the sole provider of visual arts tuition in these towns as it had been ten to twenty years ago. The new workshops supplied services not available through local sources such as TAFE Colleges or Universities.

Isolation and 'cultural deprivation' as seen in western tours no longer existed along the coastal strip. It now had a thriving cultural network, much of which had been set up by the Queensland Division of the Arts Council in the 1970s and many students had reached a level of skill where the 'how to' workshops previously supplied by Flying Arts were no longer relevant. Students in the coastal towns lacked creative art training by professional artists at an advanced level. The professionalism of the new residential workshops ensured their eligibility for funding.

However, with few TAFE colleges in rural towns, the west was a different story. To lobby the need for Flying Arts in the west, a letter was sent to Leneen Forde, Governor of Queensland and patron of the school, which noted that there were approximately 700 active members attending workshops and of these 655 were women. It emphasised that, for women living in the west, the pursuit of creative art was far more than mere recreation. Over and above homemaking, their daily schedules included mustering, cattle trucking, shearing, harvesting and driving hundreds of kilometres each week to meet school buses. Despite years of drought these women always made time to attend Flying Arts workshops. It indicated the seriousness of their need for creative activities and social contact with professional artists and like-minded fellow students.

## Drought hits Queensland

During the early 1990s, Queensland suffered a crippling drought, reputed to be the worst since Federation, and high attendances indicated there was a real need for the social regeneration supplied by the Flying Arts workshops.

Many of the western women disenfranchised by the new Arts Queensland policies lived on properties and had families and they needed the relief from anxiety which they found through creative art. Kim Mahood believed that the people that Arts Queensland did not want to fund were the stabilising backbone of rural communities.

Her advice to students was serious but humorous when she encouraged them to lobby politicians over government discrimination: 'As long as the government-run urban bureaucracies (GRUBS) are policing the equity distribution in the bush it might be worthwhile to identify your own position. It may turn out that instead of an equity group, you have a power base. Half a dozen rampaging MADGHOLS (marginalised amateur dilettantes or grey-haired old ladies) could surely be a match for a GRUB or two.'

Despite the debate about eligibility, Arts Queensland continued to fund Flying Arts and the core program of creative art workshops remained active. In 1993, 140 workshops were conducted in 41 centres throughout rural Queensland. In its first years at USQ the new management committee were making every effort to revitalise the school.

## The Australian Flying Arts School becomes Flying Arts Inc.

With Arts Queensland requesting the organization adopt a name which did not include the word 'school'– in March 1994 the name was changed to 'Flying Arts Inc.' It indicated a new image in the changing policy environment.

The core objective of sending professional artists to students in regional and remote areas of Queensland remained unchanged, but there was a shift to a broader client base.

This was defined in terms of limited current access to professional development in the arts in regional Queensland rather than in terms of geographical isolation. It would be a new planning and budgeting structure driven by client need allied with a market-oriented approach to staffing and administration.

To emphasise a change in policy, Professor Leon Cantrell, as president of Flying Arts, welcomed a new General Manager – Christine Campbell.

Although Christine came from a background in performing arts she was chosen from the thirty-one candidates who applied. The future was a challenge and it was believed she was the most suitable person to guide Flying Arts into a new era. In the following years their judgement proved sound.

Diversity of tutors was another avenue being considered. In recent years Queensland artists had been given employment priority, but in the interests of more professional regional groups, it was believed Flying Arts had to collaborate with other institutions and organizations to supply national and international touring artists.

As the drought continued it began to affect attendances. Allied with this, costs were rising. With a deficit of nearly $25,000, reducing accumulated funds to approximately $7000, the new direction of Flying Arts paid off when Arts Queensland approved its annual grant of $172,000 for 1994 and Shell Company renewed its sponsorship. Their confidence in Flying Arts was welcome, but for the organisation to survive, only two annual workshops could be planned for future years.

To continue to serve regional Queensland, Flying Arts needed to widen its student base. In 1993 the State government formed the Queensland Indigenous Committee for Visual Arts (QICVA) to unite indigenous groups throughout Queensland.

With Aboriginal artist Judy Watson on its team, Flying Arts began working with QICVA to provide a comprehensive touring program for Aboriginal and Torres Strait Island artists. The program was tried on the same basis as touring programs to other western centres. Workshops were held at Boulia, Burketown, Mt. Isa, Doomadgee, Normanton, Injinoo, Thursday Island and Darnley Island.

Flying Arts was already teaching Europeans and Islanders on Thursday Island when the State government requested more interaction with Aboriginal and Islander people. Lynette Griffith, Thursday Island Centre Representative, wrote of the special need that the organization filled for them:

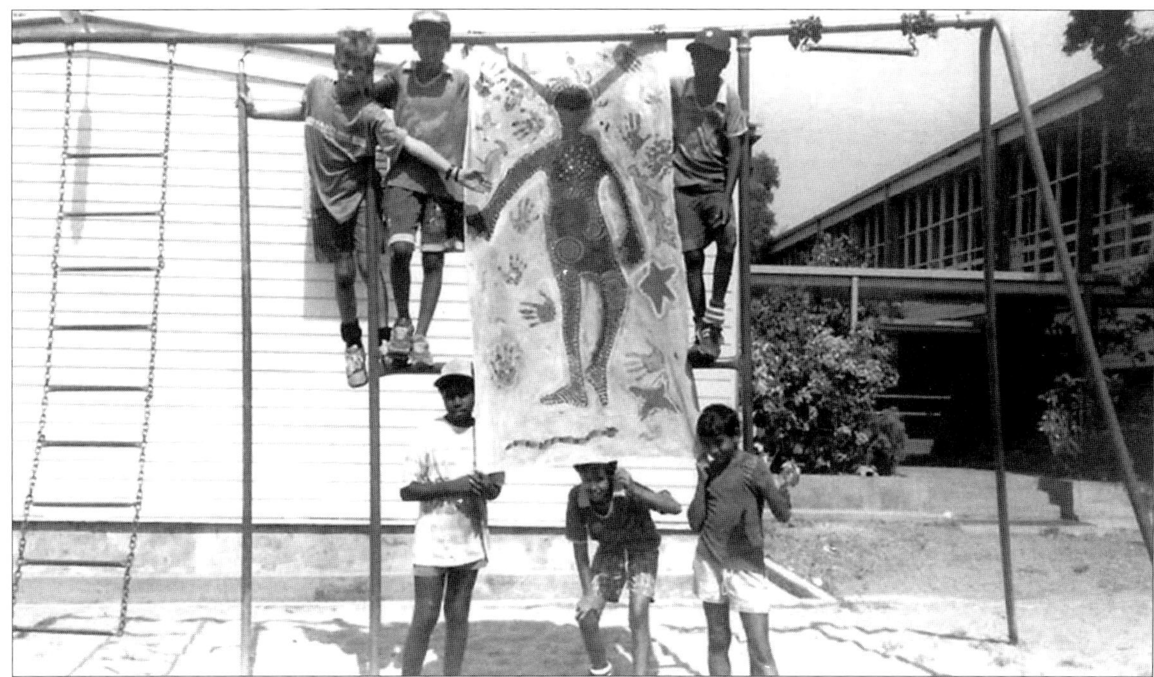

Students at Normanton High School Courtesy Flying Arts archives

'We all wait anxiously for Flying Arts to arrive. Our contact with 'those people from the South' (everything being south of here) is important to us. For two days people come together, often from outer islands, to share creative experiences and generally have a great time.

'Not only is it an artistic experience but an opportunity to yarn and catch up. . . .The Flying Arts tutors are always really helpful, leaving behind many good ideas and setting people at the start of new pathways to explore.

'By making an effort to meet on a regular basis people are more inclined to go down that path, explore their ideas, communicate new ideas to others, with everyone feeding off each other.'

Her story is a prime example of the social regeneration in isolated communities which came about through the Flying Arts creative workshops. Their presence was critical for many parts of regional Queensland. Craft workshops were also needed in some centres.

### Craft fights for survival

In the late 1980s, despite a drop in attendances in many centres, craft remained important for a number of people in rural Queensland. Funding for craft was not favoured by government institutions as, in 1987, the Australia Council's amalgamation of the Crafts and Visual Arts Board resulted in only one third of grants going to crafts.

Since then industry support for craft had diminished even more, both privately and publicly, at national, state and local level.

However, not everyone agreed with the trend away from craft. At a conference at the Adelaide University, Japanese-born British potter, Takeshi Yasuda, spoke of the importance of touch and the unfortunate decline of craft in urban areas: 'Visual arts have become simply visual. Painting, sculpture and crafts, in fact almost all aspects of our lives, have been impoverished by the primacy we place on the visual at the expense of the other senses, especially the sense of touch.'

Flying Arts knew that many people living in the west agreed with him. To these people craft was an important leisure pursuit, particularly silversmithing, ceramics, quilting and woodwork and their work was often very creative, incorporating a unique local flavour.

Added to this, a large percentage of people in western Queensland could not justify a hobby or professional activity that was unable to pay for itself; and with tourism becoming significant for the survival of small western towns, craftwork was even a growth industry in some areas.

Although craft had not always been a success, Flying Arts knew that some workshops were still needed. It applied for RADF funding to host a craft residency at Creek Farm, Alpha, with workshops in silversmithing, ceramics, woodturning and photography. Although the application was successful, to stay within Arts Queensland guidelines, professional development seminars on the marketing of work had also to be supplied.

To demonstrate its support for craft, USQ acquired work from Flying Arts ceramist tutors Fiona Fell, Gwynn Hanssen Piggott and Mary Lou Hogarth for its own collection.

**Technology comes to the west**

Flying Arts sought out other avenues.
If funding for craft was in decline, technology was booming, and satellite dishes now made TV available in the remotest parts of the country.

It allowed a broad spectrum of popular culture to be accessible to outback communities and was being heralded as the panacea for the problems of distance. The Open Learning Network had grown to forty centres, twenty-five of which had a two-way electronic communication system capable of transmitting images.

In conjunction with its electronic communication system, the State government was eager for electronic technology to be taken up by all rural centres and took responsibility for the state's arts industry policy – training and creative aspects as well as marketing the multimedia industry.

Arts Queensland sponsored visits by internationally recognised multimedia artists for people in regional Queensland and held a series of basic and specialised seminars.

Computer and Internet access to multimedia arts community groups was available for all as a new program initiative. Arts Queensland held evening forums to discuss a report on Multimedia and the Arts, it emphasised creativity as the key to the growth of the multimedia industry.
Regional arts communities were encouraged to be more involved in the creation of content, and the formation of policy in their area.

Workshops on the use of technology, predominantly video and computers, were held in Townsville and Cairns; and the creation of a non-material realm for art was embraced with enthusiasm by a number of regional artists.

Artists everywhere were using digital communications systems such as 'virtual' classrooms, conference spaces, digital magazines and electronic galleries. An Australian based electronic network especially for artists called 'Artsnet' was connected to technology and information.

Reproductions of the landscape – not of the variety created with paint and placed in frames, but images from space satellites and programs such as Landsat, were used in place of traditional representations.

Through USQ, Flying Arts embraced the new technology and began its own on-line seminars.

In late November 1994, Paul Brown, a consultant with Griffith University's Information Services, co-ordinated Flying Arts' first Art and Technology workshops on two Brisbane university campuses – Nathan and the Queensland College of Art at Morningside.
It gave students the chance to experiment with image manipulation.

Graphic designer and educator, Paul Cleveland, showed students the potential of Photoshop for artworkers. At the workshops Flying Arts launched its first full-colour issue of the Flying Arts *Gazette* online. It was available to all members with access to a computer.

With Telstra taking electronic communication to the west, from 1996 it was possible for people living in geographical isolation to keep in touch with the outside world using email.

Chris Capel, living on a sheepstation 100 kilometres north-west of Longreach, was thrilled when she became part of the first Telstra email trial. Rural women around Queensland were given Internet facilities and asked to communicate with each other and researchers based at QUT.

The Telstra trial was a boon for Flying Arts members, it allowed closer contact with people on the Flying Arts network. Unfortunately, in those early days members from remote communities in western or northern Queensland paid upwards of $12 per hour for poor quality internet access via an AUSPAC service. Responding to complaints, Telstra offered them a $5 per-hour service.

Although it was a wonderful addition to life in the west, electronic technology was still rather more expensive and less dependable than in the city. Nevertheless it led to exciting developments for Flying Arts students who could now access information online.

Flying Arts became a provider in this new field and lobbied for funds from the Australia Foundation for Culture and the Humanities to develop electronic communications through a project named *ReSiting: Regions Online with Flying Arts Inc.*

In conjunction with its traditional methods of workshops and seminars, email and the Internet had become its modern means of communication.

Despite the advantages of new technology, Flying Arts tutor Kim Mahood had reservations about the developments. She felt that traditional forms of artmaking would always be more popular in rural areas and wanted artist conducted creative art workshops to remain at the core of Flying Arts services. From experience she believed that 'the cultures of regional and remote Australia had a degree of rootedness which provided a significant counterpoint to the information being received via communication satellite'.

Although the changes were significant, money remained a priority for Flying Arts' core program of hands-on workshops, with both State and Federal governments urging non-profit arts organizations to create new funding sources.

To hold workshops for its traditional members, Flying Arts looked for more corporate sponsors.

Shell Australia was still a major sponsor and in June 1995 it was joined by Media Link International, a second sponsor which undertook public relations, advertising and marketing services to the value of $1000 per month for twelve months.

Minter Ellison Lawyers was another new sponsor. An Australia-wide organization, Minter Ellison became a permanent sponsor, assisting with legal services and newsletters.

Other sponsors quickly followed. Through lobbying from centre representatives in country towns, the Gaming Machine Community Benefit Fund became a sponsor when it agreed to provide $10,000 towards the cost of office computing equipment.

Centre representative, Rosemary Anderson from Tabubil (the OK Tedi Mining centre), persuaded BHP (at its expense) to fly artist/tutors from Horn Island to Tabubil in their executive jet to conduct two-day workshop for both expatriate and indigenous people, it was the first Flying Arts tour into Papua New Guinea.

In addition, Diann Lui, centre representative for Thursday Island, advised that Uzu Air would sponsor Flying Arts ceramist, Mary Lou Hogarth, for flights to Darnley Island for all the tours during the year.

The efforts of centre representatives in gaining sponsors demonstrated the enthusiasm and determination of women living in remote towns who assisted Flying Arts. The dedication of its volunteer country representatives, which dated back to 1971 when the school began, had always been the strength behind Flying Arts' activities.

Consequently, in 1995, owing to the generosity of more than twenty sponsors, the total cash and in-kind contribution was more than $75,000, which enabled the school to supply three tours to all centres.

There was even a surplus of nearly $35,000 in that year.

Following the three 1995 tours, in 1996 members wanted a permanent return to three workshops. As Kim Mahood predicted, new technology was exciting, but nothing could replace the personal contact and tutorial support on which the organization had been founded 25 years previously. Members put a high value on the unique opportunity the school provided for social regeneration, through face to face contact with visiting artists, to challenge their artistic practice through lively debate.

Although Flying Arts agreed that three workshops was the most desirable form of art education, at this stage government assistance allowed for only two visits a year, and private enterprise could not guarantee future funding.

The following year, 1996, was an important milestone for Flying Arts. Twenty-five years had passed since Mervyn Moriarty launched the organization back in 1971 and, to commemorate the event, Shell Australia sponsored a second touring exhibition, the '3x8+1' Exhibition.

The exhibition consisted of works by 8 Flying Arts tutors and 8 current members. The third 8 represented emerging artists who were post-graduate students from the Visual Arts Faculties of four of the regional and metropolitan universities associated with Flying Arts Inc.

The Universities that assisted in the exhibition were: QUT – Susi Muddiman, assistant curator at QUT was a driving force behind the development of the 3x8+1 touring exhibition; USQ as host to Flying Arts, gave assistance through its Faculty of the Arts; Griffith University Morningside Campus, and James Cook University of North Queensland also participated.

In addition, Southern Cross University (Lismore) made available its Art Museum Director to act as professional curator, conducting workshops in Professional Presentation for regional members.

The 'plus one' was work by Mervyn Moriarty who, in recognition of his past services to Flying Arts, was invited to Queensland to hold a special workshop – fourteen years after he left the school in 1982.

The willingness of so many sponsors and others to assist with Flying Arts projects demonstrated the high regard in which the organisation was held throughout the state.

### Visual Arts Experience Week (VAEW) – Flying Arts changes direction.

In the 1997/8 State budget, regional Queensland and youth became part of new government arts development initiatives:

* Funding to individual artists and arts groups was increased by 15 percent to $105 million.
* Additional funding was promised to all Queenslanders to improve Internet access.
* There would be significant increases to the Regional Arts Development Fund between 1997 and the year 2000.
* More than half a million dollars was to be allocated as part of a new Youth Cultural Policy.

Although it meant a change of direction for Flying Arts (e.g. bringing young people to Brisbane instead of sending artists to the bush), it saw the government youth policies as a new way of receiving extra funding as well as expanding its services.

In 1997 the feature project of Flying Arts was Visual Arts Experience Week, (VAEW). To implement what was an ambitious undertaking involving the whole of Queensland, it sought the support of other Brisbane art organizations to hold VAEW during the winter school vacation. VAEW was to be a pilot for what was hoped would become an annual Brisbane residency for young people in years 10, 11 and 12 studying art at high schools throughout the state.

Flying Arts gained the support of a number of sponsors for the project. Named *'Metropolis' a Visual Arts Experience Week*, their generosity allowed sixty-eight regional secondary students to come to Brisbane for an installation-based workshop with New Farm artist Peter Dwyer at Brisbane Girls' Grammar School. Young people came by bus, train and air from centres as far away as Weipa, Mt. Isa, Charters Towers, Longreach, Mackay and Cairns.

Coordinator Steven Carson acknowledged that VAEW was an experimental creative approach to learning. Following student participation in core workshops, which included 2D and 3D art and technology, they attended a program of gallery and museum visits, a walking tour of the New Farm/Fortitude Valley art precinct, and art industry talks.

With the success of VAEW in 1997, the following year it was again held at the Brisbane Girls Grammar School. The cost of $375 per student was paid for by sponsors. It covered accommodation, meals, workshops, materials and excursions. Special guest tutor was Judy Watson.

The *Courier Mail* supported the project through Factor X, the *Sunday Mail's* youth supplement, and ran a logo design competition for secondary students from regional centres seeking scholarships to attend the Flying Arts' youth residency.

### 1999 VAEW Scholarship

**Overall Winner: Heidi Green – The University of Southern Queensland Flying Arts Scholarship**

Heidi's stunning design will form the inspiration for future VAEW promotional material.

*In this logo, I have used an eye which transforms into a feeling, seven fingered hand, in the centre of which is the pupil of the eye. The logo shows that, throughout the seven days, art which is witnessed will become more than a visual stimulus as the pupil is immersed in the very experience that art should be*

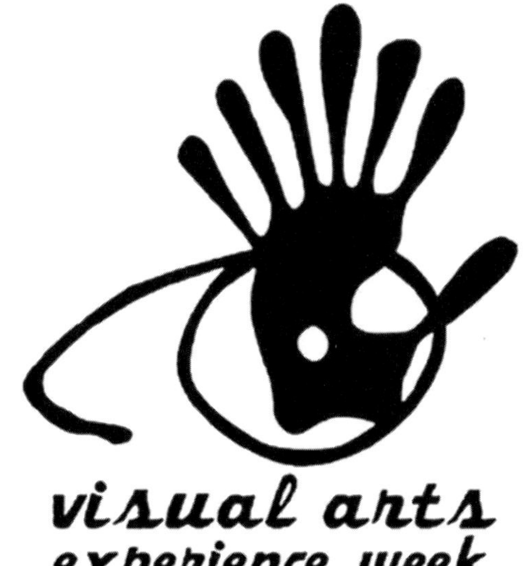


VAEW Winning Logo – Flying Arts *Gazette* No. 80 September 1999.

For the originality of her design, Heidi Green won a scholarship to the University of Southern Queensland.

The input of young people into selecting a logo demonstrated their enthusiasm for the project and eleven scholarships were awarded through Queensland's art industry in 1999.

In 2001 VAEW became *'Experience the Arts'*(ETA) when it expanded to include installation, photography, multimedia and street art for high school students coming from all parts of regional Queensland.

Held at QUT's Kelvin Grove campus, the lessons introduced students to life drawing, colour, composition and assemblage.

Classes were followed by visits to universities and galleries for talks with professional artists.

Surveys indicated that, as with Flying Arts' regional touring program, a significant benefit coming from ETA was the opportunity for young people to socialise with others who shared their passion for the arts.

69 people attended ETA that year, and the city joined the country when friendships and contacts were forged between regional and metropolitan areas.

As evidence of the success of the project, the 2001 ETA was assisted by two previous students who were now studying art at a tertiary level in Brisbane.

Another major project working with youth came through the Exhibition Development Fund, which funded *The Art of Transition* administered by the Regional Galleries Association of Queensland.

A touring exhibition, it was a combination of members' works and the documentation of Flying Arts activities by student photographer, Michelle Deanshaw, from Cooloola Institute of TAFE, with a number of works by VAEW students being featured in the documentary.

Anne Lord (previously a Flying Arts student, now teaching at James Cook University) selected members' works for the exhibition.

Support from NQX Freight System and the Gaming Machine Community Benefit Fund enabled exhibiting artists to enjoy a year-long tour of their work throughout regional Queensland and Northern Territory.

In December 1998 *The Art of Transition* opened at the Murranjirra Gallery at Tennant Creek. It was the first time that work from Flying Arts students was exhibited in the Northern Territory.

Flying Arts took advantage of any funding opportunities which enabled it to diversify its activities. In 1997 a regional summit was held at the University of Southern Queensland to discuss federal government funding coming into Queensland and Flying Arts was asked to participate.

Over the 1997/8 and 1998/9 financial years, Federal government funds totalling $900,000 were coming to Arts Queensland, via the Australia Council for the Arts, to stage arts and cultural summits affecting regional Queensland. The aim was to determine priorities and identify community projects.

When professional artists were needed, Flying Arts was nominated, becoming a service provider for two of the nine federally funded projects in south-west Queensland. The first was assisting with production of a library of street banners in Warwick to be loaned to small towns

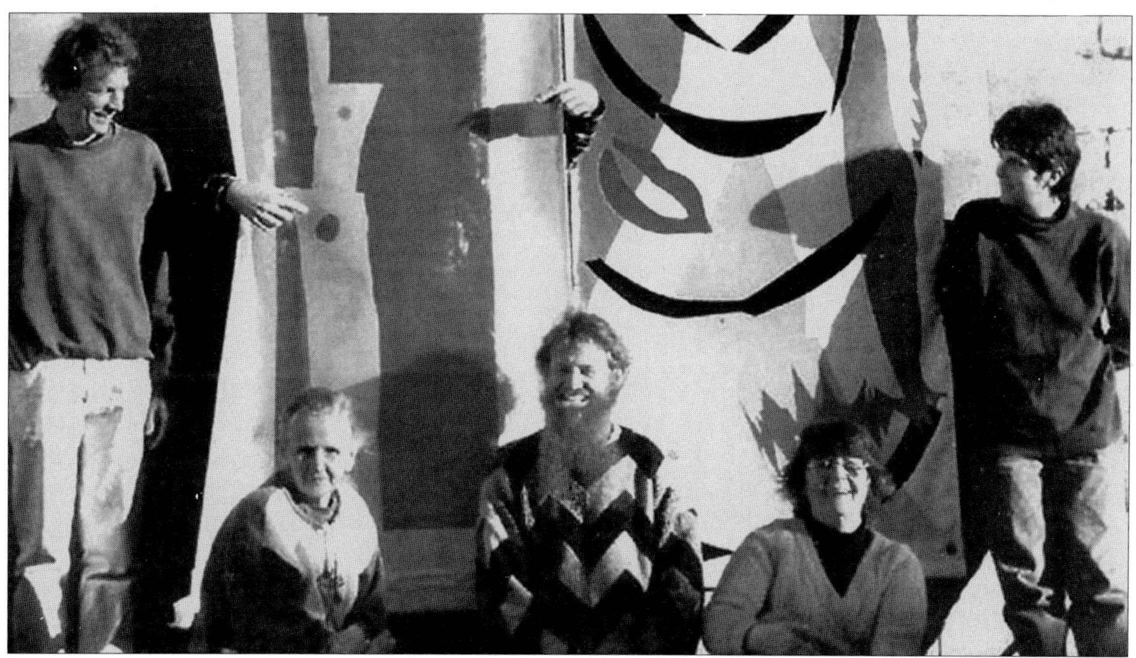

Participants in Warwick community's RAF Project *Today, Tomorrow, Together* with two of 20 locally designed and created street banners Flying Arts 1999 Annual Report

in the near south-west for festival events.

The second was a cybermural at Myall Park Botanic garden near Glenmorgan, an innovative combination of art, botany and technology.

Due to rising costs, in 1999 Flying Arts abandoned its tradition of hiring planes to fly artists to regional Queensland. Small planes supplied by outside carriers were used to conduct sequential 'studio' workshops in central Queensland but, for the far north, it was more economical and comfortable – if not quite so colourful or exhilarating – to use standard commercial flights.

With better roads, in conjunction with its southern Queensland and northern New South Wales tours, cars now serve the south-west.

With small planes no longer being hired, long standing sponsor Shell Australia, which in the past had supplied the organization with fuel, could no longer support Flying Arts. A new sponsor was needed to fund the annual exhibition and the state-wide art awards. The QCL Group of Companies quickly offered its services.

Online courses were becoming increasingly important to Flying Arts members and, in the new millennium, the use of computer technology became a priority. A 'foundation' course was tried in 2000 setting a precedent for a whole new way of delivering art experiences to remote areas. Through Griffith University and the Queensland College of Art, Flying Arts went online with an updated art-education course.

The course was designed for members of all ages wishing to acquire or revise basic art skills. As a series of virtual workshops on the Internet, the course was designed for self-study, allowing members to work at their own pace in their own time.

Through email it provided an online forum with lively and informative exchanges of ideas between participants. The internet would never replace traditional 'hands on' workshops, but it greatly assisted study between visits.

In February 2000, Arts Queensland recognised the valuable contribution made by Flying Arts workshops to art education in both coastal towns and the west. It funded the re-introduction of foundation workshops catering for beginners and others wishing to revise or learn specific techniques.

In conjunction with beginners' classes, Flying Arts now provided master classes in all areas of the visual arts and craft including basketry, jewellery making, machine embroidery and public art with local, national and international artists available as tutors.

In addition, online visual arts and professional development modules accessible to all would be available from February, 2001.

2001 was the thirtieth birthday of Flying Arts. In recognition, QCL increased its artist's award from $2000 to $5000. Added to it was a host of special prizes, including bursaries for Queensland and interstate artists whose residencies were sponsored by new partners and supporters.

That year a new corporate partner, CS Energy, toured a second exhibition - the *Thirty Years Exhibition*. As a 'birthday' exhibition it featured works of particular significance to Flying Arts' history.

Honouring Mervyn Moriarty as the founder who began it all back in 1971, he was invited to Queensland to display his art, give a presentation, and hold a workshop.

In the thirty years since 1971, the small ripple set in motion by Mervyn Moriarty when he took art education to the culture-starved people of the bush, has grown into a huge flow of cultural activity available to all who live in every part of the State.

In the new millennium Flying Arts is a significant force fostering creativity in regional Queensland.

***It is to be hoped this short history of Flying Arts highlights the valuable contribution the organization has made to the lives of people living in rural and regional Queensland and that its focus on unleashing the creative forces in people is seen as essential for the wellbeing of those whose lives are spent battling drought, floods and isolation.***

## 1990s Workshop photographs. Courtesy Flying Arts Archives

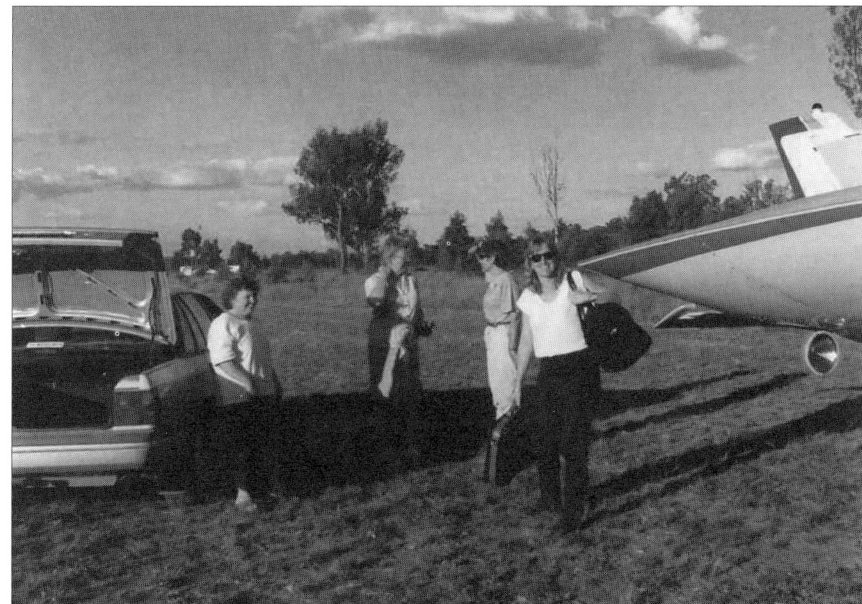

Wendy Greaves and tutors being met by Centre Reps Central Tour (St. George) 1994

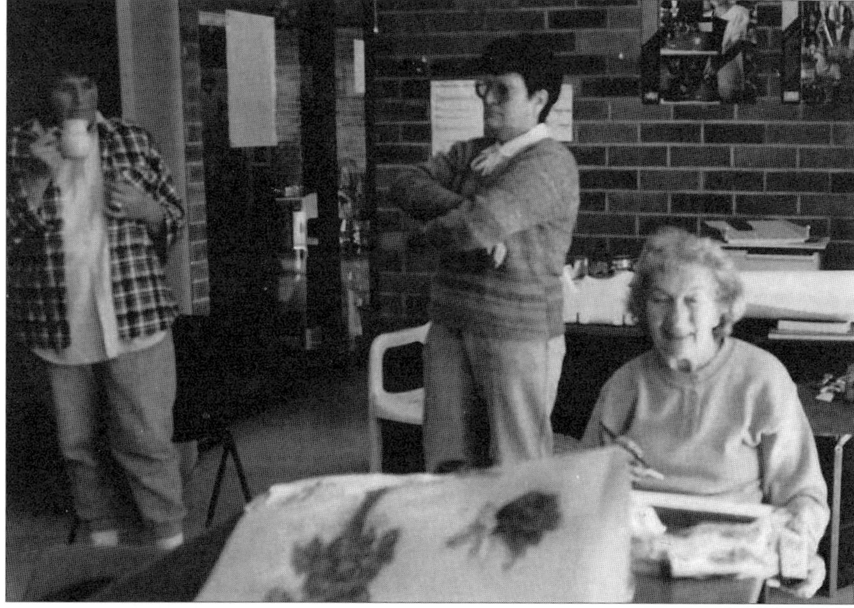

Two Fays and Kath Whittaker at Toowoomba

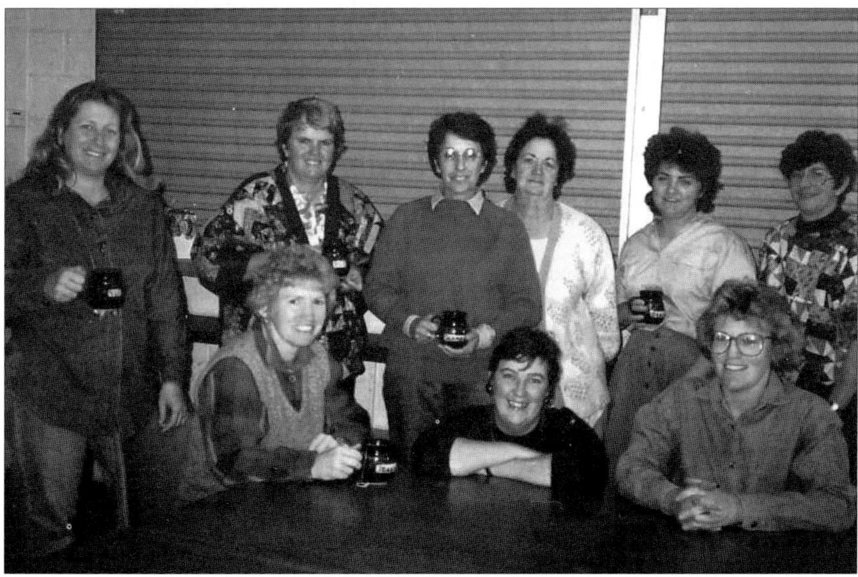

Baralaba Group

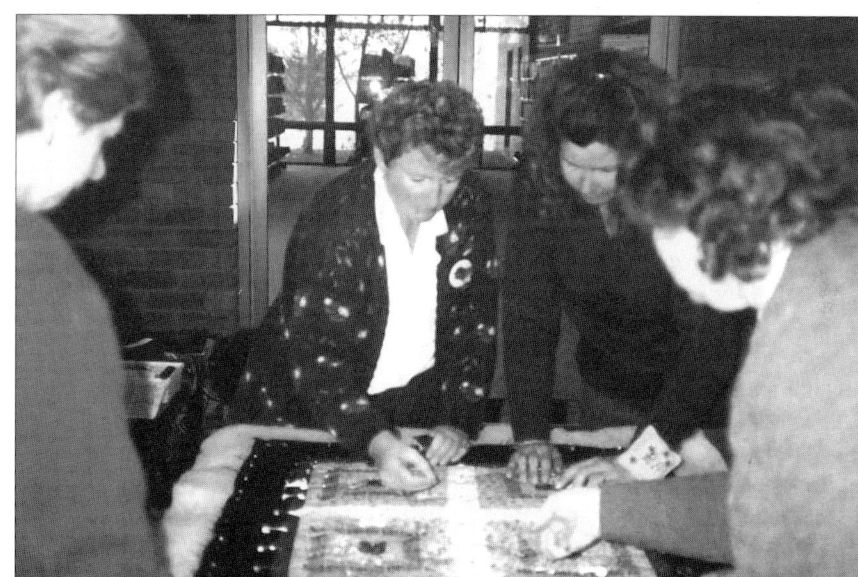

Calliope Group at a Gladstone Workshop

# Known Tutors who travelled with Flying Arts between 1971 and 2001

**1971 - school named Eastaus until 1974**

| | | |
|---|---|---|
| Mervyn Moriarty | Painting. | Until 1982 |

**Sole tutor until 1974 - with AFAS for 12 years.**

**Known guest tutors:**

| | |
|---|---|
| Clifton Pugh | Painting 1974 |
| Keith Looby | " |
| Piers Bateman | " |
| Colin Lanceley | " |

**1974 Name change to Australian Flying Arts School**

| | | |
|---|---|---|
| Mervyn Moriarty | Painting | |
| Bela Ivanyi | " | 4 years left 1978 |

**Known Guest Tutors**

| | |
|---|---|
| Guy Warren | Painting |
| Mitch Johnson | " |
| Rex Coleman | Potter |
| Vic Greenway | " |

**1977**

| | |
|---|---|
| Mervyn Moriarty | Painting |
| Bela Ivanyi | " |
| Ivan Englund | Pottery |
| Jean Jacques Vaschalde | " |
| Warren Moorfoot | " |
| Kevin Grealy | " |

**1978 - Australian Flying Art School Kelvin Grove**

**Tutors from Kelvin Grove**

| | |
|---|---|
| Kevin Grealy | Pottery |
| Robert Hinwood | Pottery |

**1978 Contd.**

| | |
|---|---|
| Mervyn Moriarty | Painting |
| Jim Aitkenhead | Painting/pottery |

**1979**

| | |
|---|---|
| Roy Churcher | Painting |
| Mervyn Moriarty | " |
| Kevin Grealy | Pottery |
| Rob Hinwood | " |

**Known Guest tutors**

| | |
|---|---|
| Paul Thomas | Painting |
| Jill Cadden | Dance western tour |
| Rhyl Shepherd | Spinning/Weaving |

**Two western Darling Downs tours**

| | |
|---|---|
| Sally L'Estrange | Painting |
| Peter Rushford | East Sydney Tech. Potter |

**1980**

| | |
|---|---|
| Mervyn Moriarty | Painting |
| Roy Churcher | " |
| Roy Oorloff | Painting |
| Rob Hinwood | Pottery |
| Rex Coleman | " |
| Ian Currie | " |
| Joan Webster | " |
| Warren Palmer | " |

**Guest tutor**

| | |
|---|---|
| Ian Smith | Painting |

**1981**

| | |
|---|---|
| Mervyn Moriarty | Painting |
| Roy Churcher | " |
| Kevin Grealy | Pottery |

**1981 Contd.**

| | |
|---|---|
| Lyndal Moor | " |
| Ian Currie | " |

**1982**

| | |
|---|---|
| Mervyn Moriarty | Painting |
| Roy Churcher | " |
| Pat Hoffie | " |
| Kevin Grealy | Pottery |
| Lyndal Moor | " |
| Lynne McDowall | " |
| Ian Currie | " |

**Moriarty leaves December 1982.**
**Kevin Grealy, Lynne McDowall resign.**

**1982 Correspondence School begins - tutors based in Brisbane, no country trips required.**

| | |
|---|---|
| Thel Merry | Batik |
| Don Braben | Screenprinting |
| Betty Crombie | Stoneware Glazes |
| Ian Currie | Stoneware Glazes |

**1983**

Coastal tours (Bundaberg, Gladstone, Rockhampton, Mackay, Innisfail, Townsville, Cairns) dropped.

| | |
|---|---|
| Roy Churcher | Painting |
| Pat Hoffie | " |
| Beverley Budgen | " |
| Betty Crombie | Pottery |

**Correspondence course teachers from KG**

**1983**

| | |
|---|---|
| Ian Currie | Pottery |
| Rob Hinwood | “ |

**Guest Tutors 1983:**

Gareth Morse — Head Dept. Painting of Art Education W.A.

Cheo Chai-Hiang. (Born in Singapore, studied at the Royal College of Art U.K., later in Italy in printmaking. Artist-in-residence at KGCAE during 1983.)

**1984**

| | |
|---|---|
| Roy Churcher | Painting |
| Beverley Budgen | “ |
| Brian Dean | “ KGCAE teacher |
| Betty Crombie | Pottery |
| Gwynn Piggott | “ |
| Ron Hurley | “ |
| | Indigenous artist recruited for Cape York |
| Jeff Shaw | Pottery |

**Guest Tutors:**

| | |
|---|---|
| Joe Furlonger | Painting |
| Ian Smith | “ |

**Correspondence Courses**

| | |
|---|---|
| Betty Crombie | Glazes |
| Beryl Taylor | “ |
| Ray Frost | Batik |
| Thel Merry | “ |
| Don Braben | Screenprinting |
| Janet De Boer | Spinning |

**1985**

| | |
|---|---|
| Brian Dean | Painting |
| Beverley Budgen | “ |
| Jani Laurence | “ |
| Wendy Allen | “ |
| Allin Dwyer | “ |
| Irene Amos | “ |
| Helen Charles | Pottery |

**1985 Contd.**

| | |
|---|---|
| Stephanie Outridge Field | “ |
| Betty Crombie | “ |

**Correspondence Courses**

| | |
|---|---|
| Betty Crombie | Stoneware Glazes |
| Ray Frost | “ |
| Thel Merry | Batik |
| Don Braben | Screenprinting |
| Janet De Boer | Spinning/Weaving |

**1986**

| | |
|---|---|
| Wendy Allen | Painting |
| Beverley Budgen | “ |
| Irene Amos | “ |
| Jani Laurence | “ |
| Allin Dwyer | “ |
| Carole Walters | “ |
| Joanne De Hage | “ |
| Mary Walduck | “ |
| Gwyn Piggott | Pottery |
| Judy Hancock | “ |
| Helen Charles | “ |
| Gillian Grigg | “ |
| Johanna de Maine | “ |
| Stephanie Outridge Field | “ |
| Janet de Boer | Spinning/Weaving |
| Sue Street | Dance |
| Sharon Boughen | “ |

**Guest Tutor**

| | |
|---|---|
| Mitsuo Shoji | Pottery |

**Correspondence Courses**

| | |
|---|---|
| Betty Crombie | Stoneware Glazes |
| Ray Frost | “ |
| Thel Merry | Batik |
| Don Braben | Screenprinting |
| Janet de Boer | Spinning/Weaving |
| Denise Johnson | Painting/Drawing |

**1987**

| | |
|---|---|
| Wendy Allen | Painting |
| Adam Rish | “ |
| Jeanne Macaskill | “ |
| Jani Laurence | Painting |
| Ron Hurley | “ Cape York |
| Barbara Zerbini | “ |
| Helen Charles | Potter |
| Gillian Grigg | “ |
| Judy Hancock | “ |
| Gwynn Piggott | “ |
| Pam Maegdefrau | “ |
| Jane Harthoorn | “ |

**Guest Tutor**

| | |
|---|---|
| Cheo Chai-Hiang | Painting |

**Correspondence Courses**

| | |
|---|---|
| Betty Crombie | Stoneware Glazes I |
| Ray Frost | Stoneware Glazes II |
| Thel Merry | Batik |
| Don Braben | Screenprinting |
| Janet De Boer | Spinning/Weaving I, II |
| Denise Johnson | Painting/Drawing |

**1988**

| | |
|---|---|
| Wendy Allen | Painting |
| Beverley Budgen | “ |
| Adam Rish | “ |
| Rod Milgate | “ |
| Vivienne Binns | “ |
| Wendy Mills | “ |
| Helen Charles | Potter |
| Gillian Grigg | “ |
| Pam Maegdefrau | “ |
| Jane Harthoorn | “ |

**Correspondence Courses 1988**

| | |
|---|---|
| Betty Crombie | Stoneware Glazes I |
| Gillian Grigg | Stoneware Glazes II |
| Thel Merry | Batik |
| Don Braben | Screenprinting |
| Janet De Boer | Spinning/Weaving I, II |
| Mary Fooks | Painting/Drawing |

**1989**

| | |
|---|---|
| Shelagh Morgan | Painter |
| Ruth Propsting | “ |
| David Burnett | “ |

**Guest Tutor**

| | |
|---|---|
| Neville Matthews | “ |
| Pam Maegdefrau | Potter |
| Jane Harthoorn | “ |
| Johanna De Maine | “ |

**Correspondence Courses 1989**

| | |
|---|---|
| Betty Crombie | Stoneware Glazes I |
| Gillian Grigg | Stoneware Glazes II |
| Thel Merry | Batik |
| Don Braben | Screenprinting |
| Janet De Boer | Spinning/Weaving I, II |
| Shelagh Morgan | Painting/Drawing |

**1990**

| | |
|---|---|
| Shelagh Morgan | Painting/Printmaking |
| Lani Weedon | Painting |
| Bonney Bombach | “ |
| Edith-Ann Murray | Pottery |
| Jeff Shaw | Pottery (NSW tour) |

**Correspondence Courses**

| | |
|---|---|
| Betty Crombie | Stoneware Glazes I |
| Gillian Grigg | Stoneware Glazes II |
| Thel Merry | Batik |
| Don Braben | Screenprinting |
| Janet De Boer | Spinning, Weaving I, II |
| Shelagh Morgan | Painting/Drawing |

**Guest Tutor**

Antjepia Gotschalk from Germany

**1991**

| | |
|---|---|
| Bonney Bombach | Painting |
| Shelagh Morgan | “ |
| Lani Weedon | “ |
| Edith-Ann Murray | Pottery |

**Demand Workshops**

| | |
|---|---|
| Virginia Jones | “ |
| Wim de Vos | Painting |

**Guest artists 1991**

| | |
|---|---|
| John Fitzwalter, | Potter |
| Julie Whitney | “ |
| Sue Leeway | Painter/photographer |
| Annette van Ham | Pottery (Holland) |

**Correspondence Courses**

| | |
|---|---|
| Gillian Grigg | Stoneware I and II |
| Thel Merry | Batik |
| Don Braben | Screenprinting |
| Janet De Boer | Spinning, Weaving I, II |
| Karen Warnock | Painting/ Drawing |

**1992**

| | |
|---|---|
| Kim Mahood, Sydney | Mixed Media |
| Lucinda Elliott | Painter/Printmaker UK & QCA |
| Jenny McDuff | Mixed Media |
| Mike Spoor | Pottery (UK) |

**Correspondence/Distance Training**

| | |
|---|---|
| Gillian Grigg | Stoneware Glazes I, II |
| Janet De Boer | Spinning, Weaving I, II |
| Karen Warnock | Painting/Drawing |

**1993**

| | |
|---|---|
| Kim Mahood | Painting, Mixed Media |
| Lucinda Elliott | Painting |
| Judy Watson | Painter (Boulia Project) |
| Fiona Fell | Pottery (Boulia Project) |

**Distance Training**

| | |
|---|---|
| Janet De Boer | Textiles |
| Glenda Nalder | Visual Arts |
| Karen Warnock | Painting/Drawing |

**Guest artist:**

Lyndall Milani

**1994**

| | |
|---|---|
| Anneke Silver | Mixed Media |
| Colin Reaney | “ |
| Jennifer McDuff | “ |
| Rowley Drysdale | Pottery |
| Mary-Lou Hogarth | “ |

**1994 Contd.**

| | |
|---|---|
| Ann Whitsed | Textiles |
| Jan Urquhart | Textiles (Quilting) |

**Guest artists:**

| | |
|---|---|
| Marion Gaemers | Basket-maker |
| Tekeshi Yasuda | Japanese-born British potter |
| Paul Brown | Computer Artist, writer |

**1995**

| | |
|---|---|
| Ann-Marce Reaney | Mixed Media |
| Colin Reaney | “ |
| Anne Lord | “ |
| Zannette Kahler | “ |
| Sam di Mauro | Pottery |
| Mary-Lou Hogarth | “ |
| Susan Flight | Textiles |
| Rosemary Lakerink | “ |

**Guest artist:**

| | |
|---|---|
| Lynnette Griffiths | Pottery (Darnley Island Torres Strait) |
| Patsy Hely | Pottery |

**1996**

| | |
|---|---|
| Steven Royster | Mixed Media (Kuranda, Richmond, Thursday Is.) |
| James Guppy | Mixed Media |
| Andrew MacDonald | Mixed Media |
| Sam di Mauro | Pottery |
| Steve Davies | “ |
| Marion Gaemers | Textiles |
| Ken Smith | “ |

**Guest artists**

| | |
|---|---|
| Wim de Vos | Intaglio Printing Workshop at Maleny. Brisbane in June |
| Jill Kinnear | Textiles Innisfail |

**Masterclass**

| | |
|---|---|
| Sue Guilfoyle | Computer Imaging |
| Ken Smith | Textiles (Rolleston.) |
| Yvonne Bouwman | Pottery (Emu Park) |

**Artists from 1996 Asia Pacific Triennial**

Nalini Malani (India) Mixed Media.
Southern tour
Francesca (Keka) Enriquez (Philippines).
Central tour
Tom Deko (New Guinea) Mixed Media.
Northern tour

**1997**

| | |
|---|---|
| Wim de Vos | Painting |
| Peter Dwyer | Painting/Drawing |
| Steven Royster | " |
| Simon Suckling | Pottery |
| Peter Thompson | " |
| Jill Kinnear | Textiles |
| Ken Smith | " |

**Guest Artists**

| | |
|---|---|
| David White | Wood, Sandstone, Sculpture |
| Di Ball | Computer Technology |

**Artists available for Masterclasses**

| | |
|---|---|
| Barbara Cheshire | Painting/Drawing |
| Karen Laird | Painting/Drawing, Pottery |
| Gary Andrews | Painting/Drawing |
| Shirley Wilkins | Pottery |

**1998**

| | |
|---|---|
| Peter Dwyer | Painting/Drawing |
| Gary Andrews | " |
| Barbara Cheshire | " |
| Karen Laird | Pottery |
| Shirley Wilkins | " |
| Wim. de Vos | Printmaker & Painting |
| Jill Kinnear | Textiles |
| Ken Smith | " |

**1999**

| | |
|---|---|
| Rachel Apelt | Painting /Drawing |
| Barbara Cheshire | " |
| Louise Taylor | Printmaking |
| Karen Laird | Pottery |
| Shirley Wilkins | " |
| Jill Kinnear | Textiles |
| Wendy Wright | " |

**1999 Demand Workshops**

| | |
|---|---|
| Seanne McArthur | Jewellery |
| Bonney Bombach | Mixed media |
| Katrina Odgers | Glass making |

**Guest Artists**

| | |
|---|---|
| N.S. Harsha | Painting (India) |
| Nguyen Minh Thanh | Pottery (Vietnam) |

**2000**

| | |
|---|---|
| Rachel Apelt | Painting /Drawing |
| Majena Mafe | " |
| Donna Confetti | " |
| Melanie Forbes | Pottery |
| Wendy Wright | Textiles |

**Special Workshops**

| | |
|---|---|
| Cathryn Lloyd, | Silk Painting /Batik |
| Tom Justice | Paper clay |
| Adele Outteridge | Creative bookmaking |
| Helen Broadhurst | Clay Sculpture/Mosaic |
| Pippin Drysdale | Ceramics masterclass |
| Lucja Ray | Painting |

**2001**

| | |
|---|---|
| Lucja Ray | Painting |
| Majena Mafe | Mixed Media, Painting |
| Heather Winter | Photography |
| Bonney Bombach | Installation, Painting |
| Melanie Forbes | Ceramics, Sculpture |
| Jenny Mulcahy | Paper Clay |
| Glenys Mann | Textiles |
| Pamela Croft | Mixed Media, Monoprinting |
| Chamay Bauer | Mixed Media, Monoprinting |

**International Textiles Artists**

| | |
|---|---|
| Marian Boontjes | Feltmaking (Holland) |
| Jeanette Appleton | Textiles (England) |
| B.J. Adams | Embroidery (USA) |
| Bina Rao & Keshav Rao | Textiles (India) |

**Special Guest**

| | |
|---|---|
| Ian Smith | Painting |

# Artist Stories:
# Following are stories from three of the early artists who flew with Flying Arts

Beginning with four paintings by Mervyn Moriarty

Bela Ivanyi

Kevin Grealy

Beverley Budgen

## Works by Mervyn Moriarty

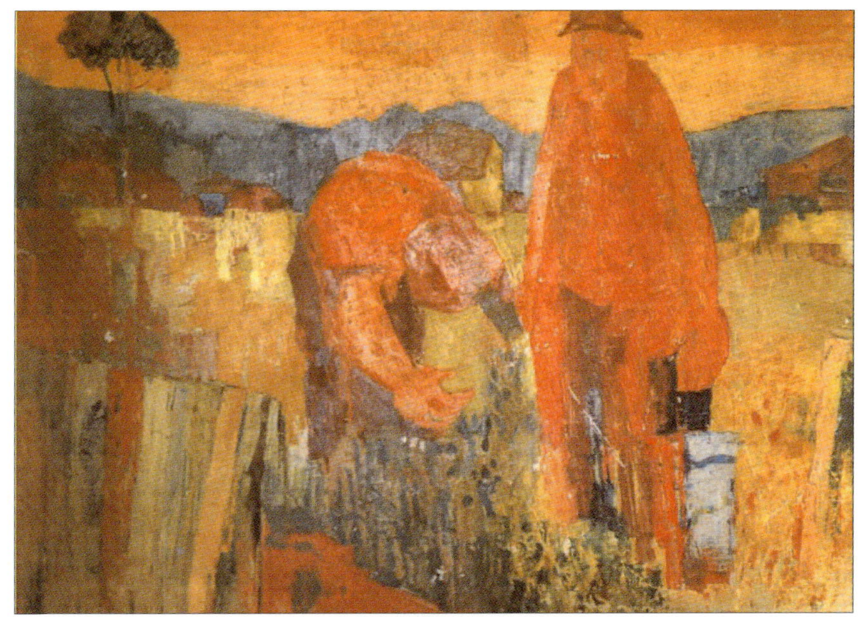

*The Pickers* 100cm x 123cm oil on prepared masonite Mervyn Moriarty

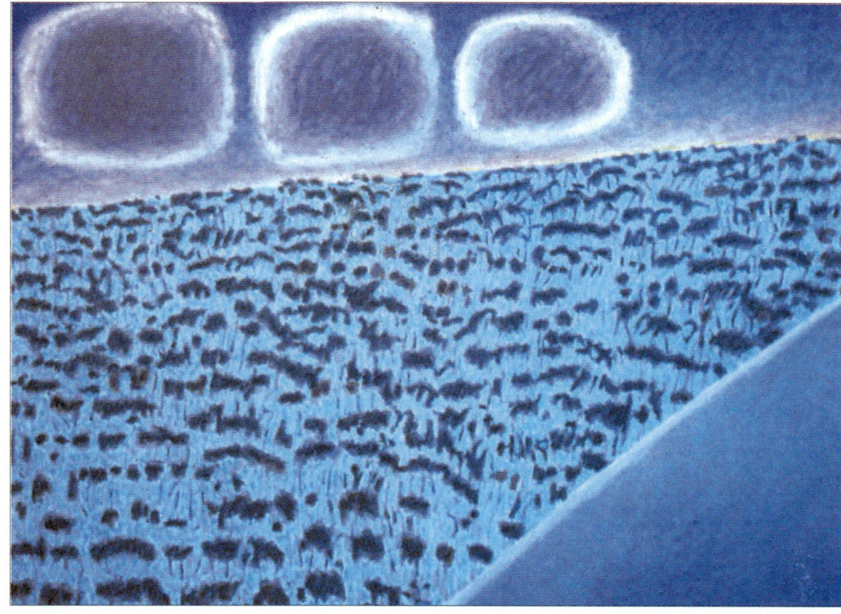

*Snow Gum forest on ridge, winter afternoon* 120cm x 160cm oil on canvas Mervyn Moriarty

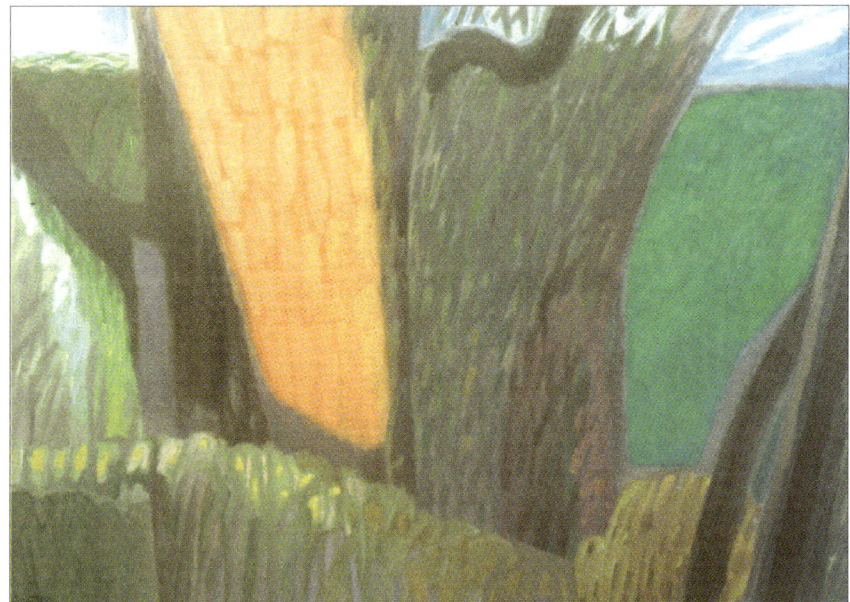

*Tree in the afternoon light* 120cm x 160 cm oil on canvas Mervyn Moriarty

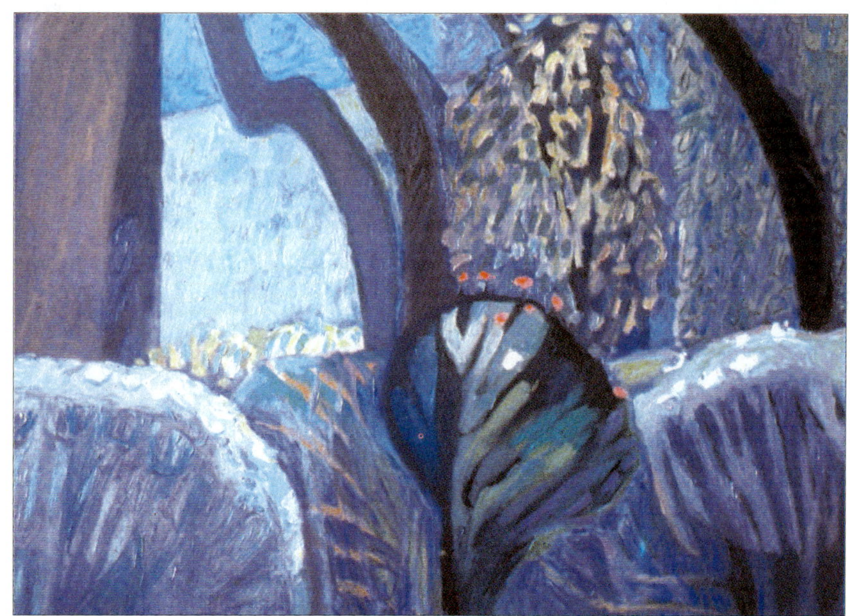

*Lynn's Rose Bush* 90cm x 120cm oil on canvas Mervyn Moriarty

## BELA IVANYI

**Worked with the Australian Flying Arts School from 1974 to 1978**

Bela fled Hungary and arrived in Australian in 1957. He trained in art at the National Art School in Sydney. After joining Eastaus he flew both the northern and western routes. When Mervyn flew west he would fly north, taking workshops to towns three times a year. For the fourth trip they would change over. Following are some reminiscences of his days with Flying Arts:

*In the towns we visited workshops were held at local cultural centres, schools or even out on a farm or station property where we taught anything from 8 to 20 students or more in a shearing shed. In the evening there would be a great cook-up and get-together with everyone talking about art and exchanging ideas.*

*I believe that isolation was a problem. In Richmond for example no-one would even attempt to paint contemporary work, it was only traditional painting which was accepted in the bush. These were the paintings that sold, no-one in those towns was interested in buying a more contemporary painting and the artists interested in modern work were only able to get the reassurance they needed to continue their efforts after the Flying Art School came to their town. The seminars held by the Flying Arts were casual but the teaching was very thorough and the school supplied good training books. The day-time seminars were complemented by casual night sessions.*

*Soon after I started with the school – before I had my own pilot's licence – I had a pilot fly me out to Richmond. The instruments were not working in the plane and when we saw the airstrip we had no idea where we were, as it was outside the township. When we landed I found a wind-up phone in a shed so phoned and asked the person on the other end "could you tell me where I am", the person at the other end promptly hung up. Finally someone came along and picked me up and took me into town where we stopped for the usual cup of coffee and cakes . After we had all been there for a little while a lady came in from the local post office who told us about this strange person who had rung her up earlier. It turned out that it was the lady who had hung up on me so we all had a laugh about that.*

*When Flying Arts started flying to the west the women living out there had little to interest them. The big thing that Flying Arts did was to get people together, and in time they had much wider interests than simply learning to paint. The initiatives they gained as a group through Flying Arts gave them confidence. In Richmond the group purchased a house in town for their own use which they totally modernised. I remember that the local chemist's wife threw a party to raise funds for the house and when it was finished they had multi-cultural evenings where her husband would recite poems from Banjo Patterson, others would read literature or sing or play music.*

*The country around Richmond was particularly flat and this probably had an effect on the art being produced. I remember that one day we all went to a property at Myuna about 30ks. out of town where there was a dam wall about 15ft high. We all climbed on to this to get a better view of the surrounding country and to look at the few trees to be seen on the horizon line. I was interested in the way that the different environment affected the landscape painting being produced.*

*Then there was the time that Keith Looby came to Jo Forster's place at Richmond. I had to leave the group with Keith as I had to attend to the plane. When I came back the group had painted a mural on the wall of a building on the property. It was a scene from the Garden of Eden with Adam and Eve and Keith Looby was absolutely amazed at the colours they had used in the mural and couldn't understand where these people were able to get the ideas for such a huge diversity of colours.*

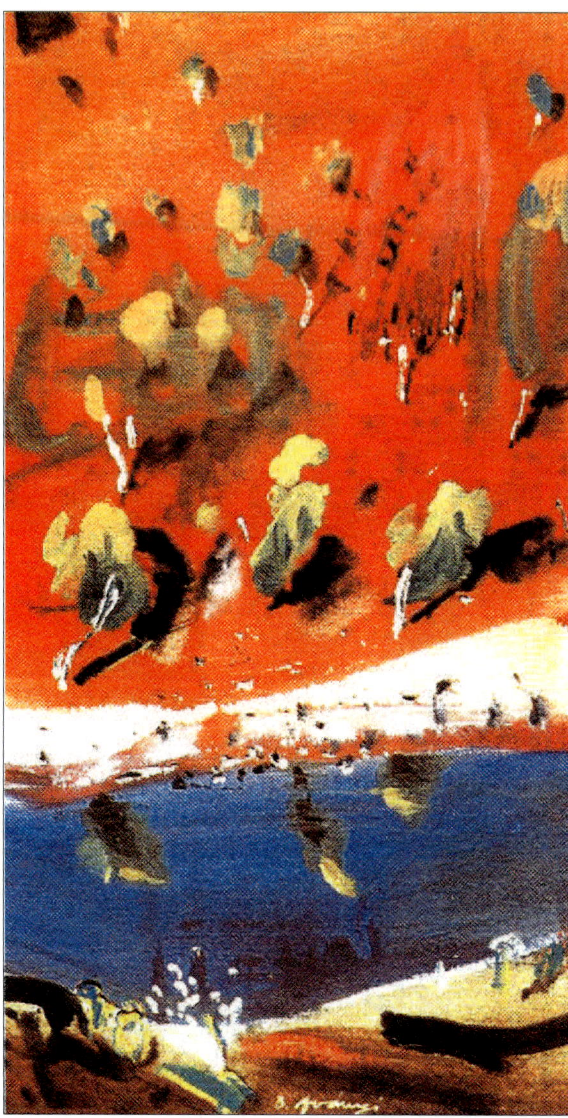

*Leichhardt River at Noon* gouache on paper 75cm x 30cm Bela Ivanyi 2000,

## KEVIN GREALY

**Taught Ceramics with the Flying Arts school from 1978 until 1982. He left when Mervyn Moriarty left the school.**

Kevin trained at the Queensland College of Art in the 1960s. In those days it followed the South Kensington type of teaching—only drawing and other skills were required—learning to be creative was not part of the curriculum. Kev remembers that William Robinson was a contemporary at the college and even he struggled to get good marks in his drawings when the work was judged by little things like a line that was not quite thick enough,

Kevin did one year's training at the Teachers College in 1960, which was all they did in those days, and he was only 18 when he began teaching pottery at one of the few high schools in regional Queensland. He thinks only Cairns, Innisfail, Townsville and Rockhampton high schools taught art in 1963. Like Mervyn Moriarty he had also attended Jon Molvig's life classes where he met other local artists. Molvig's classes broadened his knowledge of creative art. From there he taught interstate in Australia as well as in Canada. This is Kevin's story:

*Prior to joining AFAS I had made many visits to some of the country towns privately, conducting weekend or weeklong workshops. It made me aware of problems which I felt AFAS was overcoming.*

*Firstly, there was no system in those centres for one workshop to lead to another workshop to take the group members forward. Instead, they would engage another guest teacher who frequently took them through the same hoops as the previous teacher. The only difference may have been in style. I felt that this was not a good use of the group's finances, nor was it advancing their knowledge.*

*Secondly, a significant portion of the group's funds were spent in airfares for the tutor from Brisbane to "X" and back to Brisbane. The Flying Arts program of progressing from one town to the next made sense economically, as did the provision of a teacher who could lead the individuals in the group towards gradual independence.*

*I eventually wrote a three-year correspondence course in ceramics for AFAS where the focus was still on each student's progress at his/her own pace. There was no formal assessment, though formative assessment was always a crucial part of each visit.*

*There was a third reason why I wanted to teach with AFAS. As a young art teacher in Innisfail in 1962-64 I had experienced isolation from other artworkers, colleagues and from tuition or visits to practising artists in their studios, as would have happened if I had remained in Brisbane. I was aware that there was a thirst for these experiences beyond the gates of Brisbane and that students would be enthusiastic learners—always a bonus for teachers—and they were. My most productive teaching and most memorable teaching experiences have not taken place in colleges, high schools and universities, but in hot tin sheds, show grounds and shearers quarters miles from Brisbane.*

*Finally, there was Mervyn Moriarty. I remembered him from Art School days, had heard of his Eastaus project, and wanted to be part of it. I believe that regionalism in art is the future that Queensland should follow. There can be a unique richness in the art of people who react to the attributes of the region they live in and work in . . . its history, geography, climate, botany, industries, legends etc. From my experiences in China, I found that regional uniqueness was more interesting than much of the urban artwork which seemed distanced from, or a memory of, its subject. In pottery it often included using local raw materials in clay and glazes. The great styles of Asian ceramics stem from coaxing success from local raw materials i.e. Yixing teapots; Jingdezhen porcelain; Shigaraki in Japan; Choson in Korea; and in Europe: Delftware in Holland; Bone China in England; Beleek in Ireland.*

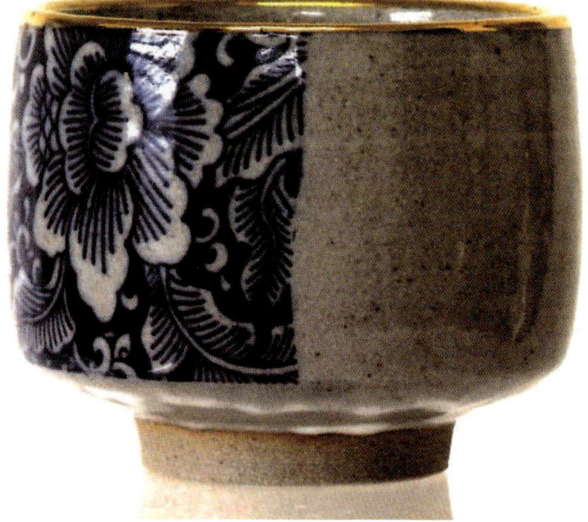

One of the many pots made by Kevin over the years. This is a Teabowl 10.5cm wide x 9cm high it was made in 2008. Woodfired stoneware celardon glaze, decal, gold lustre on rim

# BEVERLEY BUDGEN

**Memories of Australian Flying Art School 1983-7**

Beverley Budgen, a Queensland artist began painting as a very young child. A foundation member of the Wednesday Group, Beverley studied with Moriarty, Churcher, Gleghorn, Ed May and John Firth-Smith. Since 1982 she has travelled widely to England, Europe and the United States. This is her story:

*Barcaldine, early morning, sitting in the Cessna 210, wondering why the pilot was taking so long to do his pre-flight check. Then instead of getting into the plane he announced that there was absolutely no fuel in the tanks – someone had, during the night, stolen the valuable AVGAS. The pottery tutor and I climbed out of the plane and sheltered in a shed beside the strip and waited for more fuel to be delivered to the plane. It took for ever to hand pump the gas, nevertheless finally we were underway.*

*Early mornings at country airstrips were always wonderfully atmospheric. Jabirus strutting mysteriously about. Fond farewells from our overnight hosts. The smells were quite often very odd. One trip to Wandoan where the strip was in use by crop dusters had us almost gagging with the acrid chemical smells oozing from the ground. Another morning, flying into a small western town we were only a few feet from the grass when from our left came a light plane. It darted in front of us and landed just yards ahead of us. It taxied away with what we later found out was an ex RAAF fighter pilot at the controls. We were too shocked to even speak.*

*None of these incidents spoilt the times with the students who in some cases drove for miles the previous day to get into the centre where we were to hold the seminar. The one lasting impression of these wonderful people of the West was just how incredibly talented they were. One particular guy who attended regularly was a grazier, artist, equestrian tutor and judge, poet, stud sheep breeder, stonemason, builder, husband and father to 5 children. The multitalented AFAS students were not a rarity but almost the norm.*

*The morning teas and lunches were legendary. Each centre had several women whose cooking would put any TV chef to shame. The hospitality was unequalled all around the State and down into northern NSW where we worked with artists in Moree and Lightning Ridge.*

*One tour to NW Qld and beyond had the pilot conferring with one of the students at the Longreach workshop, Sally Ogg. She asked us if we would like to stopover at their station in Winton on our way south from Mt Isa. The pilot discovered that their airstrip was too short for our plane and we had to decline the invitation. Within the hour we heard that her husband would extend their airstrip to accommodate the Cessna, and a week later we landed, to be greeted by the beaming owners whose first words were "It just feels as though God has landed!"*

*Baralaba centre was always wonderful as we stayed in an old Queenslander on Auda Maclean's property "Coolum". The old place was next door to the homestead and had been the Maclean family's original home. Coolum had a river running through and near the homestead was a billabong filled with lotus blooming. Dinner each night was in the homestead. We were supplied with torches and some alarming advice – "Remember, stamp your feet on your way across to dinner as we have lots of snakes at the moment!"*

*Nights around the dinner table with our hosts were filled with stories of crocodiles in the swimming pool, tales of min min lights, polo meets, tennis tournaments, strange shaped boulders and on and on.*

*Once at "Clarenden", a station just outside Blackall, during dinner amid gales of laughter we were invited to try on our host's coronet. Our host, Ian Wehl, had just inherited a German title of Baronet. After dinner, entertainment at a station in Winton could include playing ping pong and then a few sets of tennis on a well lit court. Endlessly wonderful hospitality.*

*I remember marvelling on arriving back in Brisbane that the inside of heavy plastic sleeves of the folio of drawings was coated in the fine dust of Western Queensland which seemed totally invisible while we were outback.*

From 1973 onwards Beverley has had 20 Solo Shows.
Her selected Group Exhibitions have been:
1954 Qld Tourist Bureau, Melbourne and Sydney.
From 1964 37 group shows : Qld Art Gallery, UQ Art Museum, Institute of Modern Art Brisbane, Brisbane City Museum, JCU Townsville, Uni SQ, and many more, both interstate and overseas.
From 1954 Beverly has won 29 major art prizes.

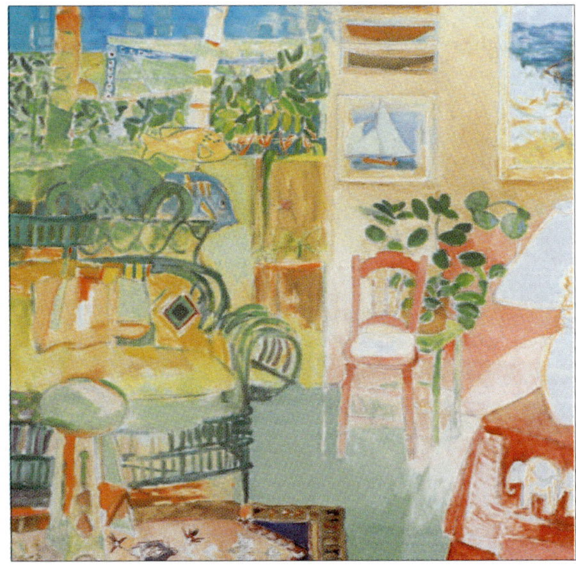

*Paradisio* Oil on canvas 36" x 36"
Beverley Budgen

## Student Stories:
## Following are stories from some of the people who trained with Mervyn Moriarty and Flying Arts between 1970 and 2001

# Student Stories from South East Queensland

## BUNDABERG

***CORALIE BUSBY, 1971***

*My mother had been an artist and I had always wanted to become one too, but I was living in a country town with my husband and family and there were no art classes or art galleries, not even a library, as the local councillors felt that now we had television people would no longer require books for reading.*

*When the Flying Art School started it brought books. Before then we would travel to Gin Gin which had a small library and they would get books in from Brisbane for us which we devoured. Later I began collecting books for my own personal use and now have quite a library of my own.*

*I started painting one day in the 1960s when there was an advertisement in the local paper asking those who were interested in forming a painting group to come along to a meeting.*

*Thus we formed our local art group and it began with still life drawing where we learnt basic skills. When Roy Churcher came to judge our annual exhibition he could see the group badly needed tuition from more advanced teachers. Roy stayed at our house and we discussed our problems. Soon after that we heard that a flying art school was being formed by his friend, Mervyn Moriarty.*

*Mervyn made contact with art groups around the country and I was the first to enrol (Mervyn and Helen put my enrolment form up on the wall of their studio). He was an excellent lecturer - we learnt so much; when he spoke we could listen to him forever. He was never boring, it was wonderful the way he could talk about art, he just made it sound so exciting and the books he wrote were a great help. Later tutors were Bela Ivanyi and Roy Churcher, they were also great teachers.*

*Then came a pottery tutor and our Bundaberg potters began producing some very fine work. We also had guest tutors from Sydney who often came along.*

*Mervyn and Helen would stay with my husband and I for the two-day workshop which was held in our garage. Our group became quite good. Several of the people who came to our seminars were already art teachers in surrounding high schools.*

*We were a more contemporary group than the original Art Society members who still held their annual exhibition, so I formed a gallery for our members in the front of my home. This was called the Allamanda Art Gallery and I ran it for Flying Art Students for eleven years.*

*For me contemporary work was always very exciting but Mervyn never tried to influence my style. One of his first remarks was that we were never to copy from pictures. We had to go out and draw from the inspiration that nature gave us; for him copying was not art and never would be.*

*In the beginning Mervyn had no financial help, he really did it on a wing and a prayer and we helped him because we knew that if he gave up we would lose such a lot.*

*Once we got a taste for art we wanted to see paintings, but Mervyn would never show us any of his work, he was so frightened that we would merely copy his style and he wanted us to develop our own individual talents. He believed that art was like handwriting, we were all different and we had to develop in our own way. So we never saw any original art until we went to Brisbane. That was the first time I had ever walked into a gallery. Firstly we went to the Johnstone gallery, and then to the Moreton gallery.*

*In those days Edgells were growing acres and acres of beans which were picked by hand so we would go out for weeks and weeks to raise the money to fly to Brisbane for our once a year gallery crawl and it was absolutely wonderful. At that time the Queensland Art Gallery was still up on Gregory Terrace.*

*By the time Mervyn left Flying Arts my husband had died and my children were grown so I packed up and left Bundaberg and went to Sydney where I studied and exhibited for eight years. During that time I went to a workshop on Long Island in New York and worked for five weeks with artists from all over the world, it was a great experience. Then I went to London and Paris to visit galleries there.*

Coralie has held solo exhibitions in Bundaberg, Rockhampton, Brisbane and Sydney. She has won prizes in Bundaberg and Gympie and is represented in public and private collections throughout Australia. Her early "Wallum" series paintings were purchased by the Bundaberg Sugar Co., the Bundaberg *News Mail* and the Biloela City Council.

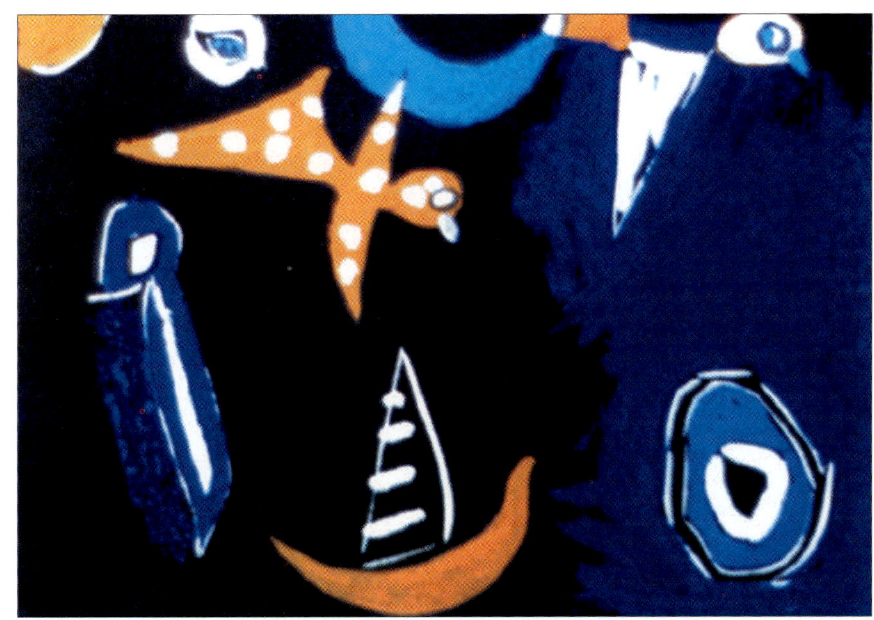

*Wynnum Night Creatures* Coralie Busby, Bundaberg

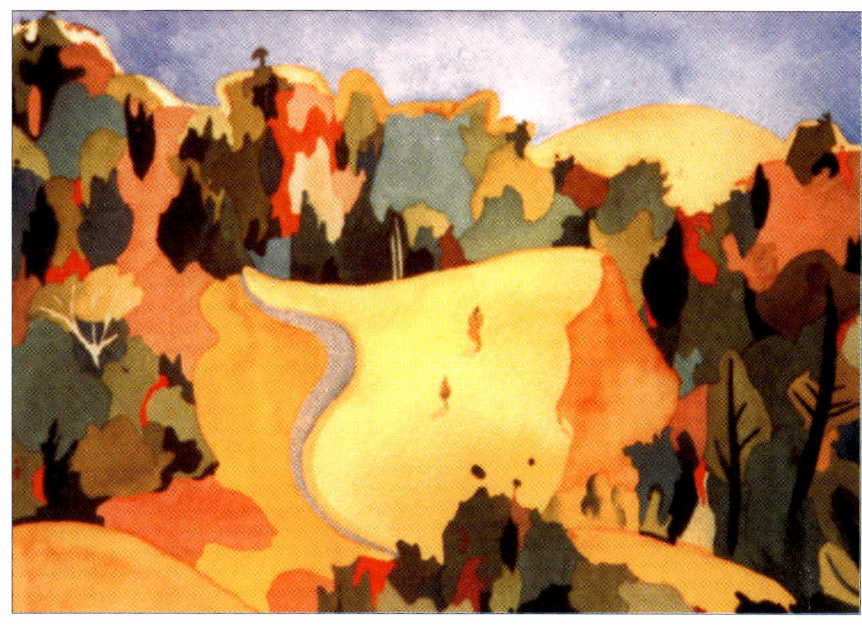

*The Bunyas watercolour 35cm x 50cm* Jack Wilson, Dalby

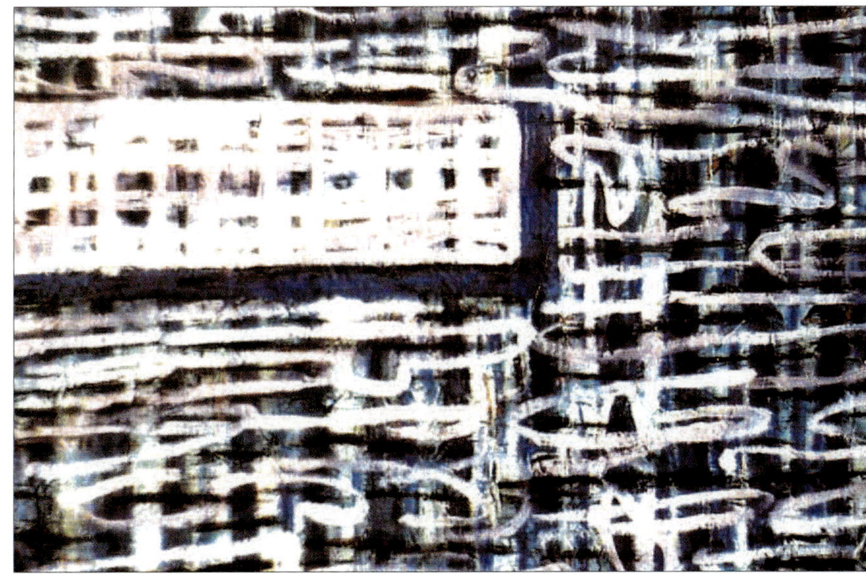

*Blue Angle* Coralie Busby, Bundaberg

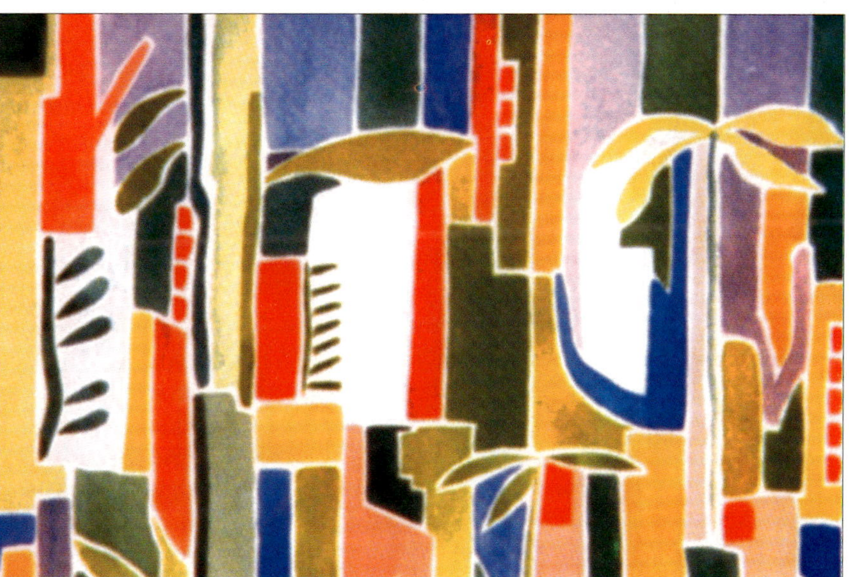

*Untitled* watercolour Jack Wilson, Dalby

## DALBY

### *JACK WILSON, 1971*

*I began painting with the Dalby Art Group in 1968 as I had always been interested in art books and galleries.*

*I joined Flying Arts when it came to Dalby in 1971 and over the years my tutors were Mervyn Moriarty, Bela Ivanyi and Roy Churcher.*

*In 1968 Mervyn Moriarty came occasionally to give lessons and seminars, until in 1971 he started up his Flying Art School, flying in to give four seminars a year. As is well known, Mervyn came as a breath of fresh air. The group owes much to his efforts.*

*Before Flying Arts, members of the Dalby Art Group would drive to the countryside for a day's painting with a bottle of red. We just copied the work of the tutors we had then, there were lots of gum trees, and creek scenes with bunyas in the background.*

*The Dalby Art Group had started in 1958 when the Adult Education Dept. sent out our first art tutor – Don Featherston, a watercolourist from Toowoomba who came up once a month, held field days and gave instruction.*

*Ron Murray, also from Toowoomba took over in 1962, teaching both oil and watercolour painting. Later on Len Blacklow, David Fowler, and Alex Roteveel held seminars and regular field days. Another was Herb Carstens. Many other artists came and gave seminars over the years.*

*In 1963 Dalby held its Centenary celebrations. To help the festivities the Art Group ran an art contest with open prize money of £130. Laurie Thomas from the Queensland Art Gallery came to judge, and gave the open oil to Irene Amos, and the watercolour to Joy Roggencamp. The prizes were non-acquisitive, but with the profits Dalby's first painting was bought from Herb Carstens. The art contest was such a success that it was decided to hold a similar contest every year. So from 1964 the Acquisitive Dalby Art Contest became an annual event.*

*These contests continued through until 1974 when the exhibitions had Open Purchase Prize Money instead. In 1979 it was decided to discontinue holding art contests altogether. There were various reasons for this, the main one being funding.*

*The Town Council gave grants towards the contests from 1977 and the Visual Arts Board of the Australia Council gave yearly grants from 1975-1979 under the Contemporary Arts Acquisition Scheme.*

*In 1971 the cultural bodies of Dalby were given a home, it was the old Bore Baths. Built in 1923 the Hot Artesian Baths were said to contain 'curative properties unexcelled in any other part of the Commonwealth.' The art group and the potters were the first tenants. The two front rooms were set aside for a gallery.*

*In the early 1970s NSW had 20 regional galleries, Victoria 16, Queensland had only two.*

*When Mervyn arrived he opened our eyes to contemporary art and a new and exciting way of looking at reality which freed us from the narrowness of traditional painting as we knew it. We were now free to use our imaginations.*

*Mervyn came as a breath of fresh air and dragged us into the 20th century.*

*Flying Arts visited us four times a year. Workshops were held at the old Arts Centre in Marble Street. In the early days we would hold the lessons in a shed at the Show Grounds, but later when Mervyn started coming, we used the old Bore Baths as our painting centre.*

*I would pick him and Helen up from the airport. If they stayed overnight it would be with Tom and Joan Gill. As well as the workshops there was always much discussion on art history and related subjects.*

*In the Eastaus period Mervyn wore casual gear – he was a true bohemian with his wild ginger hair and beard. Sometimes we would have lunch at the RSL and we would have to warn some of his accompanying artists to wear shoes and shirts when we went to eat there.*

*My watercolours are now in the Dalby Regional Gallery and the Global Arts Link at Ipswich.*
[Today known as the Ipswich Regional Gallery.]

## DALBY

### *KATHRYN BRIMBLECOMBE-FOX, 1971*

*I grew up with my two younger brothers on my parent's grain farm 11 miles outside Dalby on the Darling Downs. This farm had been developed by my grandfather Wilfred Brimblecombe who was also the Federal Member for Maranoa for sixteen years during the 1950-1960s. I went to local Dalby schools before attending boarding school at Fairholme in Toowoomba.*

*I had painted since early childhood and had met with success at local, regional and state art competitions. When I was twelve I started attending Flying Arts. Both my mother Elsie Brimblecombe and grandmother, Enid Ross, painted. I was thrilled when my grandmother suggested I attend the classes with her.*

*I also studied art at school and completed a BA [double major Art History] at the University of Queensland in 1980. I worked at the National Gallery in Canberra as a curatorial assistant for a year after graduation, married in 1982 and moved to Goondiwindi, where I attended Flying Arts [off and on] until 1998-99. I moved to Brisbane in 2000.*

*My early tutors were Mervyn Moriarty and Jock Clutterbuck. Flying Arts toured Dalby about four times a year, Goondiwindi two to three times a year. Workshops at Goondiwindi were held in an old woolshed. However, we often ended up outside to talk and work.*

*During the early days we were encouraged to bring recent paintings to the class. Mervyn or the visiting artist he had with him would then discuss the work with us as a group. Thus, three quarters of the first day would be spent talking about each other's work. This was very useful because it provided an opportunity for self-reflection and critical feedback. The classes were a time for experimentation rather than producing a complete work. As a child I found Flying Arts a challenge.*

*Flying Arts did not visit very often but the fact that they came at all was fantastic. It was also great for local artists to be shown at the local art exhibitions with professional artists from further afield. I think Dalby was pretty unusual in that respect. I seemed to be the only 'kid' who actually went along to Flying Arts.*

*I know Gertrude Langer came to Dalby but I am not sure how often. She saw my work and I think she gave me a couple of prizes, as did Irene Amos. I also received a prize from Ron Radford in my late teens at one of the local art society art competitions.*

*I think Roy Churcher came to Dalby, I certainly remember him coming to Goondiwindi. He was a good talker. When he came to Goondiwindi he would sit around and talk with us. Some people just wanted to paint whereas I really liked the connection with the city artists.*

*I remember Mervyn's art books which he had written as a teaching tool. They provided a different art education to the one I received at secondary school. Art education in primary school in those days was non-existent. Mervyn's books contained many exercises on 'looking' which I really enjoyed. The process, experimentation and what was essentially play were important components of our lessons.*

*Many people travelled in from out of town to attend Flying Arts workshops. People would give up their whole weekend to paint and sit around talking. In Goondiwindi some people travelled for a couple of hours to get to town for the lessons. In both Dalby and Goondiwindi mainly women attended classes. However, there were a couple of men [I especially remember Jack Wilson] in Dalby who attended regularly. Many of these people who knew me as a child have continued to show an interest in my career.*

*I have received prizes in a number of art competitions over the years. One memorable competition was in 1977 when I won first prize in the open section of the Queen's Silver Jubilee Art Competition. I received my prize from Queen Elizabeth II at Government House. My work is now in the Stanthorpe Regional Gallery, Ipswich City Collection, Dalby Regional Gallery and various corporate and private collections in Australia, UK, USA, Korea and the UAE. I have exhibited overseas and extensively in south east Queensland.*

*Flying Arts was and is an important offering for rural and regional communities.*

*Skittles* mixed media *on paper 56cm x 74cm*
Kathryn Brimblecombe-Fox, Dalby

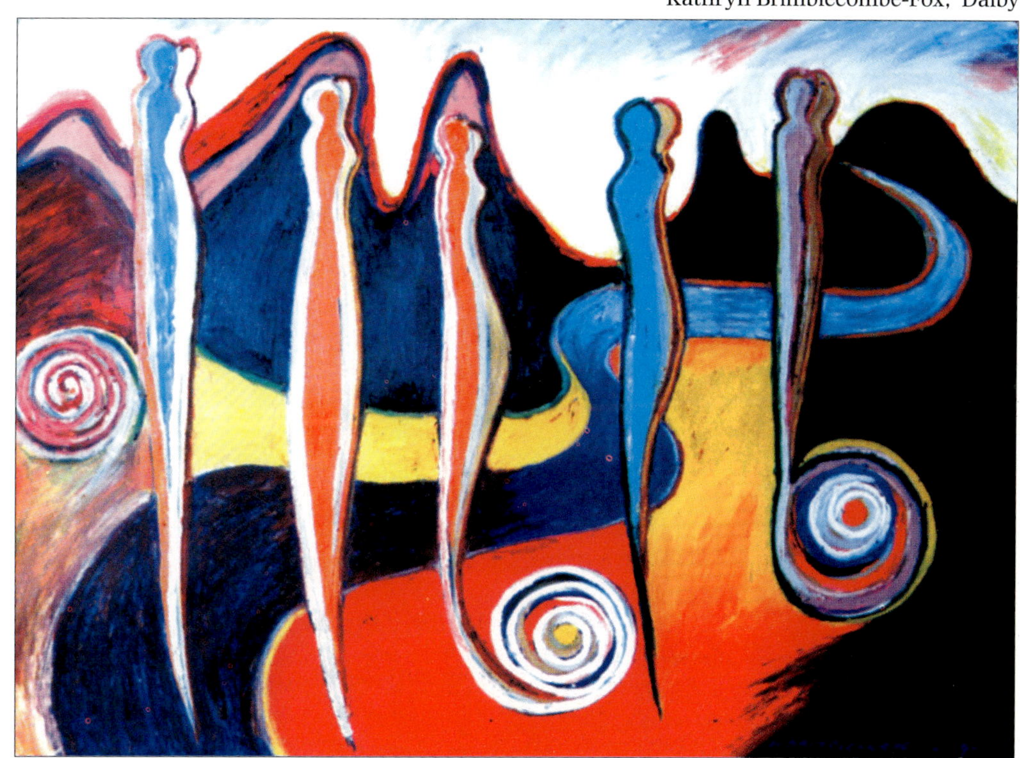

# DALBY

## *MAREE CAMERON, 1976*

*I am a self taught artist who began painting with the Australian Flying Arts School in 1976. I won my first prize for a portrait, followed by a Minister for the Arts Encouragement Award in 1987, which allowed me to spend a week in Longreach with Flying Arts tutor Warren Palmer.*

*Others who have touched my painting career are Mervyn Moriarty, Irene Amos, Trevor Weeks, Wendy Allen and Pat Hoffie, while Jeanne Macaskill has commented on my papers.*

*In 1997 I won the Arts Queensland Award, which enabled me to attend McGregor Winter School at The University of Southern Queensland in Toowoomba. My first public solo exhibition was held on 20 June 1995. Since then I have had twelve solo exhibitions.*

*Time is never wasted when it comes to ART. I am now passing on my techniques and experience by teaching the Durong 'Big Scrub Art Group' and another small group in Jondaryan. I have also taken five other artists to the Jondaryan Woolshed to promote the Heritage Complex. It was so successful that our group was asked to sketch and paint the Oakey War Museum. Presently I am the Rep. For Flying Arts in Dalby.*

*My story began in Charleville where I was born on 10th February 1951 and where I spent my childhood. After that I went to Boarding School at All Hallows in Brisbane. My mother insisted I do a commercial course but the shorthand class was next to the art room so I was always watching them at work and I wanted to join them.*

*Then I met, courted and married my husband Jim and we moved to the Tambo area in 1971 where we stayed until 1989. We had two children Robert and Sandra.*

*We were living on an old cattle property and for the first fifteen years we had no phone, power or mail service.*

*Around 1975-76 I began to paint in my spare time and I became involved with the Flying Art School.*

*Mervyn Moriarty used to come out by plane from Brisbane and bring a potter with him to hold workshops in the bush so, like our city cousins, we did not miss out on the latest techniques.*

*I attended all the painting workshops and for the first ten years I painted in oils but never exhibited because I thought I wasn't good enough. Then in 1985 I won my first portrait prize at the Charleville Show, it was the first time I had ever sold a painting. In 2006 I won 2nd prize at the Royal Toowoomba Show for my self-portrait, so I knew that I was making progress with my work.*

*But the highlight for me was my portrait of R.M. Williams. He was 90 when I painted him and I had two sittings with him. I remember taking the portrait back for his approval and he studied it for what seemed ages and then he said: "There is only one thing I don't like Maree, it's the skin on my arms – it's not dark enough. I'm like an Aboriginal – make me darker."*

*After I made the change he thought it was great and wanted me to take it to Canberra's Portrait Museum. I told him that I was flat out getting past Brisbane and I finally gave it to our son.*

*In 1987 I won the then Minister for Arts (Mr. Brian Austin) Award. This was an Encouragement Award of $500 which was a lot of money in those days. It enabled me to attend my first Summer School in Longreach with fellow artist Jenny Kelly.*

*In 1997 I won the Bell Chimes Art Award. Then in 1999 I won the Arts Queensland Award and was able to attend the Winter School in Toowoomba.*

*During that year I was also one of fifteen chosen from all over Queensland, from Cairns to the border, to participate in internet trials for a course called INDELTA through Flying Arts in Brisbane and the University of Southern Queensland in Toowoomba. Our tutors were from Griffith University. It was a success and in 2007 the course was passed on to the TAFE colleges.*

*In 2006 I had my first showing with six other Regional artists at the Graydon Gallery in Brisbane. It was wonderful to meet up with a fellow artist from Blackall who had painted with me thirty years ago and find that we were both still painting and were exhibiting our work together in Brisbane.*

*My next project is a Bell Art Calendar in the making. It is due to be released on 23rd September 2007. I have two pieces in the calendar. Also, Arts West at Blackall have a Fabrication Competition in which I have another piece. They will be displayed in the Winton Waltzing Matilda Gallery.*

*There are five categories in the competition – painting, sculpture, pottery, textiles and silversmithing. Each category has a prize of $500 and each entry will receive a piece of the same roll of fabric on which to produce a masterpiece, and so our journey goes on.*

*I have two pieces in the Brisbane Exhibition opening on 9th August 2007 and entries in the Flying Arts Regional Awards and I have just held my twelfth solo exhibition at the Dalby Regional Gallery. In 2008 I will be exhibiting at the Kingaroy Gallery and in 2009 at the White Gums Gallery in Chinchilla.*

*I am still discovering new techniques and styles to express my feelings and relay the excitement of my world through fantasy and colour.*

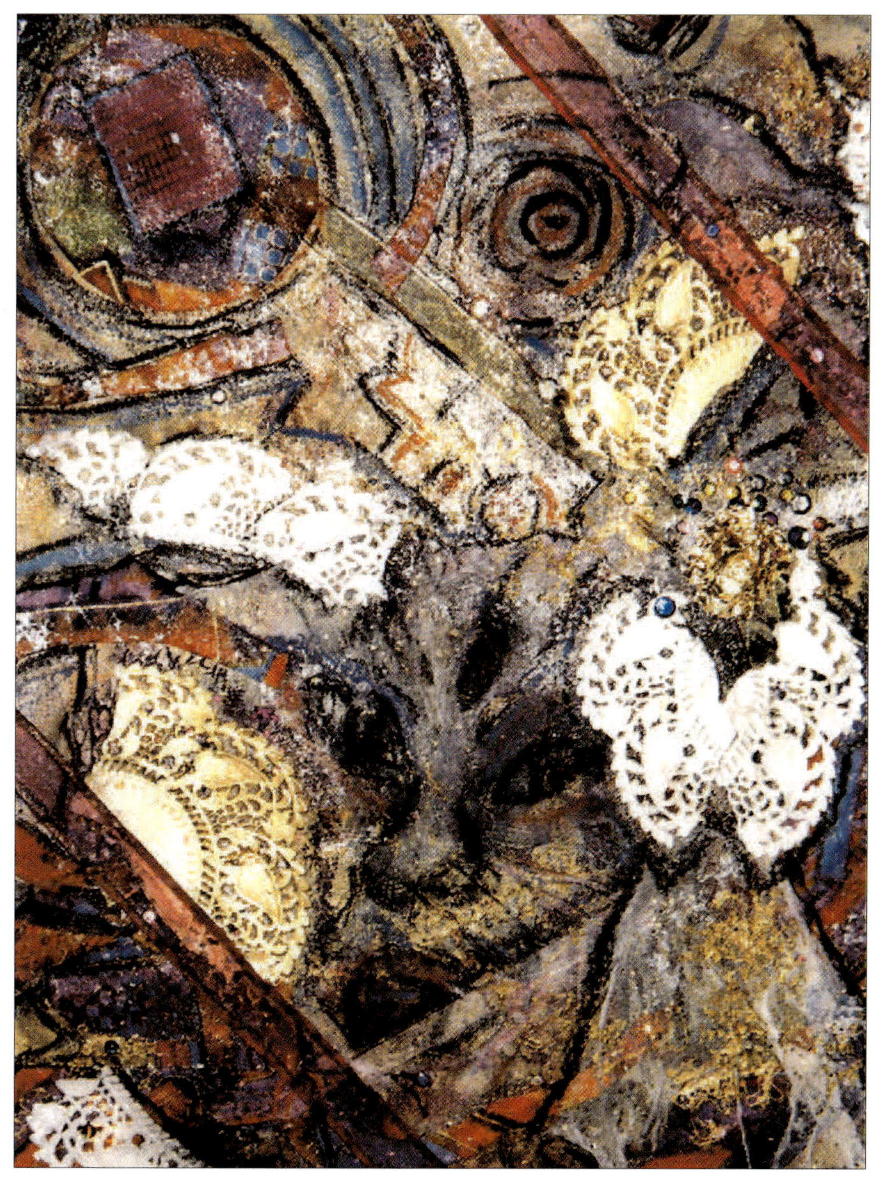

*A Spiritual Encounter*   Maree Cameron, Dalby
Patchwork

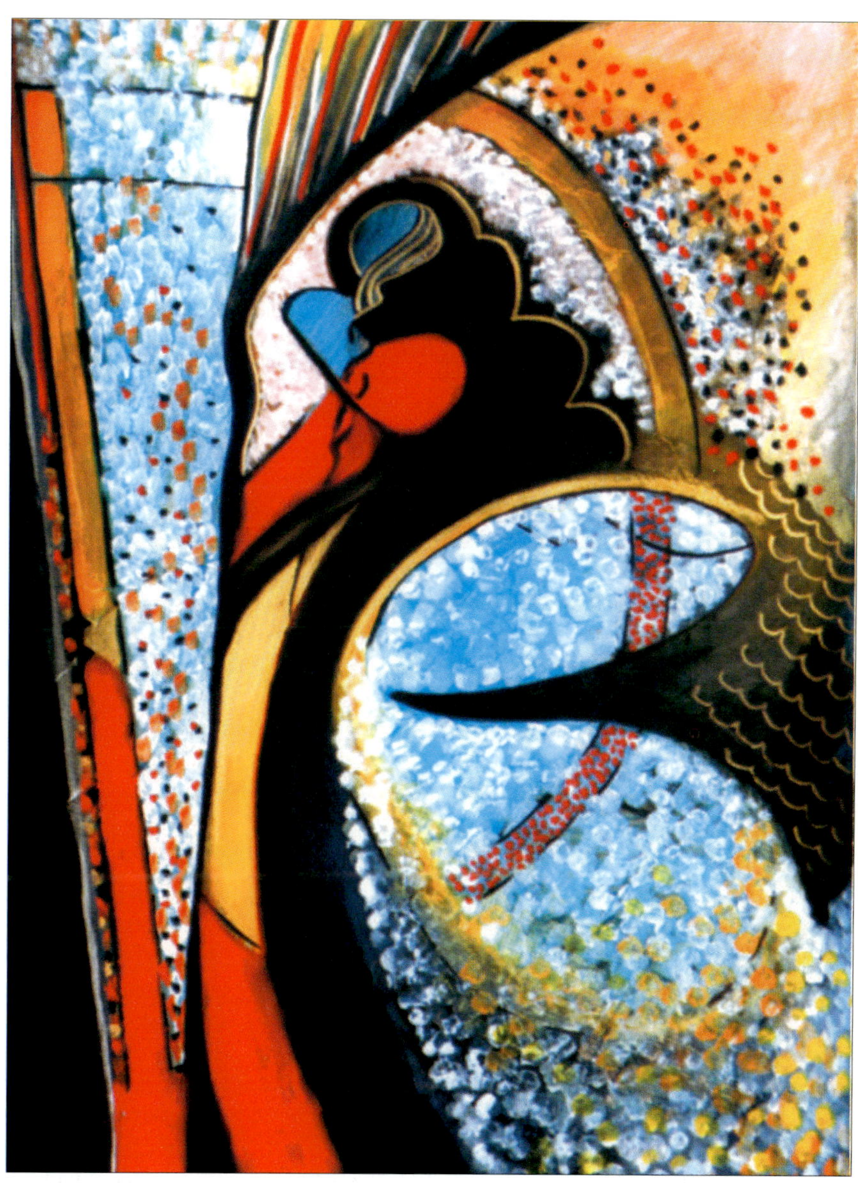

*Take Flight*   mixed media on paper   Kathryn Brimblecombe-Fox, Dalby

## DALBY

### *ROBYN BAUER, 1970S*

*I started going to art workshops in Dalby when I was about ten. This would have been around 1968. They were organised by the Dalby Art Group which was incredibly active even before Flying Arts came along. They had workshops with David Fowler and Herb Carstens from Toowoomba and they had other people who came to teach us art as well. Dalby had an acquisitive art prize every year then and I remember Roy Churcher came to judge it. He taught us on the weekend he came.*

*Then Mervyn came to Dalby and a few years later he brought Bela Ivanyi. I don't remember Clifton Pugh. I went to Mervyn's workshops when he had Helen with him. In those days the Dalby Art Centre was in a building down on Myall Creek and Mervyn would take everyone down to the creek. We looked at bark and trees and looked in the dirt and we began by drawing in the dirt. He was an incredibly imposing figure for a ten, eleven or twelve year old.*

*Mervyn was very sparing with his comments. He didn't just praise things, he would stand there next to you for ten minutes watching you doing something which I found a bit intimidating. But he was obviously trying to work out what I was trying to do and then he would say something or make a suggestion.*

*I particularly remember Bela's class because he was talking about the huge works he was doing on watercolour paper and he told us we had to be careful when working on paper. If we made just one simple mark wrong we could ruin the whole thing. If that happened we'd have to start on a fresh piece of paper and it could cost a fortune in materials.*

*But it was Mervyn who came on a regular basis and kept alive my passion for art. Years later, around 1980 when I was twenty-two I was working at the Queensland Art Gallery as Education Officer. It so happened that I had to organise an exhibition called the 'In Touch' Exhibition for the year of the disabled. When we took that exhibition out west with the Flying Art School Mervyn was our pilot.*

*I remember there was a woman named Peta Parer on the trip and she was one of the first volunteer guides. She was into Distance Education for Kindergartens, so while she was talking to people about that Mervyn was taking his Flying Arts classes and I was looking after the exhibition from the Queensland Art Gallery. We flew it to Julia Creek, Mt. Isa and Moura I think. In all there were about five or six places we went to.*

*I always thought of Mervyn as this bohemian, red wine drinking person larger than life because he was so big and I thought he was a bit scary. But when I actually saw him flying I was absolutely amazed at how meticulous he was, how careful he was, When he was in the air he concentrated only on his flying and he had that reputation of being a really good pilot. I was so young when I flew with him. It was just after I was married that I had to do that trip.*

*Afterwards I had a studio in the city and once again Mervyn became part of my career. He had studios in Eagle Street at the Brisbane Eastaus Art School and a few of us also had studios there. As well as myself there was Jim Edwards, Marit Hegge and Michael Richards who subsequently became the 'Courier Mail' art critic and wrote plays and various things. We called ourselves the Eagle Street Artists although we did show our work in the Eastaus gallery, so in a way we were associated with Eastaus. I remember I had an exhibition with Jamie Maclean and Helen Campbell and Mervyn opened it.*

*Mervyn also did a bit of teaching at Eagle Street when he was not flying out bush. I think he took what are now called 'Master Classes' and I went along to a few of those. By this time I was teaching the children's classes for Eastaus.*

*Sheelah Mee was one of my tutors while I was at Eagle Street, also Paul Griffin. Irene Amos did workshops there as well. That was the time when I was at the University of Queensland and living at Duchesne College so I would catch the bus in to the Master Classes with Sheelah. I remember that Sheelah was favourably reviewed by Gertrude Langer when she held an exhibition in the Eastaus gallery.*

*Gertrude also reviewed my work when I had my exhibition at Eastaus and she gave me a good review in the 'Courier Mail'. Later I did some reviews myself; when Michael Richards went overseas I took his job as 'Courier Mail' art critic for a while. Those were the days – no-one does that any more.*

Robyn now operates a gallery in Paddington, Brisbane, and apart from private collections her work can be found in the Dalby Regional Gallery and the Wide Bay Gallery.

## THARGOMINDAH

### *DONNA HOBBS, 2001*

*I have only been involved with Flying Arts at the Bulloo Shire for the past three years. In that time we have undertaken the services of a Raku Pottery tutor - Mark Warne. This is the only time Flying Arts have visited Thargo during my time. The class was held in the town hall. There are no professional artists within this pottery group. I did not attend the workshop myself, I simply organised it as the RADF Liaison Officer.*

*Thargomindah has a pottery group of whom most members attended the Raku workshop (12 participants). There was a pottery group many years ago, but I am unsure of its history. Our nearest art training school would probably be Dalby - 700km east of Thargomindah.*

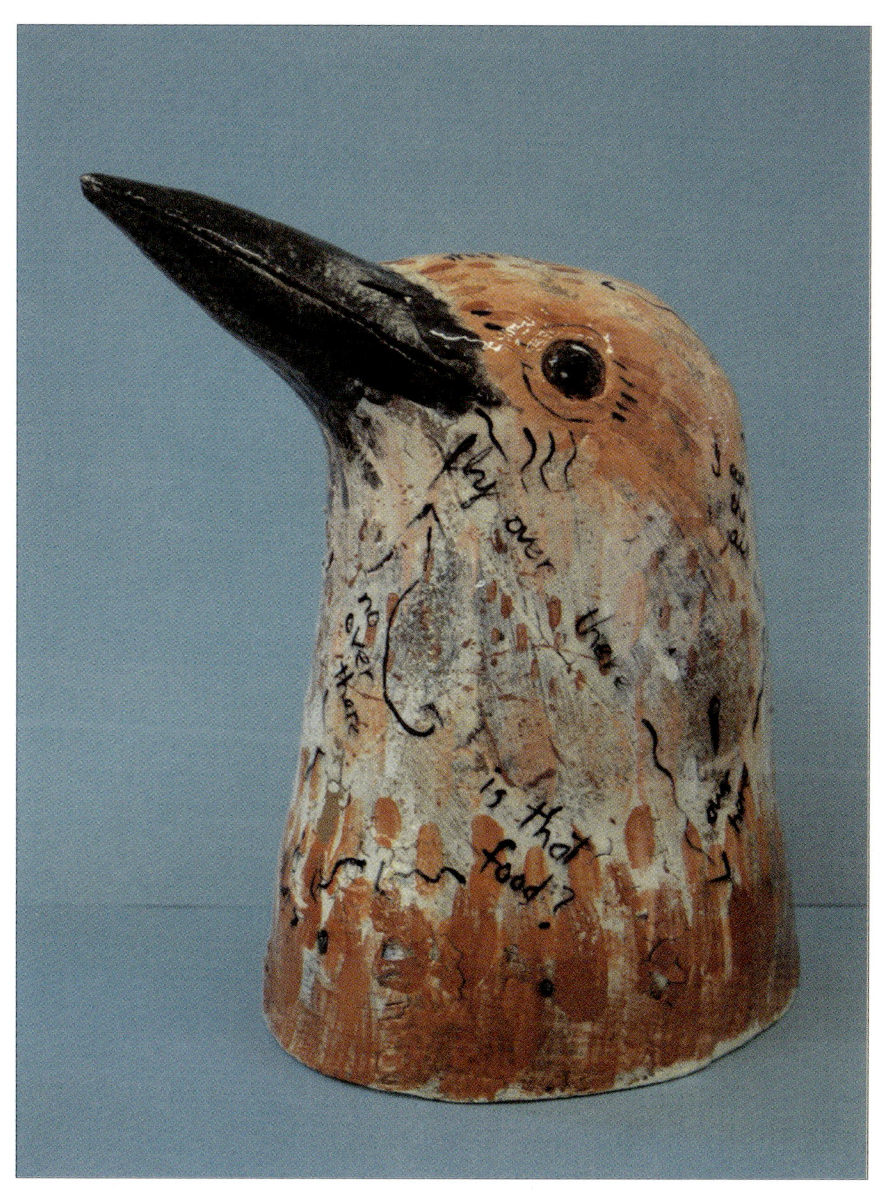


*Bird Thoughts* glazed buff raku clay 40cm high Robyn Bauer, Dalby

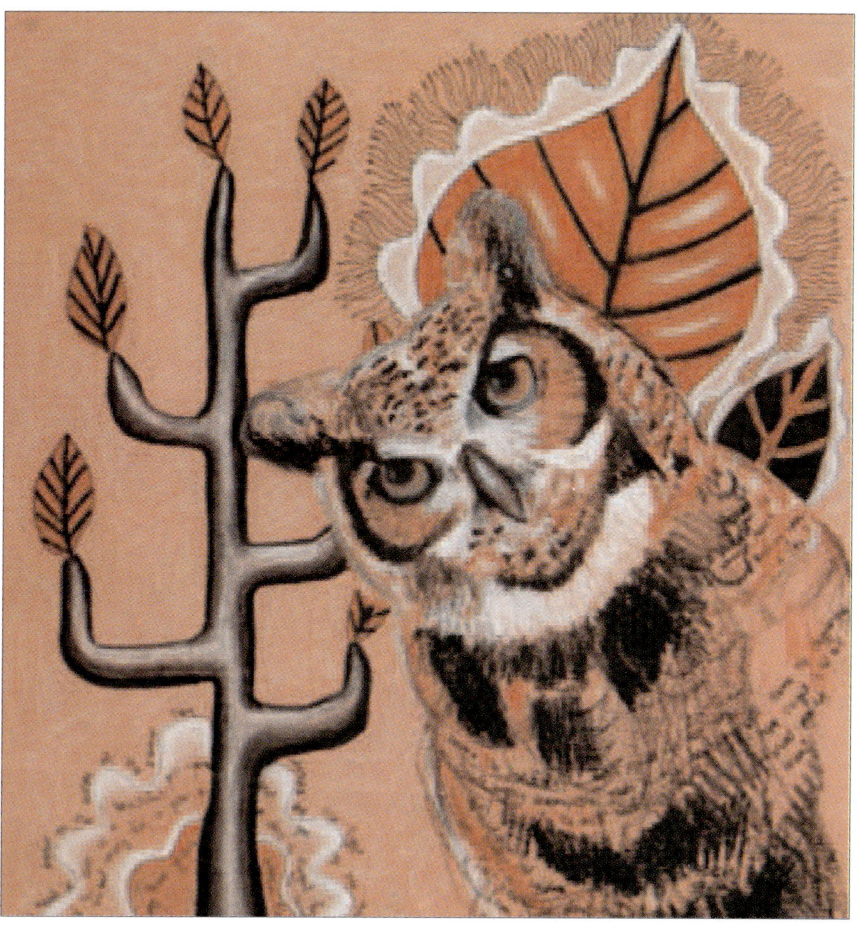

*The Great Wing Beat (Owl)* Ink and charcoal on paper 35cm x 35cm
Robyn Bauer, Dalby

## GOONDIWINDI

### *PAT GARNER, 1971*

*In 1971 a group of friends with like-minded art interests formed an art group, the first in Goondiwindi, to foster painting and to share our knowledge with each other. We also needed a group of people who could mount art exhibitions for the various community activities beginning to take shape, e.g. the Spring Festival and Annual Show. Most importantly we were looking into matters of tutors.*

*After much discussion I wrote to Penny Murphy on 'Meandarra' around August 1972 for information on Mervyn Moriarty and the 'Eastaus Art School'.*
*I then wrote to him and in November a call came from Mervyn saying that he was dropping in to meet the group to discuss our request and would I pick him up from the airstrip. He wished to see our facilities.*

*We had an annexe on the eastern side of the theatre, in a central position off the main street, it was large and airy with plenty of light and came to us courtesy of the local Council.*

*The visit was a particularly good one. Mervyn was impressed with the venue and as our group had more than sixteen people in it we would be able to have a two-day seminar and he would start us with his first western tour in 1973.*

*Mervyn complemented his classes with twenty-four books of written lessons to match the classes; they were sent to us on joining. We found them very comprehensive, they were a credit to him. We felt his courses equal to art courses people received in the city.*

*So began our association with Eastaus. I was given the role of Centre Rep. for Goondiwindi, a role I thoroughly enjoyed.*
*In 1975 we welcomed Bela Ivanyi as our new tutor. He alternated with Mervyn.*

*1976 and our classes continued. Mervyn's visits now included a potter, John Vasdrall. The potters occupied the southern end of the Annexe. Dianne Cairns was their Rep.*

*Through all the funding problems during these years our classes never faltered in content. We received excellent tutoring from our dedicated and committed teachers and our art understanding grew and flourished.*

*In 1977 funding was again difficult and we feared the school would be forced to close. However, the students all rallied behind Mervyn with letters of support. We lobbied members of parliament and finally we were offered a lifeline in the form of the Kelvin Grove College.*

*In my five years as Centre Rep we were given a solid foundation in art practice and sound advice through deep and meaningful sessions of philosophy in which we hung on every word.*

*Mervyn was a guru to the art-starved bush and Bela complemented Mervyn's mystical ways with a more practical and down to earth approach.*

*They are often remembered by members of our group. We all admired their teaching methods, their ability and their commitment and dedication.*

*Mervyn must go down in history for his courage in developing his remarkable dream of the first flying art school in the world. WE DIPS OUR LID TO YOU MERVYN MORIARTY...*

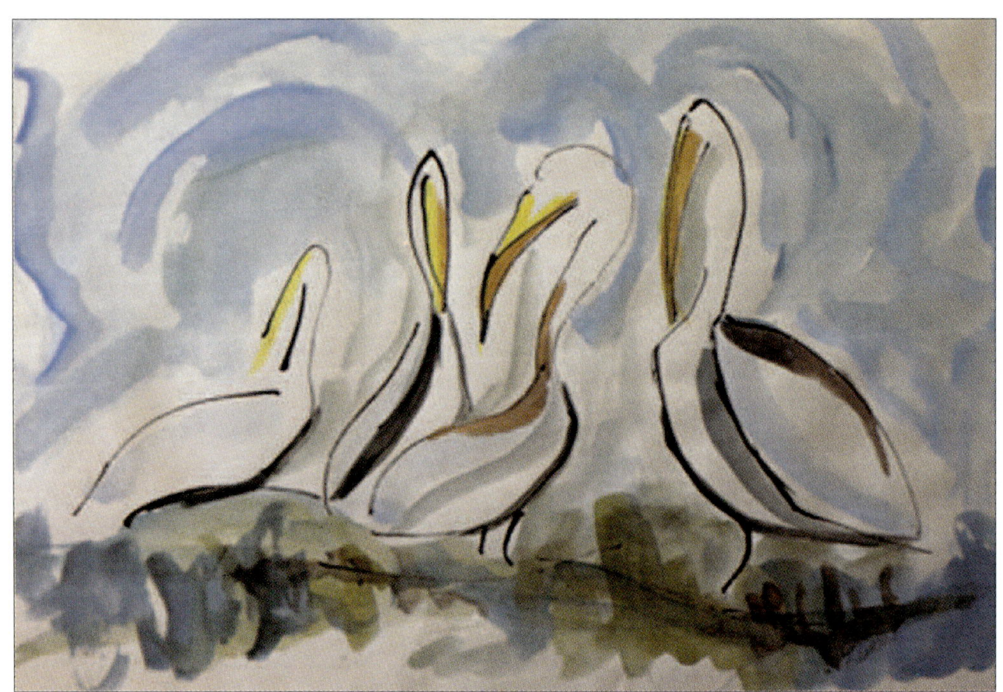

*Pelicans* watercolour Pat Garner Goondiwindi

# GOONDIWINDI

## *JOCELYN CAMERON, 1974-1981*

*I trained with Flying Arts from 1974-1981. I always had an interest in art and received a few lessons from visiting artist Tony Shielbeck. My Flying Arts tutors were Mervyn Moriarty, Bela Ivanyi and Roy Churcher who came four times a year.*

*Workshops were held at the Civic Centre annexe, an old shed just out of town. One of my paintings was used as a design for a wall installation and now hangs in the Goondiwindi Cultural Centre. It received a Highly Commended in a National art competition.*

*It was my tuition through Flying Arts which gave me my success. Mervyn showed me how to approach the subject with freshness and originality.*

*The Goondiwindi & District Creative Art Group was established in 1969 and the group worked in the shearer's quarters at 'Jindabyne', Bungunya. A few friends who were into craft brought their spinning wheels, easels and painting equipment along.*

*Over 60 people from the surrounding districts attended the first four days and they all helped each other to learn the three basic subjects - painting, pottery, spinning and weaving. At the classes they also did some floral art and natural dyeing.*

*It was thought that Goondiwindi's population was too small to support a cultural centre but Mr. Creedy, Director of Cultural Activities in Queensland, decided that the self-help efforts of the group deserved financial assistance and gave the group a series of annual grants towards tuition and equipment.*

*Early in 1970 we were successfully launched at the Goondiwindi Showgrounds, then the venue became the High School for the next 18 months until they had enough numbers to rent the Annexe of the Civic Theatre in the main street of Goondiwindi.*

*The annexe and adjoining kitchen was used as a workshop area for all subjects. It was also the base for the local potters who used the outside carpark for their two kilns.*

*A generous grant for building renovations from the Dept. of Education allowed the group to establish workbenches, screens, lights, blackboard, etc. which would become part of the future Goondiwindi Cultural Centre.*

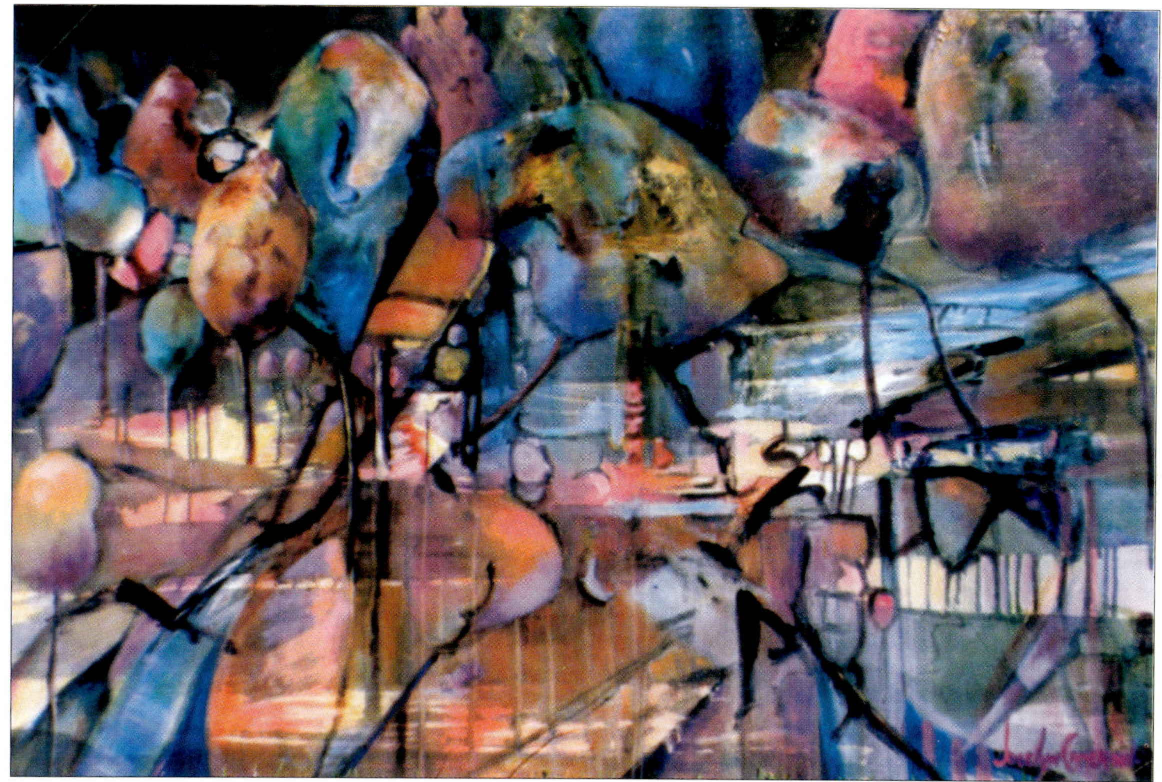

*And Then the Rain Came* acrylic on board 105cm x 125cm Jocelyn Cameron, Goondiwindi

## GOONDIWINDI/ST.GEORGE

### *JUDITH BANKS, 1972*

*My first training in art was at school and I passed my senior art examinations. My teacher was a Miss Wilde who was a student of Rubery Bennett. Then I drove to Goondiwindi where I first attended Flying Arts for two years going along to six or seven classes. At St. George I continued to go to the Flying Arts workshops. In 1974 the Council provided us with an Arts & Crafts cottage.*

*The visits of Mervyn Moriarty to Goondiwindi and St. George lifted our spirits. It brought those of us with similar interests together which was so important to all of us who live on properties.*

*I travelled for three hours over dusty, bumpy roads to get to Goondiwindi for his workshops because I found myself stimulated into a different mind-set.*

*For me it could only be described as a life-changing experience. I know it changed my life and I'll always be grateful to Mervyn for the beginning of a great journey.*

*Mervyn's emphasis in the early classes was on colour – getting to know the colour wheel and learning how to mix colours to get the required shade or tone. When we were painting outdoors he emphasised the seeing – looking to find the relative tones and then recording little vignettes of scenes which moved or delighted us. He heightened our awareness immensely and his visits widened our outback horizons.*

*He showed us slides of famous contemporary artists and encouraged us to try to find new ways to depict our own world and we left behind that general tendency to depict the scene photographically or 'traditionally'.*

*Being exposed to slides of Matisse, Cézanne, and the other impressionists we were encouraged to explore our own painting and we were free to experiment.*

*Lots of Mervyn's students were successful at local shows. After he came the standard noticeably changed for the better. In 1978 I won first prize of $500 at the Charleville Art Show, also first prize of $500 in Brisbane at the Royal Agricultural Show in the Open Semi-abstract section. Both were judged by prestigious artists.*

*In 1978 I moved to the Gold Coast where I opened a small gallery where a group of local painters joined me. Mervyn came to tutor us a couple of times. My work is now in the Tweed River Regional Gallery.*

## MONTO

### *KATHERINE FORSYTH, 1990s*

*Born and bred in the rural town of Monto, I was exposed to extensive landscapes and expressive buildings. These I admired for their natural and man-made beauty.*

*What held my thoughts and interest was the difference between the traditional styles and the modern art movement.*

*Resources led me to artists such as Fred Williams, the 'Fauves' - Raoul Dufy and Matisse, but Picasso captivated me most in my younger years with the simplicity and solidity found in his work.*

*Enthusiastic teachers assisted me in finishing my schooling years with a progressive folio and accreditations such as Youth Week Poster Designer and the Australia Day 1993 Cultural Award.*

*Wishing to continue my Art studies I enrolled in an intensive year at the Hervey Bay Senior College, where meeting with other ambitious artists and the exploration of the media, such as photography and jewellery, gave my art a new direction. The year widened my knowledge of other art movements and media.*

*Art is like a diary entry, very personal: It may be a year or a second of one's life. As I paint, sketch or construct a piece, I do not know exactly what I am portraying until the end. I look and look and finally I will see. I have based some paintings solely on a feeling. Each stroke is an experiment, a step forward, be it wrong or right.*

*Art for me is like discovering the world twice, seeing things others might not like - a tone, line or a simple suggestion of something else. Each work is a signpost for another, giving way to each other, like putting together a jigsaw.*

*Now, through Flying Arts, I can converse and exchange with other artists and try more new media possibilities. It's important to know what other artists are involved in. Currently I am studying photography, which is a medium that is more instant and points out to me perspectives I don't see when painting. Observing other artworks is similar to reading another dialect. All this intrigues and inspires me. Art is best described by Brett Whitely as a "Difficult Pleasure".*

*To be nearer the arts and available work I moved to Brisbane in 1996. There I was able to continue studies in art completing a Diploma whilst working full time in a creative industry. Since being married I have travelled overseas many times and currently we are building a ceramic studio at home. I still paint which will always be my first love, I firmly believe that art has made my life more full. I continue to go back to Monto to pass onto others what I have learnt just as the people from Flying Arts once did for me.*

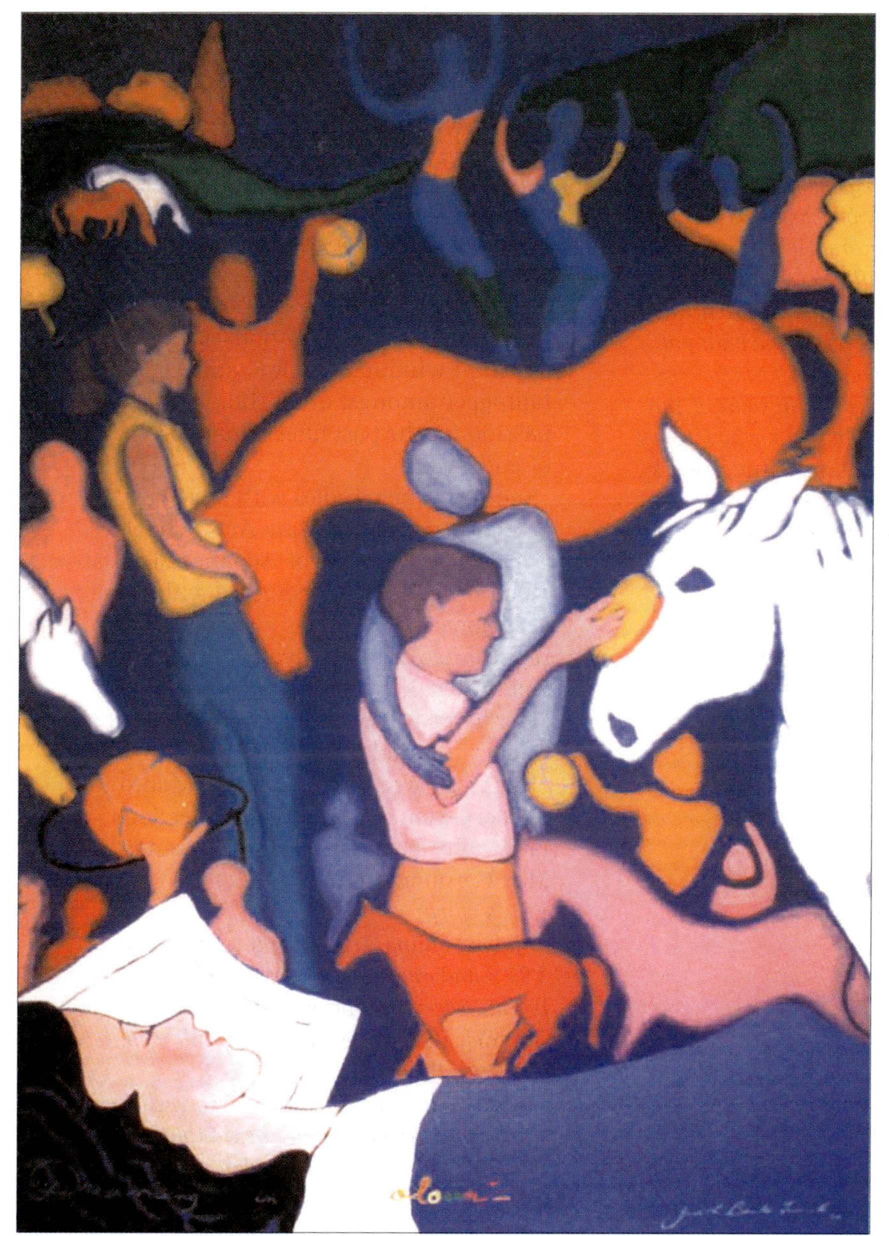

*Dreaming in Colour*
Acrylic on canvas
102cm x 92cm
Judith Banks,
Goondiwindi

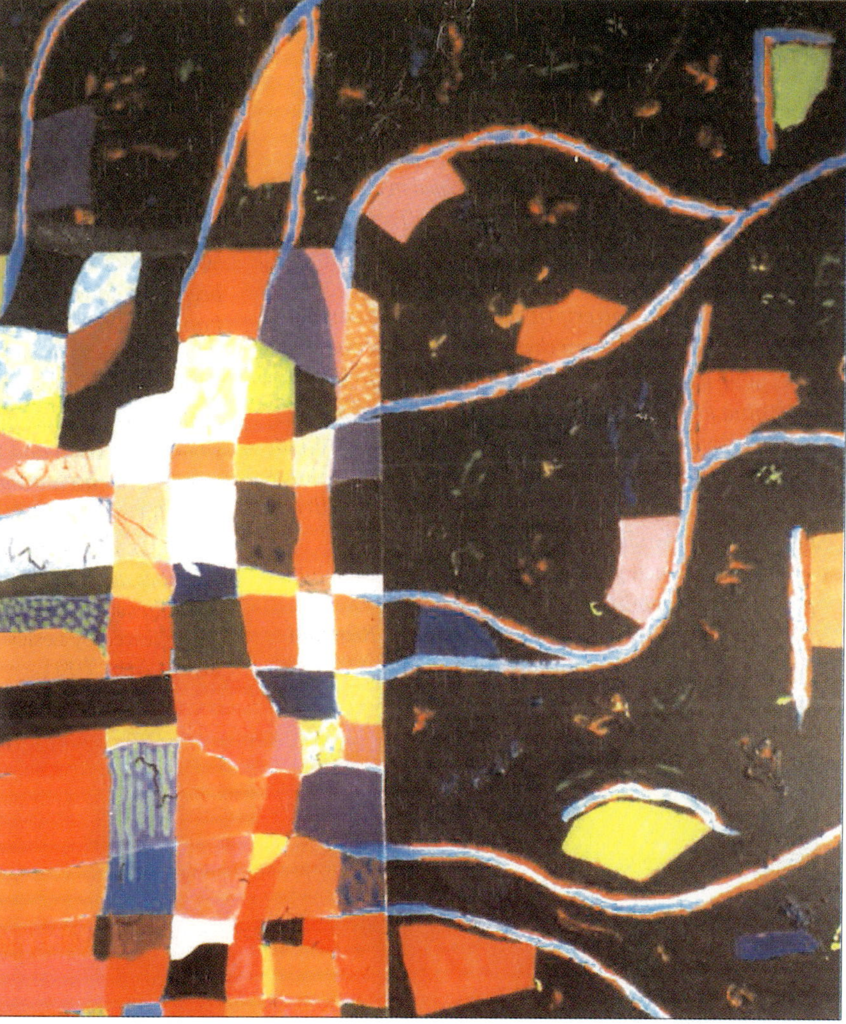

*Vestiges of Vivaldi*
Acrylic on canvas 102cm x 92cm
Judith Banks, Goondiwindi

## GLADSTONE

### *MARY NORRIS, 1978*

*I started with Flying Arts in the late 1970s. In those days there was no-one else teaching pottery.*

*The Gladstone Potters Group was formed in 1973. We met in a house that is currently called the 'Potters Place'.*

*Our Flying Arts tutors were Kev. Grealy, Helen Charles, Yvonne Bouwman and many others.*

*Kevin developed pottery tuition books. The course books would come before the lesson so you could read it at your leisure. There was nowhere here to buy anything for pottery until we set up our own shop.*

*When Kevin was coming there was always hilarity in the group and there would be a function at night. He would play his guitar and sing and would stay with one of the student families.*

*Nowdays I teach young mums and dads and young people with disabilities.*

*My work is represented in the Gladstone Regional Art Gallery Collection although I am not an exhibition person. My pottery is displayed and sold at the Potters Place Gallery where I teach and work on my own pieces. I have won an award in Gladstone's Martin Hanson Memorial Art Exhibition.*

*I have been a Flying Arts Regional Coordinator and have attended most pottery workshops held in the area.*

*I think the Flying Arts tutors, Helen Charles and Yvonne Bouwman, have influenced me the most because I do very little wheelwork, I concentrate on handbuilding. I learnt that every hand built pot didn't have to be made by coil.*

*You can almost see the coils still in some of my early work because nobody showed me how to get them out. Helen and Yvonne demonstrated work where you can hardly see the coils.*

*We did our first salt firing at Gladstone with Kevin Grealy with a funny little antiquated kiln. We now have a really large one which we fire with diesel and wood.*

Interviewed by Lesley Jenkins, Oral Historian for Flying Arts, 2001.

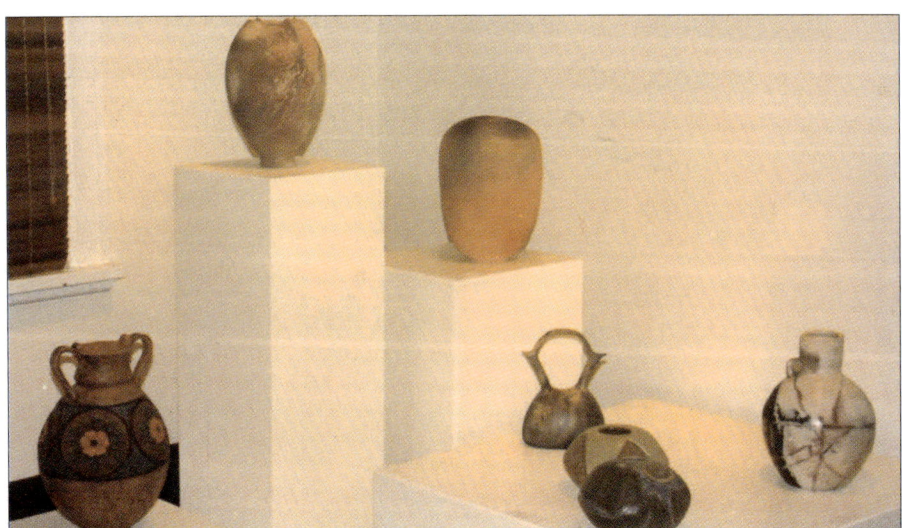

Some pots by Mary Norris

## BILOELA

### *ELLIE NEILSEN, 1979*

Ellie was born in Brisbane in 1927. She considers herself a modern painter in acrylic, a printmaker and a muralist.

She lives on a property in the Capricorn region's Banana shire, between Biloela and Monto. Over the years she has worked as a governess, stationhand, housekeeper, cook, assistant windmill repairer, and eartagger and tailtagger amongst other things, but her true passion for the past fifteen years has been the art of etching.

She began her studies with Mervyn Moriarty and the Australian Flying Arts School and at the Capricornia Institute of Advanced Education.

Ellie's work is wry, tempered with humour and very appealing. She has won many awards and is represented in both private and public collections.

Her first solo exhibition was at the Allamanda Gallery in Bundaberg in 1981 and 1982.

Her work is represented in the Monto Kindergarten and in private collections.

Biography from *Artists & Galleries Australia*, Max Germaine, 1984.

*Ellie's story:*

*I joined Flying Arts when it came to Monto in 1979 and my tutors over the years were Bela Ivanyi, Mervyn Moriarty, Irene Amos, Roy Oorloff, Beverley Budgen, Jeanne Macaskill, Wendy Mills and Ruth Propsting.*

*We came to live in Monto at 'Rawbelle' which was a big cattle property and I heard that Flying Arts travelled to Monto and Theodore teaching painting and drawing, but it wasn't until we moved closer to Theodore that I was able to attend.*

*My first tutor was Bela Ivanyi. Because I didn't understand what it was to be creative in those days I remember I became annoyed with him for chastising a lady for copying from photographs.*

*There were other influences besides Flying Arts but it was the only consistent school. I think Mervyn managed to get through to me that painting is not just a matter of getting the paint down. Even if they are only random marks you have to think about them before you make them.*

*I only ever had Mervyn once as a tutor because I came in right at the end of his time. I always worked loosely and thought it was awful but Irene Amos made me realise that painting loosely might be a good thing after all. I think, looking back, that my work was more representational than anything else.*

*I was introduced to etching by Peter Indans at the Institute at Rockhampton and I liked the way marks were made on the plate.*

*From the beginning I went to every workshop. Bev. Budgen, Jeanne Macaskill, Wendy Mills and Ruth Propsting were also important to the development of my work.*

*I just picked up every workshop I could go to. I went to Flying Arts and McGregor, Armidale, Irene Amos, and John Rigby when I was coming out of using only black and white or sepia and cream. That was all I could do in etching and I wanted to learn colour.*

*There were just a huge number of people that had input and they were all very generous with their time and their friendship. I remember saying that it wasn't a good idea to send the same tutor for two years because you started to paint like they did and it was better to sample the work of a range of tutors so that you didn't become the clone of anybody.*

*I have maintained my membership with Flying Arts, not only for what I can learn, but for the friendships forged with both other members and the tutors who travel out to hold the workshops.*

*Highlights of my artistic career include a six week fellowship to a Master Printmakers course at Studio Camnitzer in Tuscany (Italy) in 1995.*

*I have had a dozen or more solo shows in Brisbane, Central Queensland and interstate, and close to forty group exhibitions.*

*Working as artist-in-residence at Studio One, Canberra (1989), and Callide Coalfields, Central Qld. in 1998 was a joy and inspiration.*

*I enjoy travelling throughout Central Queensland as well as further afield, conducting workshops for both primary and secondary students in the techniques of etching, creative drawing and printmaking without a press.*

*In April 2003 my husband and I moved to Morayfield, near Redcliffe. I have become involved in the RADF committee again and am also on the management of the Bribie Island Community Arts Centre.*

In 1994 and in 1999 Ellie was the recipient of an Australia Day Award for services to the arts in her local community.

In July 1997 Ellie was one of five members appointed for their relevant artistic experience to the new Peer Assessment Panel for Arts Queensland for Visual Arts, Craft and Design, responsible for the initial assessment and ranking of applications for funding to the Queensland Government through The Arts Office.

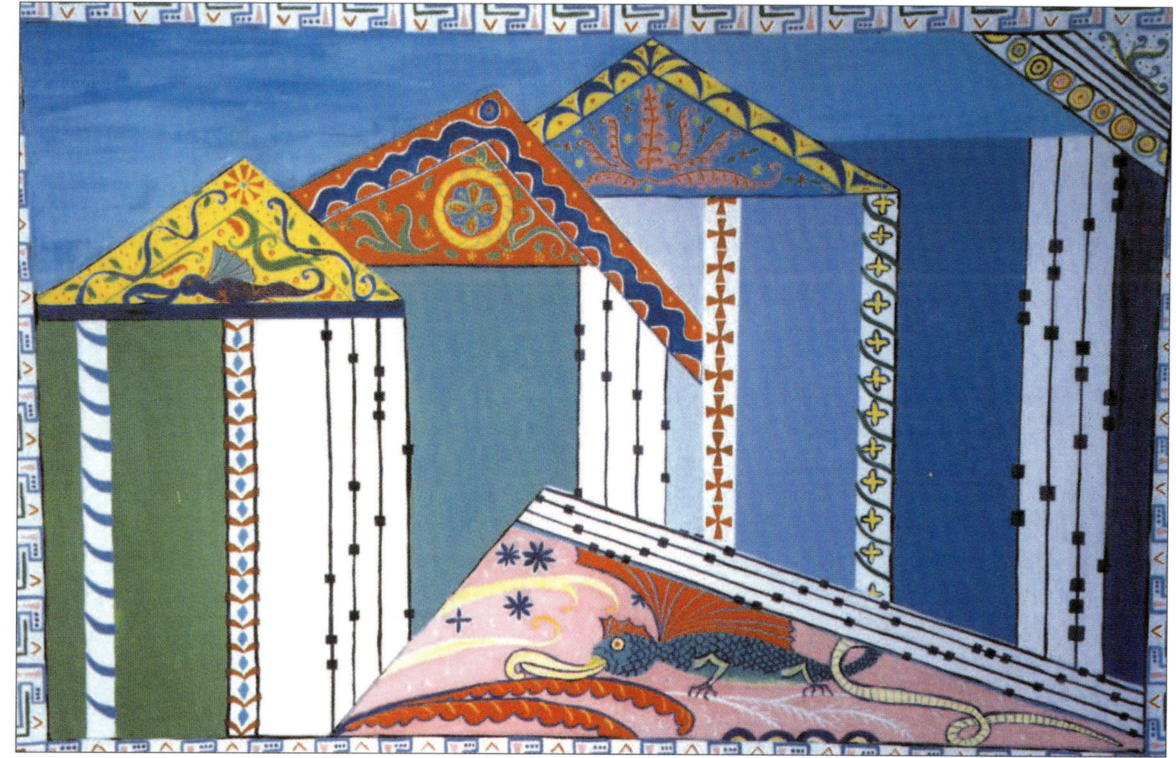

*Sienna Shapes* 60cm x 90cm acrylic on canvas Ellie Neilsen, Biloela

# EIDSVOLD

## *JEAN MESNER, 1970s*

'Jean Messner from Eidsvold is one regional artist whose association with Flying Arts will see her work being exhibited in galleries throughout the State and beyond. Jean's work, *Figure of a Country Woman*, is presently on tour throughout Queensland and northern New South Wales as part of the exhibition, *Shell Australia's 3x8+1: 25 Years of Flying Arts.'*

*Central and North Burnett Times* 3 October, 1996.

Jean Mesner started with Flying Arts in the 1970s. In 1996 she won first prize in the Flying Arts touring exhibition 3x8+1: 25 years of Flying Arts. Her prize winning image, *Figure of a Country Woman*, has been used to promote Flying Arts. This is her story:

*My mother used to tell everyone how I drew a recognisable human figure when I was fifteen months old. She made up her mind then that I would grow up to be a famous artist, but I don't think I've fulfilled her dream.*

*Kind friends and relatives kept our little bush family well supplied with crayons and those tin boxes of doubtful water colours that children use. Paper of a sort was always there as my father was a freelance writer in his spare time and ordered writing pads by the gross, though brushes were a problem. They had a habit of rolling down the cracks in our low-set verandah, to be lost forever, and I remember that, desperate for a brush, I made one with hen's feathers pushed through a quill. It worked, but not very well. I was about eleven then, and beginning to be frustrated with the available art supplies.*

*Later I learned to use pastels, but the high school I attended, Clayfield College, had no art course at the time, so I was sent to Saturday morning classes at the Brisbane Technical College where we drew beer and wine bottles, using charcoal. The next year I attended full-time art classes at the Technical College where apart from two hours of geometrical drawing a week and some lettering, we drew beer and wine bottles using charcoal; not a spur to my enthusiasm, though I still draw a good bottle.*

*In 1938 my family let me go to a relative in Sydney where I attended the East Sydney Technical College. I did life drawing, a little freehand, lettering, and one term of Design which I really loved. I would have liked to stay and work for my diploma, but money was short so I had to return home.*

*The following year I began work in Jackson & O'Sullivan's art department, earning the princely sum of fifteen shillings a week. I began with retouching negatives and graduated to doing graphs and meter charts, a very exacting job. I was also gofer and tea-girl, but it was interesting and I learned a lot about printing. I was there for two and a half years and then my allergies, unheard of then but very real, took over and I became quite ill.*

*Apart from making the family's Christmas cards I had done no work at home during this time, though there was quite a lot of pressure.*

*My grandfather wanted me to do political cartoons for the papers; for Mother, pretty little greeting cards were the way to go.*

*Past experience had made me detest water colours, and the smell of oils was quite sickening to me, so I decided to give up art altogether, with the good excuse of ill-health, and went off to the bush to become a governess.*

*I hardly gave art a thought for thirty years as I married and raised a family of five, later working as a dressmaker. It was only then, when we moved to Dalby on my husband's retirement, that I heard of Mervyn Moriarty's Flying Art School and decided to join. It was a wonderful eye-opener to me and I learned a lot. I found that acrylic paints, which hadn't been invented when I was young, were very kind to my allergies.*

*For two wonderful years I really enjoyed painting and learned a lot, but then my husband became ill and we moved to Brisbane where he died.*

*When I remarried in 1977 and came to Eidsvold I found that attending Flying Arts entailed a lot of travelling and nights away from home, and I only attended sporadically.*

*I joined the closest art group and began exhibiting in local shows, but I am a very private person and have a curious reluctance to display my work. Then, bored with endless traditional landscapes, I let the art lapse again and took up creative writing with very moderate success.*

*Art called me again in 1993 and I attended Lucinda Elliott's seminars in Monto, really enjoying them. I had trouble with cataracts and missed the following year, but went back to be tutored by Ann-Maree Reaney in '95, and at last found the medium that really suits me - mixed media. I love it! Not too much paint - still a bugbear - but fabric, string, paper, you name it.*

*Marvellous! Thank you Flying Arts. I've left it pretty late, but I'm having fun!.*

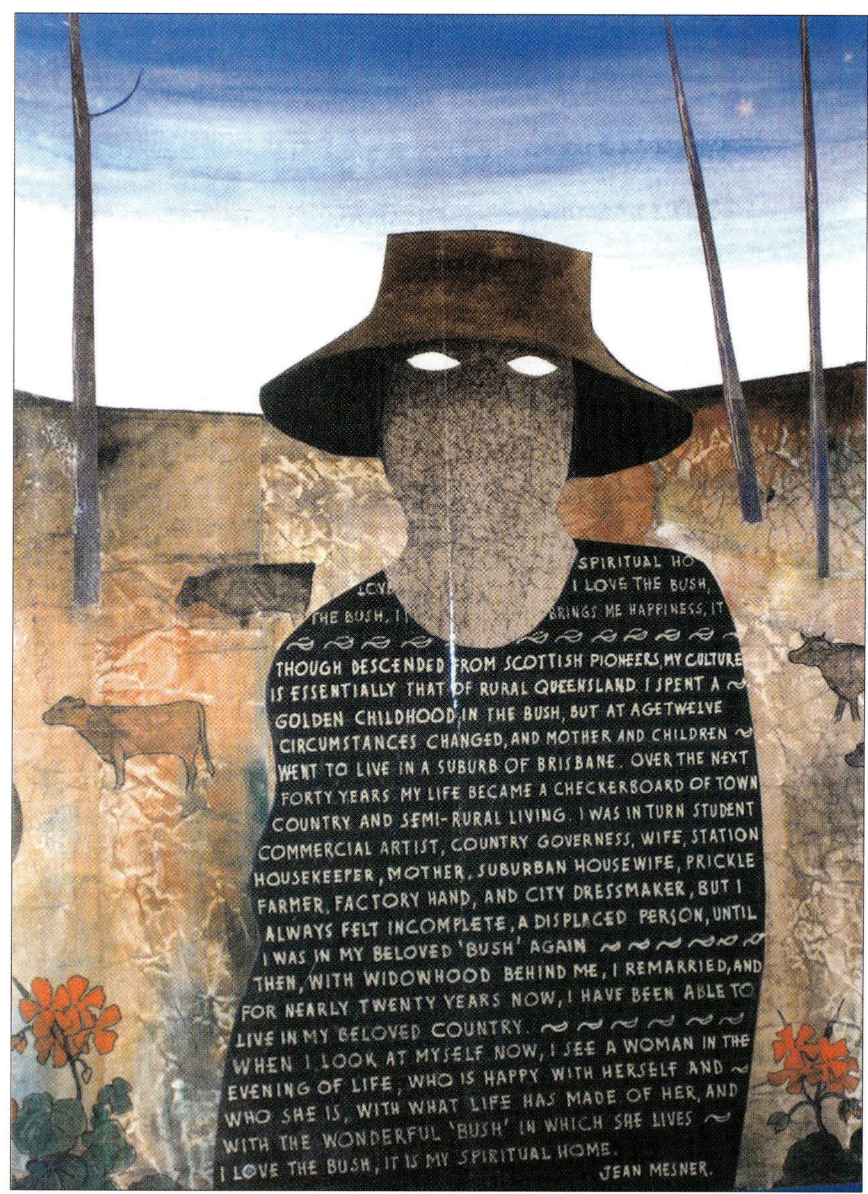


*Figure of a Country Woman* Jean Mesner, Eidsvold

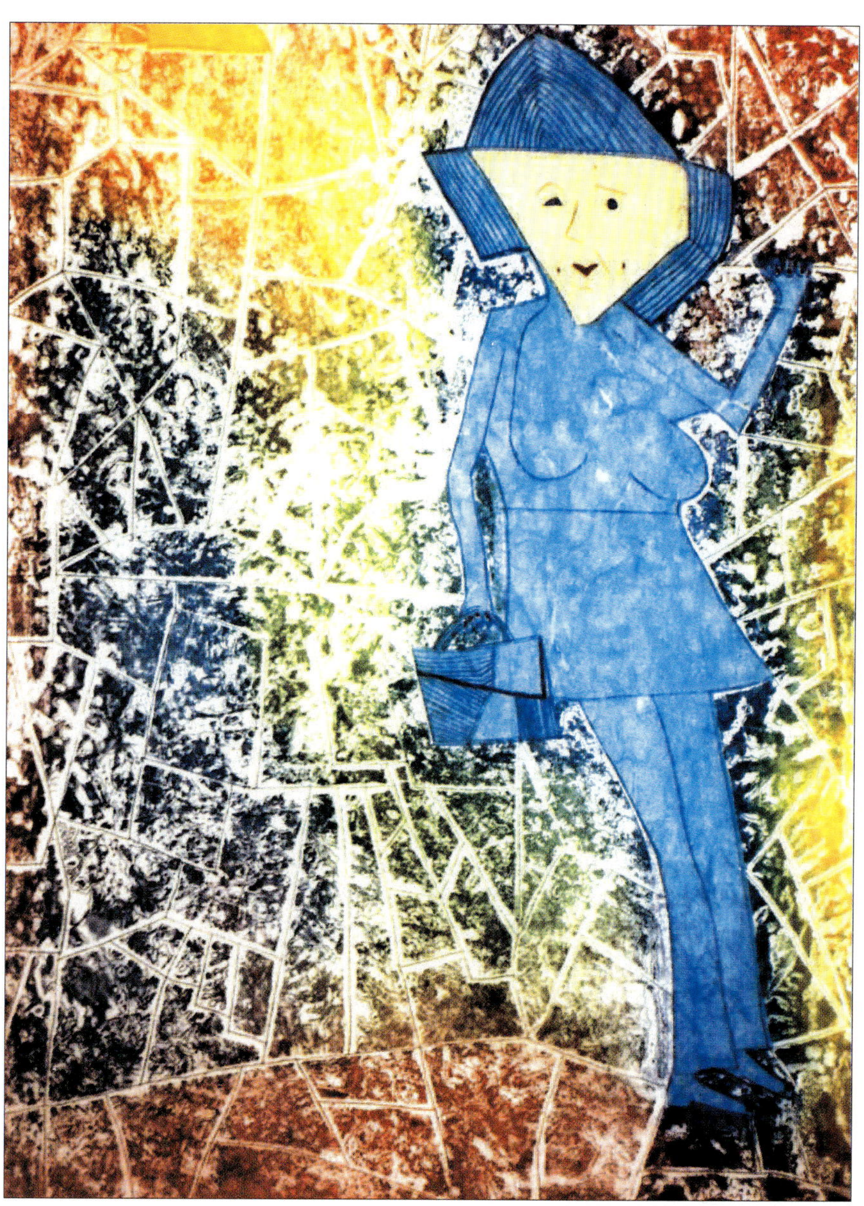

*Waiting at the Bus Stop* 50cm x 33cm etching chine' colle Ellie Neilsen, Biloela

# Student stories from South West Queensland

## GLENMORGAN

### *JANIS SOMERVILLE, 1971*

*I began as a member of the Glenmorgan Art Group in 1970 and went through to 1978. During this time I was introduced to Eastaus and the inspirational influence of Mervyn Moriarty.*

*In the early days the Glenmorgan Art Group was quite small. We'd put our children in a play pen under the trees while we painted just a short distance away.*

*We had heard about Eastaus and were at the point where we were very frustrated with our art. We had been working in watercolours with two local painters who were our mentors. They could show us techniques but they were conservative painters and were just reproducing landscapes. We loved the landscapes but some of us were hungrier for other things.*

*Mervyn came to teach us four times a year, he stayed for two days and two nights, he slept in the shearer's quarters. In those days it was blue ribbon national party country, it was very, very conservative, a red-neck area. The dominating factor for the local farmers was the use of the land and the use of resources. Mervyn had a completely different idea.*

*I left Glenmorgan and moved to Brisbane. After some years I felt very stuck there. I felt I'd gone as far as I could. So I sought out opportunities in other countries as an artist-in-residence.*

*First I moved to Indonesia with a three-month residence and ended up staying for a year. Indonesia had a fundamentalist government at that time and contemporary artists were constantly under threat because of their work. I was sympathetic to the young women, the way they were treated in their culture, especially in art school.*

*I decided to curate a show of Indonesian women artists. Later I worked for the Indonesian Art Delegation to the ASEAN Art Forum. After Indonesia I worked in Singapore and later in Japan and Thailand.*

*I then had a residency in Italy supported by the Australia Council. Thena residency in England and Germany.*

*In 1997, during my time in Germany I co-founded 'ART at WORK' with Pip Cozens. We were working almost every day in the streets somewhere with our form of performance art.*

*We were working directly with ordinary people. We looked at many local issues that affected the quality of life, then I used my experience and my artistic vision to enable participants and my audience to understand a range of life threatening environmental and social issues.*

*All this was started in Germany and now we have a small group in Belgium and one in England.*

*I go back to so many things that Mervyn taught me and I feel I can really do something with it now. I know how to make it work. It took a long time, but I think to be a late bloomer is the best thing anyway.*

Janis Somerville died in Brisbane.
30th August 2004

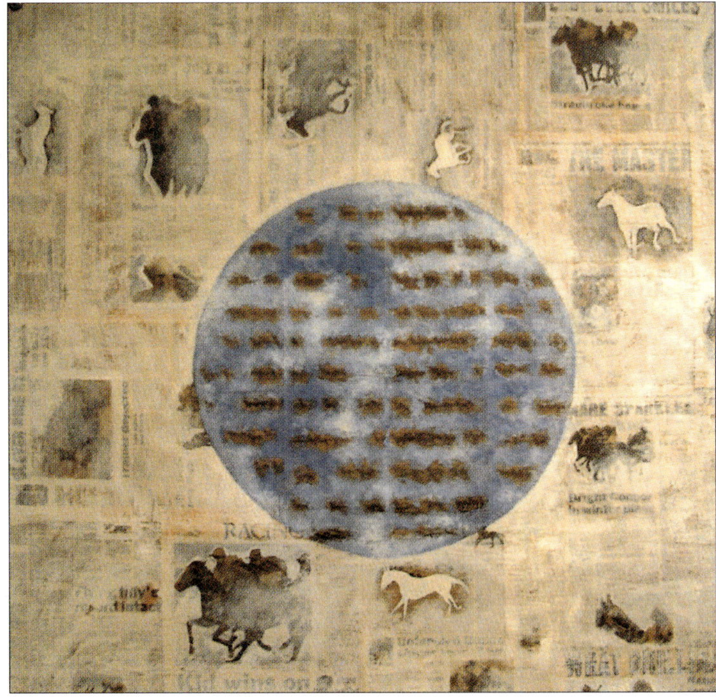

*Untitled* Janis Somerville, Glenmorgan

## GLENMORGAN

### *CAROL McCORMACK, 1972*

Carol began her early life in the bush near Hughenden and now lives on a Droughtmaster stud cattle property at Glenmorgan. She is a foundation member of the Glenmorgan Art Group and has been a member of the Flying Art School since 1972. She is an established artist who has had several exhibitions in Brisbane, Toowoomba and Regional Galleries. . .

*I came to Glenmorgan in 1968 and the Glenmorgan Art Group started in about 1969 with five or six founding members.*

*I think we must have heard through the Meandarra Arts Council that some funding was available for groups joining Mervyn's Eastaus Flying Arts School which at that stage had been going for at least a year.*

*I remember going over as a group to Surat and listening to someone from what was the equivalent of Arts Queensland who was speaking about regular seminars and a structured course.*

*We put our names down and had our first Flying Art seminars at Dorothy and Dave Gordon's home at Myall Park.*

*I suppose what appealed to me most was Mervyn's analysis of how a painting was constructed – you don't look and blob. Even the most abstract art has form and composition and an underlying colour scheme which you have to plan.*

*There was something in his teaching process that really opened a door for me. I could then understand what I'd been brought up to think was 'weird' art. For the generation of teachers, my parents, and other people who influenced me, Impressionism was acceptable, but they couldn't cope with Sidney Nolan and the brilliant art that was happening at the time.*

*I suppose I didn't know much about it, or try to understand it. Suddenly everything Mervyn said fell into place. In art, there is no 'how-to' and you're only limited by what you can dream up.*

*Place is still the most important theme in my work, though it is not always my place. I did a lot of 'home' paintings in the drought of the early '90s, an enormously significant event in our lives that needed recording.*

Interview by Lesley Jenkins, Oral Historian, for Flying Arts. 2001.

Carol is now a director of the well-known Myall Park Botanic Garden which Dave later excised from his grazing property and gave it to the community.

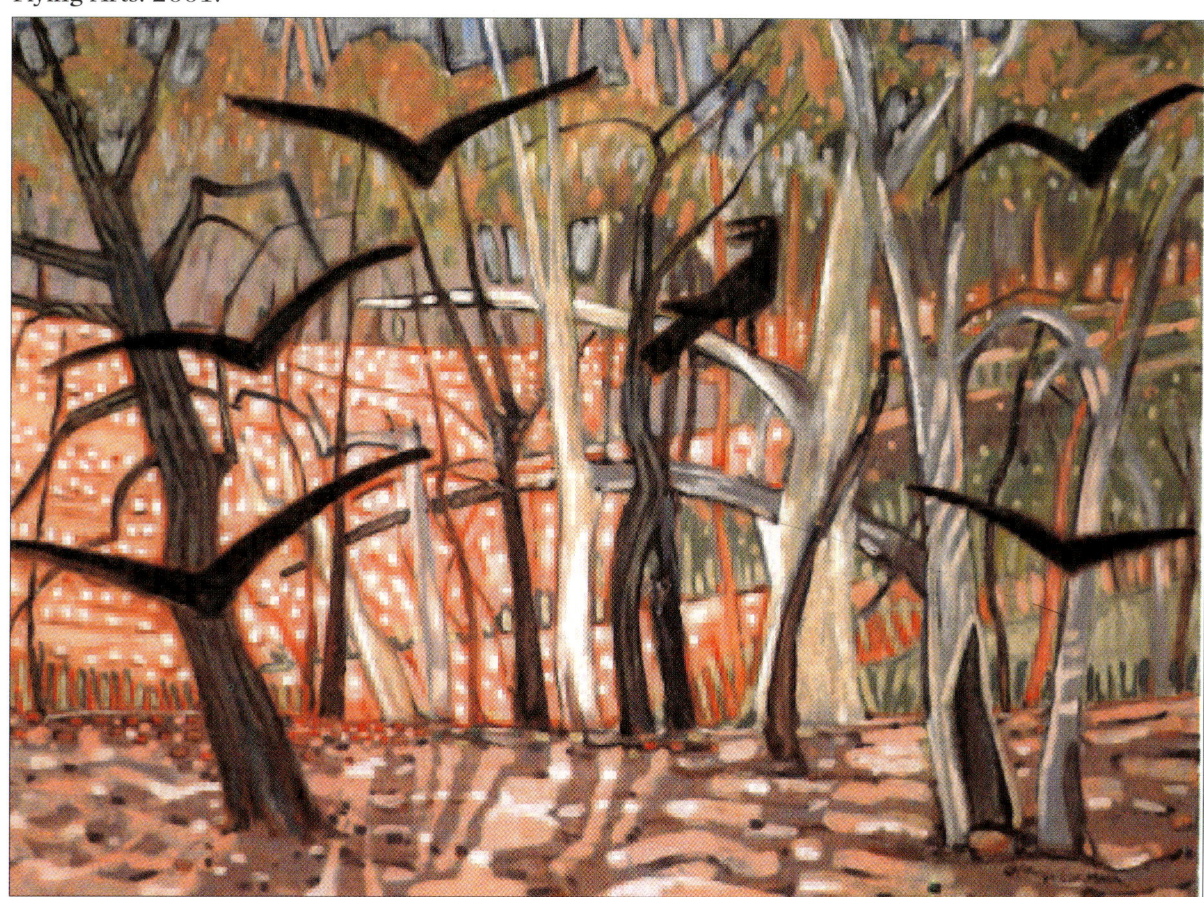

*Currajong Creek at Bundabar* 120cm x 95cm Oil on canvas Carol McCormack, Glenmorgan

# YARAKA
## *BETTY TURNER, 1980s*

Betty Turner is a wife, mother, artist and community worker. She has been her children's school teacher, a Flying Doctor campaigner and farmhand and could have been a clothes designer of note.

*I live on a 40,000 acre sheep property called 'Merriman', west of Yaraka in lower western Queensland. The family property is drought declared and life is far from easy.*

*My earliest school education was carried out in the country until such time as I was old enough to be sent away to boarding school at St. Hilda's at Southport during the Second World War.*

*I found that I had all the necessary qualifications to tackle professional dress designing and enrolled at McCabe's Academy in Brisbane. Then I married a young ex-serviceman.*

*After ten years of marriage we had two children. My husband was successful in drawing a land ballot for property in the Yaraka region and we moved west and set up home. This time was perhaps the hardest of my life as the land was completely unimproved. We lived in an 18'x10' boundary rider's hut, used a kerosene stove, and carted water in buckets from a nearby creek.*

*Thirty-eight years and three children later I am still living in rural Queensland.*

*I was instrumental in seeing the establishment of the Yaraka State School and I am a key member of my local Church community.*

*Today, after my family have grown up and allowed me more time to devote to other interests, there are two things which figure prominently in my life - my commitment to the Church, and my love of art.*

*My initial involvement with painting and the Australian Flying Arts School was less of a conscious decision to develop an artistic talent and more of an act of making up numbers at the first AFAS school into Blackall. Since that time however, I have developed a passion for learning and extending my interest in art.*

*I see my art as a challenge as well as an extension of myself - it brings me closer to other country women and offers me the opportunity to travel to different parts of the country.*

*In April 1988 I hosted a workshop at the family property with tutor Beverley Budgen. She opened the shearers' quarters to house the many women from regions such as Roma and Quilpie who expected to learn more about the art of painting – a workshop which is yet another opportunity for us to learn and grow in the company of each other.*
Farmers & Graziers Magazine April-May 1988.

Roy Churcher said of Betty that with her interest and her commitment to extend herself he would be prepared to travel to Blackall to teach, even if she was the only student.

*Fort Douglas on Merriman Station* oil on canvas Betty Turner

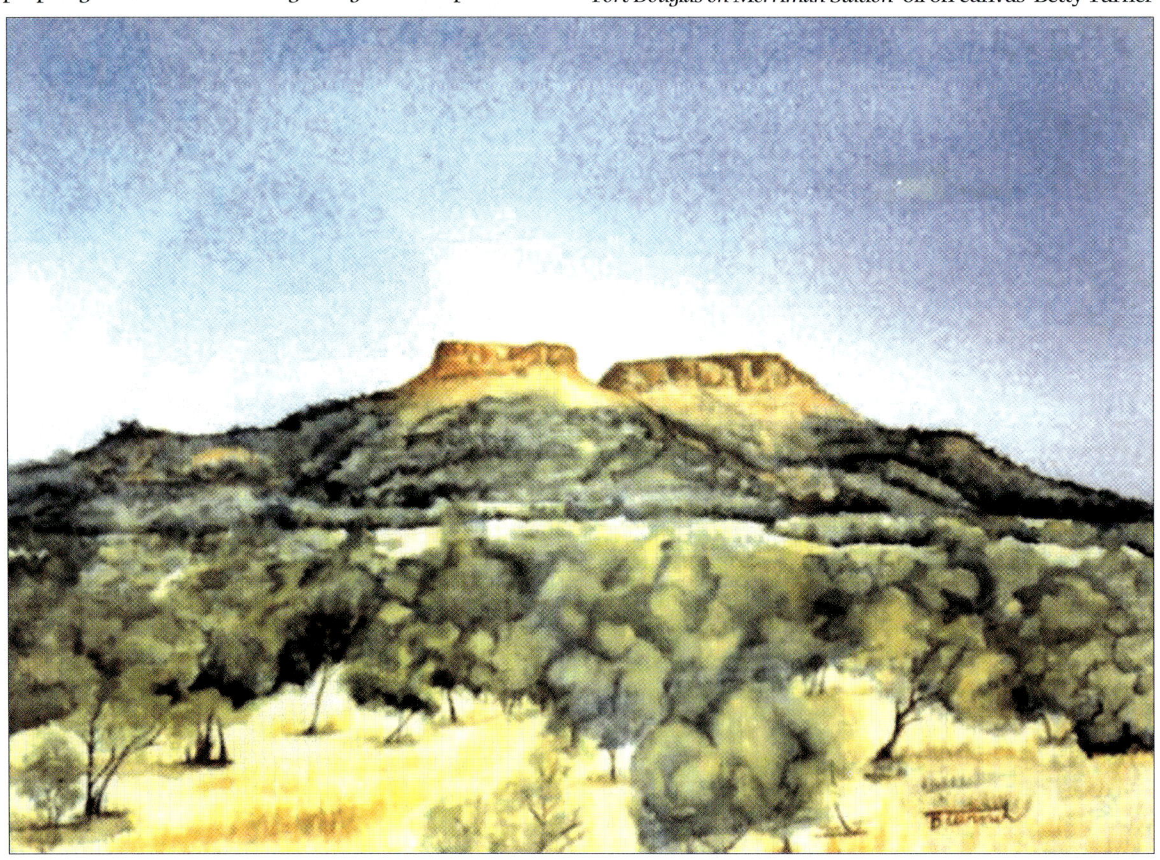

# QUILPIE

## *CHAR SPEEDY, 1971*

Char learned water-colour painting at High School (Somerville House) to Junior in Brisbane and worked at colouring photographs with oil paints in Brisbane for two years.

Her tutors were Caroline Barker and Pat Prentice (at school) and Mervyn Moriarty and Kelvin Grove tutors with Flying Arts which came four times a year. Workshops were at the Art & Craft Centre in Brolga Street Quilpie, later the building was bought by the Quilpie Cultural Society. Quilpie now has two galleries. The Museum Gallery opened in 1997 and the Outback Gallery (private) in 2000. This is her story:

*A group of interested people formed the 'Quilpie Cultural Society' in 1971 with pottery classes. The society also had a library. We raised some money and had a Mrs. Cameron come to Quilpie from Brisbane who taught us about clay, kilns, firing, glazing etc.*

*Some of us who were interested in drawing and painting formed an art group and had an art teacher come out from Brisbane.*

*Mervyn contacted us, I think he may have heard about us from the Arts Council and we accepted his offer to fly out four times a year, he would teach painting and another artist would come with him to teach pottery. I think he taught at Roma and Charleville along the way.*

*We had to paint in oils as acrylics dried too quickly in this climate. We mostly did landscapes and would go out into the bush. He was really great with teaching the mixing of colours. When he finished we carried on with tutors from the Kelvin Grove campus with both pottery and painting for many years.*

*Mervyn and his group always stayed in our building, he preferred that to the hotel. Some students were from the town but most were from the country and would drive miles for the lessons. He didn't give us homework as such, but expected us to bring in some work for constructive criticism. Some of my work is in Brisbane, Roma, Charleville and the local hospital and school in Quilpie.*

*At one stage a television crew came to Quilpie to do a documentary on the local artists. Mervyn chose a painting of mine and criticised it quite dramatically. This upset a new student who suggested I hit him over the head with the painting.*

*Since then our members have taught beginners in Eulo, Thargominda, Eromanga, Adavale, Windorah and Quilpie. This is beneficial for beginners as some are unable to cope with professional tutors and like to practice their chosen craft at a local level.*

*My greatest challenge came when I was asked to teach at the Quilpie State school for one term. I was offered a grant so I accepted.*

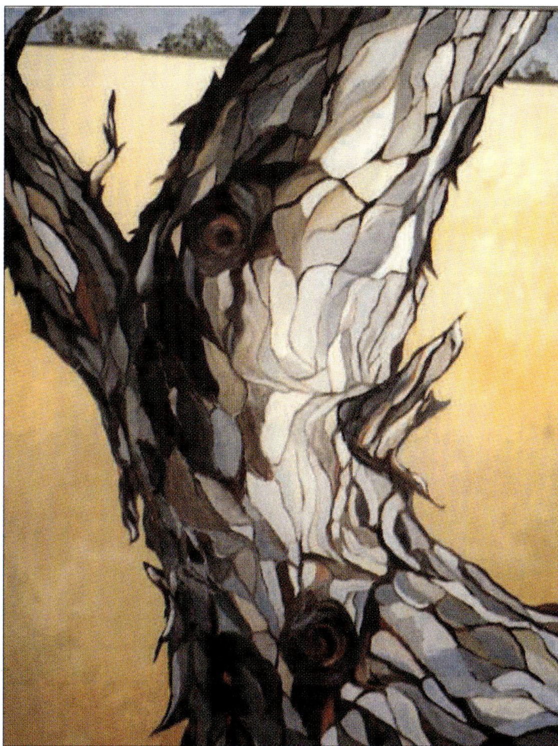

*Stained glass Gidgee Tree* Char Speedy, Quilpie

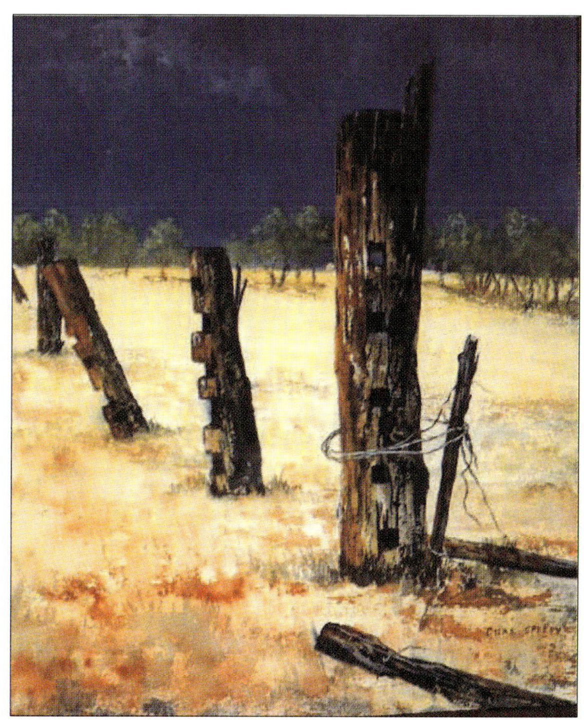

*Old cattle yards on our property at South Comongin*

Watercolour
Char Speedy, Quilpie

## QUILPIE
### BETH TULLY, 1974-1982

*I have very fond memories of the time when Mervyn and his Australian Flying Art School visited Quilpie. A.F.A.S. was seen by many of us then as the cultural equivalent of the Royal Flying Doctor Service.*

*Mervyn Moriarty first visited our group in Quilpie in the mid 1970s. His idea was to bring art to the people of regional Queensland – and that he certainly did. His vision of Flying Arts became a leading force in advancing arts practice throughout Queensland.*

*His mission was to provide innovative opportunities for artistic experience, development and achievement, especially for those with limited access to any art schools, thereby meeting the needs of isolated art practitioners like those of us who lived way out west in Quilpie. He certainly achieved this and I for one am eternally thankful.*

*My home in the Quilpie district was on a sheep station. Before marrying I had worked in the Parliamentary Library in Brisbane, so life was very different, and when Merv came he brought a new dimension to it. I was in my early forties when he first arrived and as I had always wanted to paint I took advantage of the wonderful opportunity he provided.*

*Our first impression of Mervyn was: "who was this Irishman with wild red hair?" He was very much the eccentric artist. He flew into Quilpie about four times a year – mostly for two days at a time. His choice of accommodation was our old building with its shearer's stretchers, and our country cooking appealed to him. He always said Quilpie was the best food – I wonder if he said this to all centres? Many a time we had political arguments with Merv as he loved to stir us up at lunch time. I remember one morning at home when I was cutting up chicken to take to our centre. When my husband saw me cutting the chicken he said to the boys at lunch time "chicken sandwiches today boys", and was sadly disappointed when it didn't arrive. When I came home that night he told me that he wanted to meet this Mervyn who was getting the chicken sandwiches he had missed out on.*

*Over the years Mervyn brought us many wonderful guest tutors. I remember Bela Ivanyi, Piers Bateman, Roy Churcher, Irene Amos and Ian Smith to name just a few; it was so wonderful to see these really good Australian artists painting our western landscape. We had such red earth and the grey-green of the trees gave them lots of inspiration. The Gray Range was not far out of Quilpie so it was no wonder that we loved our local landscape.*

*Mervyn could be a harsh critic. One time the ABC Big Country crew came to Quilpie and Mervyn flew in that morning and had us all line up our paintings on the footpath. One he called a monstrosity, but he was quite encouraging about some of the others. He truly was a wonderful teacher and he left lessons for us to study between visits. They were excellent. He was a superb colour teacher and consequently I have never had any trouble mixing colours.*

*My desire was to paint with water colour and when I asked his advice about this he said to learn to paint with oils first and then I could change. I did this and my love of watercolour is still strong today.*

*For a few years I was on the board of the Australian Flying Art School with Joy Wehl of Blackall who was the other country representative at the time. The years I spent with A.F.A.S. were indeed a very happy and fulfilling time for which I am truly thankful.*

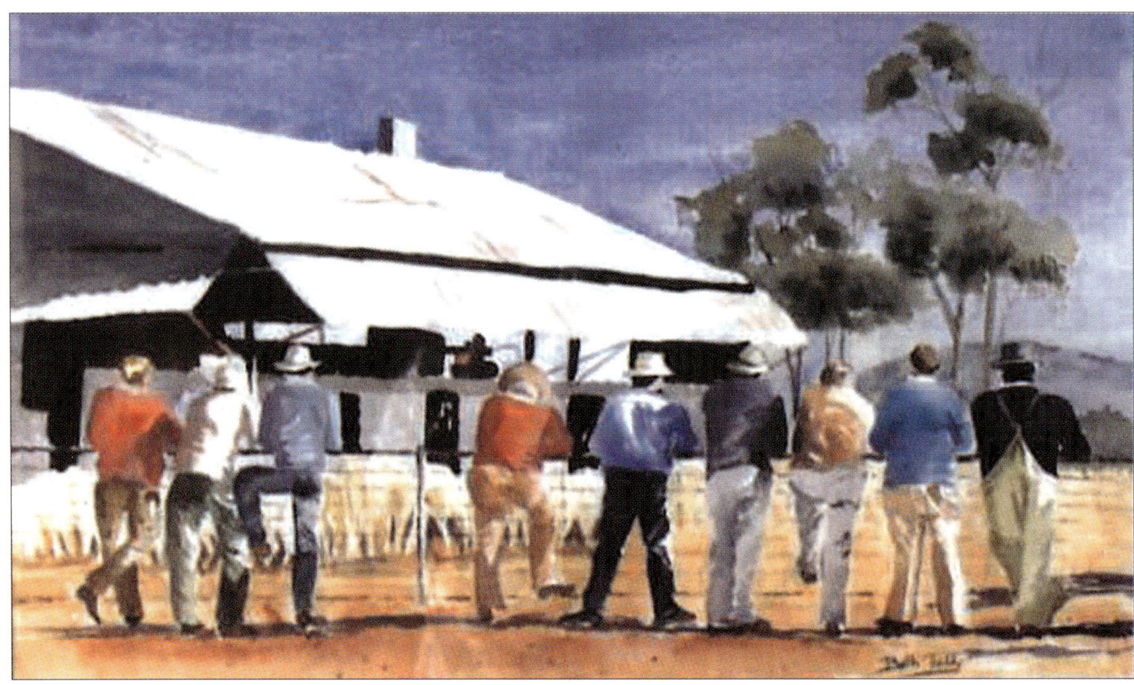

*Men's business* 37cm x 56 cm, watercolour on paper Beth Tully, Quilpie

# Student Stories from Central Queensland

## BLACKALL

### *JAN GALL, 1971 + 1996*

*More than 25 years ago, there were almost no opportunities for budding artists in the bush to work with professionals. I was fortunate enough to belong to a group who got together once a week under the tutelage of Jan Douglas-Shaw, who was living in Blackall at the time.*

*Then, I think it was in 1969, we heard of this red-headed artist called Mervyn Moriarty who was travelling out west, by road at this stage, to teach.*

*With Jan's encouragement, several of us decided to spread our wings and so we went to Barcaldine for a two-day workshop with him.*

*This was a very big adventure in those days. To leave one's home, husband and children behind and stay overnight in another town was enough, but little did we realise just how big an adventure it would be.*

*Mervyn's ideas impacted upon us and our horizons were broadened beyond our wildest dreams. Enraptured, we then invited him to Blackall so the other local painting enthusiasts could share in our find.*

*It was around this time that Mervyn had the idea of using an aeroplane to cover the huge distances of the outback, and the Australian Flying Arts School was born.*

*Today the people of the west enjoy any number of opportunities to learn and develop their artistic talents, but this was not always the case and I would like to pay tribute to Mervyn Moriarty for being at the vanguard of this development, and for having the initiative and the courage to become a pilot for this purpose – our knight in shining armour at the time.*

*To my knowledge, Flying Arts is still the only organisation using air travel to enable tutors to tour.*

*After a long period of involvement in other things I have recently returned to creative activities, this time experimenting with natural fibres and textiles. I have discovered that my room-mate from the Barcaldine adventure is also back with Flying Arts in Wee Waa.*

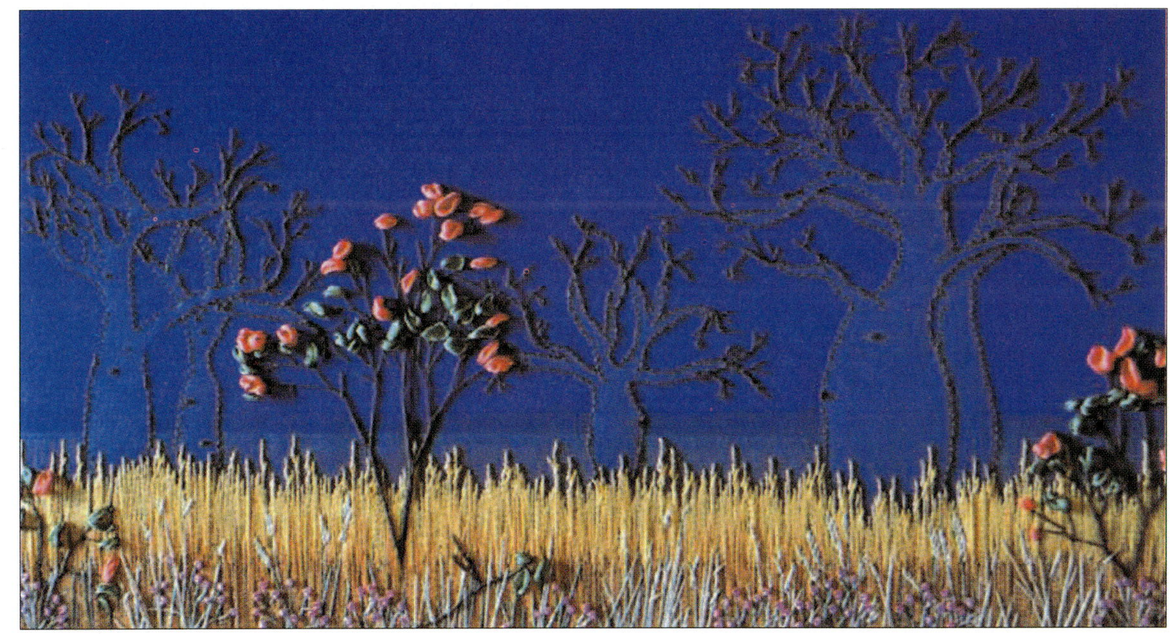

*Kimberley Garden* Embroidery 14cm x 25cm Jan Gall, Blackall

## ROCKHAMPTON

### *RITA KERSHAW, 1971*

Rita has been a pivotal member of the Flying Arts Rockhampton Group from its beginnings and later, in introducing contemporary art to Rockhampton. In 1972 Mervyn Moriarty made these comments about one of her paintings, *Walk on the Beach*. "It is jumping for joy on the beach - it is a great painting with lovely line. Bars join up beautifully, to put more line in would overstate. The most powerful sensations of the sea edge I've ever seen." Rita's story:

*I started painting by going to adult education. The first classes were held in the RQAS hall in Victoria Park. The Council had leased a corner of the park to us and we had shifted a small hall to the park for our use. At first the hall was crowded but later the attendances fell off. We had about twenty students. I remember our first guest tutor at the Eastaus classes was Clifton Pugh in 1973.*

*Our favourite outside drawing spot was at six-mile, a rather wild picnic spot on the Fitzroy River. There were huge paper bark trees there and plenty of shade in Rockhampton's summer.*

*At that time Eastaus was a group of members from within RQAS. However, there was friction from other members of RQAS and Mervyn and the President had a falling out. In the meantime the Council had bought an old warehouse now known as Walter Reid Arts Centre and RQAS were given space there and sold their hall to the Contract Bridge Club. We then rented the Wandal Tumbling Club when Mervyn visited about four times a year (the hall has since burnt down).*

*Then Bela Ivanyi from Cairns was appointed an alternative tutor. He and Mervyn were opposites with the same feeling for art and we loved both of them but some used to say there were Bela centres and Mervyn centres.*

*Alec Thompson took over as rep. for a short while and then Joyce Mullins and I took over. When Joyce left for Brisbane I continued until the Flying Arts School from Kelvin Grove stopped coming to centres along the coast.*

*In the meantime there was a name change to the Australian Flying Arts School. We worked for a while in a room I hired in the National Fitness Rooms and then got space on the top floor of Walter Reid's Art Centre and completely left RQAS. We now called ourselves 'Central Queensland Contemporary Artists' and paid rent to the Rockhampton City Council. We did not charge rent to Flying Arts School and all the tutors, guest tutors and pilots were billeted.*

*Other guest tutors were Roy Churcher, David Aspden, Keith Looby and then we had Pat Hoffie, Adam Rich, Irene Amos, Beverly Budgen and others, but some came after 1978.*

*In 1975 Eastaus had an exhibition in Brisbane in their old office space in Eagle Street and a number of us went down for the opening.*

*Mervyn brought slides with him when he came to Rockhampton and we usually all got together for dinner at night and then went back to our area for a slide showing.*

*He also showed slides of students when he toured from other areas, and sometimes a couple of paintings. One year he was allowed to give students throughout Queensland five entries to a large Exhibition in Brisbane. I remember I was given one of them.*

*We were sent two study books each three months for the course. The homework was done and commented on by Mervyn before we started new lessons. The ones who did all the books received a certificate at the end of the two-year course.*

*The numbers kept high for a number of years and we were one of the strongest centres. The money we paid helped to keep small groups going.*

*We continued to improve and had a couple of exhibitions. The feeling by us all was that Mervyn was something special and we did worry about his health and his problems in keeping the school going.*

*When we first started going along to Flying Arts we had people from Emerald and Gladstone coming here. If it looked like the plane couldn't come in, we would all be ringing up to see if Mervyn could get through in the little aircraft.*

*We would all be sitting here waiting for him and some of us would go out to the 'drome' to pick him up. One day we went out there and there was something wrong with the plane. It was circling above the airfield and the ambulance and fire brigade were following it round and round on the ground. Luckily it was nothing much as he came down alright. Sometimes the small plane would be held up by fog or rain in Brisbane but usually it got through eventually.*

*Many of our group in those days came from outside areas, Comet, Emerald, Baralaba, Yeppoon, etc. so there would be many phone calls wondering when the plane would arrive. The officer in the tower one week-end got so many phone calls he said: "who's this Moriarty?"*

*Bela was an impetuous pilot. I spent a few times taking him to answer questions to the Air Traffic Control. Once he flew in the flight path of the large planes.*

*Then there was Cooee Bay: Bela felt we needed longer than a two-day seminar and he organised a ten-day seminar at Tinaroo N.Q. in 1976 and Highfields S.Q. in 1977. These proved very popular and it introduced us to each other and we all formed a special bond. The next year was Central Queensland and Gloria and I found a National Fitness camp at Yeppoon. We were in the middle of organising it when*

*Kelvin Grove took over AFAS. Unfortunately they were not interested in the ten-day seminar so Bela said, "let's do it ourselves."*

*It proved to be a fantastic ten days and is still as strong as ever after twenty-six years. I retired as organiser after twenty-two years, but Cooee Bay still goes on with some of the old Eastaus Group still turning up.*

*Most of us win many competitions and are represented in local galleries and overseas. We put a book together in 2001 and it was published at C.Q. University. It shows how far we have come from small beginnings. Many of us now are professional artists and all give praise to Mervyn and his Eastaus school for giving us something that so enriched our lives.*

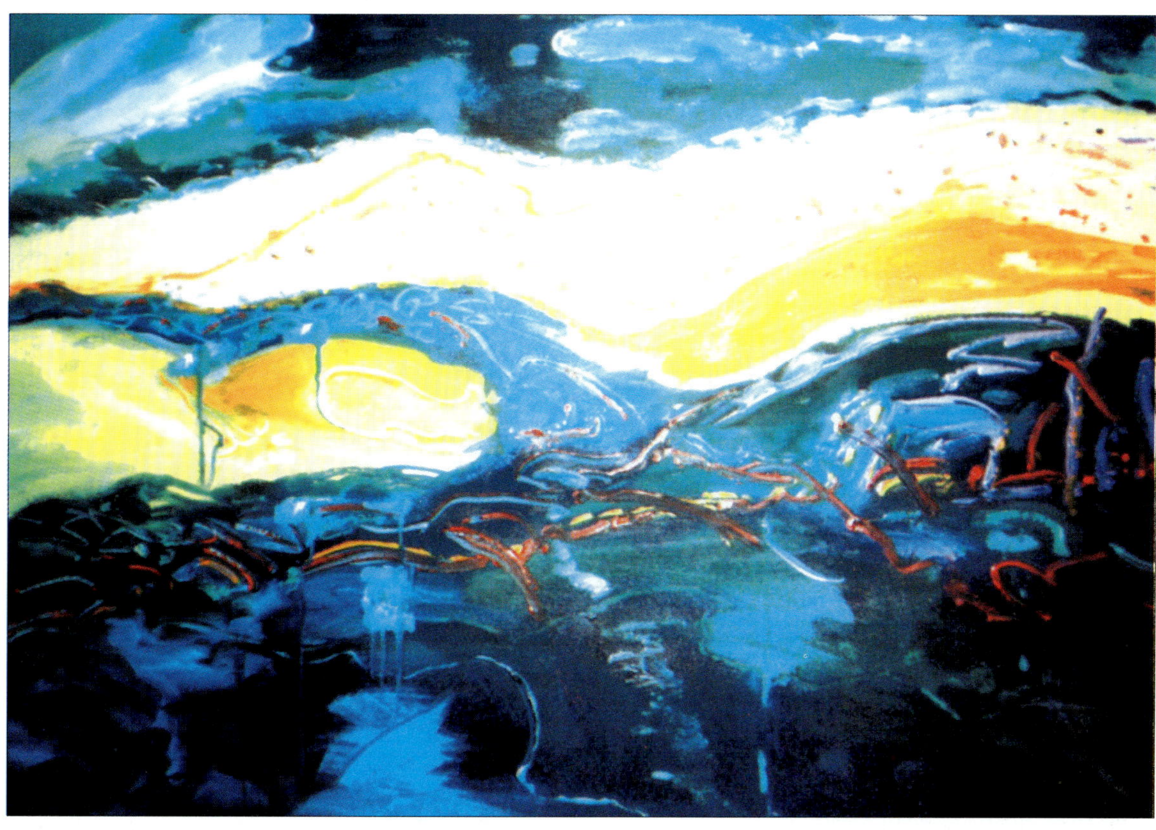

*Sandy Point* 1991 Acrylic on canvas 90cm x 120cm Rita Kershaw, Rockhampton

## ROLLESTON

### *BLOSS HICKSON,* 1990s

Flying Arts tutor Lucinda Elliott wrote:
"I first met Bloss Hickson in 1992, on a Flying Arts visit to Rolleston. Bloss runs a property and spends much of her time in isolation. Her time is filled with developing Landcare, publishing the local rag, running the local Art group, supporting environmental and local issues, and rearing beef cattle. The isolation, self reliance and practical application of personal philosophy, makes Bloss and many other country people impressive. I found myself constantly in awe of these people who quietly move mountains."
This is Bloss' story:

*Painting is one of my greatest pleasures. Nothing is more exciting than an exhilarating landscape lying before you and a reason to sit there all day! I love the bush and every fascinating relationship within its complex makeup.*

*The preservation of the bush is probably the greatest driving force in my life and painting it, my personal contribution to its immortality.*

*I wish I had more spare hours to paint, but life doesn't dish them out.*

*Thanks to the frequent returns of Lucinda Elliott and Flying Arts our art is kept alive, its value reinforced and our keen little art group inspired. I still remember her first class in the Rolleston Hall. She had us painting self portraits and quite successful ones as I recall. She is a most enthusiastic teacher.*

## BARALABA
### *AUDA MACLEAN, 1971*

*I was born in Baralaba, Central Queensland and have lived within a thirty mile radius of here all my life, so I suppose I am a local of the area.*

*At about the age of eleven we moved to a property six miles from Rannes and as there were no school buses then, my sister and I had correspondence lessons until we went to boarding school.*

*My lessons were often interrupted by mustering - I was Dad's right hand man and together we did all the mustering, branding, etc.*

*During this period, with no other children to play with, my sister Clare and I drew a lot, and also found clay in the creek bank and created motley characters with chook feathers for hair and little seeds for eyes, which we dried in the sun - I still have some of them. Clare later went on to become a painter and sculptor.*

*Two people helped me along the way - my grandfather, who had been a painter and photographer, gave me some watercolours, and an elderly friend, who was an artist but was going blind, gave me her oil paints. I spent hours teaching myself to use these.*

*My drawing was put on hold for some years during my late teens when I married and had small children. However the urge to start painting and drawing again returned just before my fourth child was born.*

*Not long after that, Mervyn Moriarty started flying to the bush to teach art so I began driving the seventy miles to Biloela to attend these seminars. The first workshop happened to be a life class - the first I had ever attended, and I was so excited about it all that when I was driving home afterwards my head was so full of what we had been doing that I missed the turnoff to Baralaba and kept going towards Rockhampton.*

*During the '80s I spent many hours painting on our property, and after completing some of these paintings, I felt I would like to show them as a collection. It seemed they would be best shown here in their environment, so this prompted the first exhibition in the old homestead here at 'Coolum'. I asked my sister Clare to include her sculpture in the exhibition.*

*Looking back over the years since the first AFAS seminars I went to, I know I would never have come this far with my art without the help and support of the AFAS tutors.*

*Being an artist involves many highs and lows and lots of soul searching and indecision. I felt lots of frustration at my failed attempts to paint in an abstract or contemporary manner. Finally with the help of a few friends (including AFAS tutors) I have had the courage to accept myself as I am and do what I do best and that is to paint people. New doors seem to have been opened to me with invitations to exhibit in Brisbane.*

*Biloela was one of the first groups to join Mervyn in the early 1970s and I drove from Baralaba to attend the workshops there. Mervyn particularly liked the Biloela group who followed him into abstraction.*

*I always liked Mervyn, he was a true artist and stimulated us all to become artists. In those days he would take us to a bush spot on the first day of the two-day seminars on a sketching trip. He came four times a year, flying in to a local airfield (most properties had their own airstrip then).*

*I organised an art group at Baralaba after Biloela folded, we needed at least seven students. Some have come and gone over the years but the art group is still working thirty years on. Today our tutors fly into Emerald on a commercial plane and then come by car to our country workshops.*

*My only training was with Flying Arts and my tutors over the years were Mervyn Moriarty, Bela Ivanyi, Bev. Budgen, Bonney Bombach, Roy Churcher, Wendy Allen, Irene Amos, Brian Dean, James Guppy, Peter Dwyer, Lucja Ray, Lucinda Elliott, Maureen Hansen, Ruth Propsting from Tasmania and Jeanne Macaskill from New Zealand.*

*Mervyn was often critical of our work but despite that he was a popular teacher and is greatly missed. Bela (who joined in 1974) has been to Baralaba a few times as a tutor.*

*Baralaba started a small art gallery at the Landcare Centre in the late 1990s, the exhibitors were mostly AFAS students.*

*AFAS has been very valuable to me in many ways - in expanding my knowledge of art, meeting other artists and the fellowship that developed in our group. It helped me to see colour, shapes and rhythms in everything, adding a new dimension to my life.*

*I have entered many art competitions and have won quite a few. I have work in regional gallery collections and in the boardroom of the Shell Company as well as in overseas collections.*

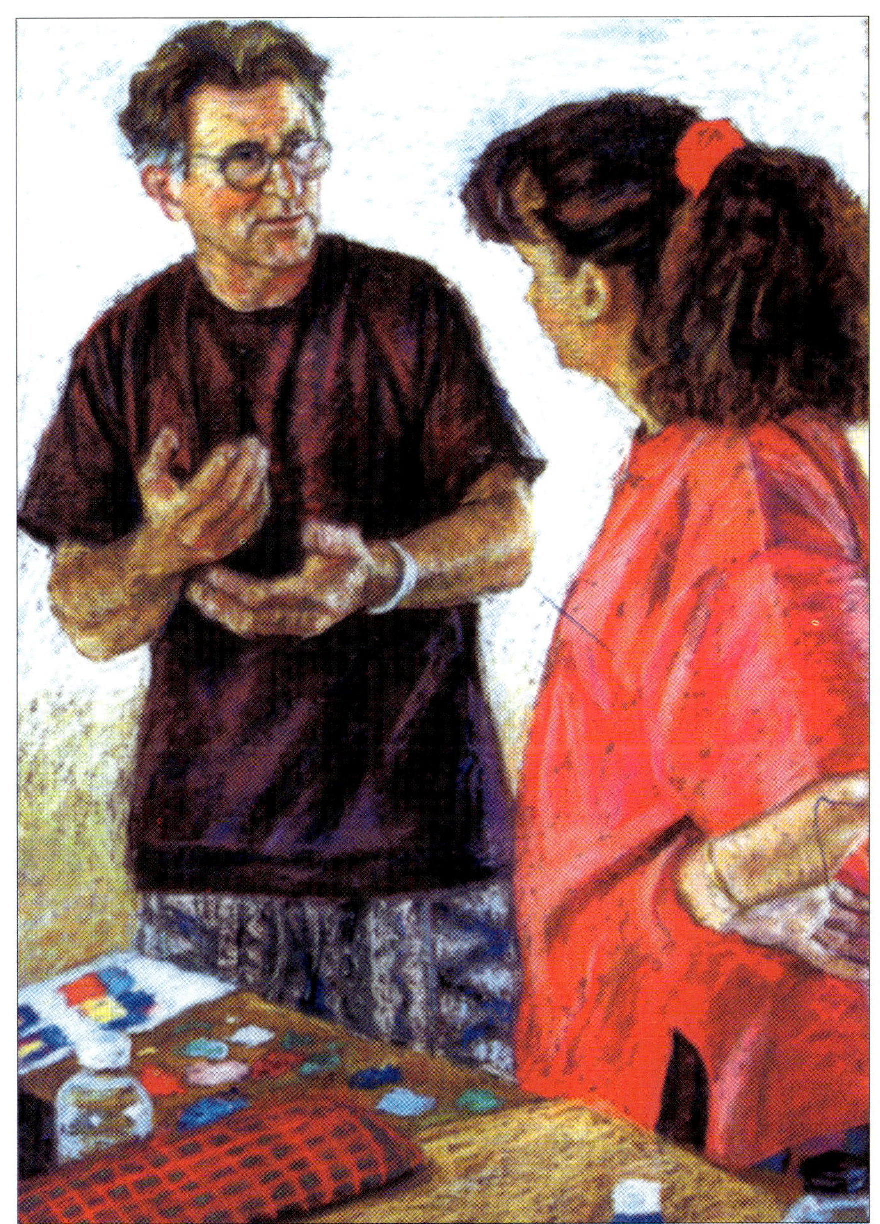

*Art Lesson* Pastel 65cm x 53cm Auda Maclean, Baralaba

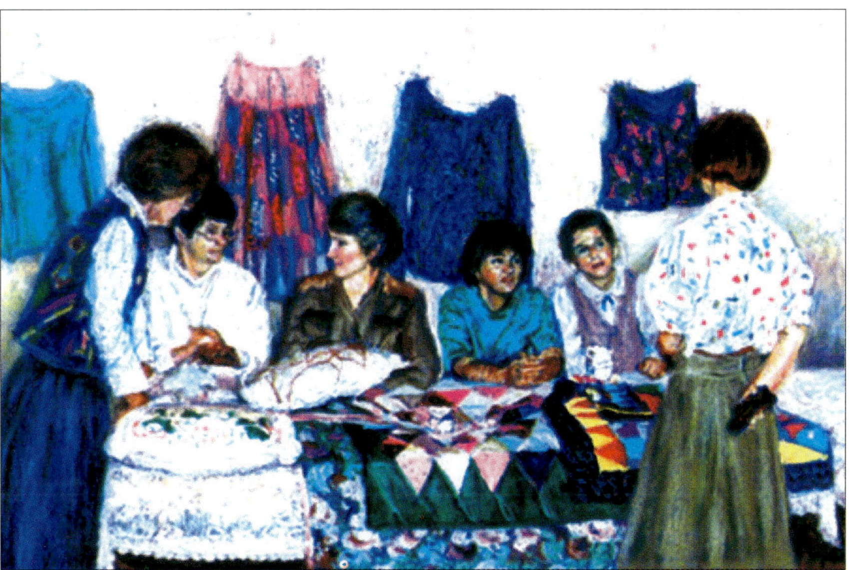

*Patchwork Stall* Pastel 34cm x 50cm Auda Maclean, Baralaba

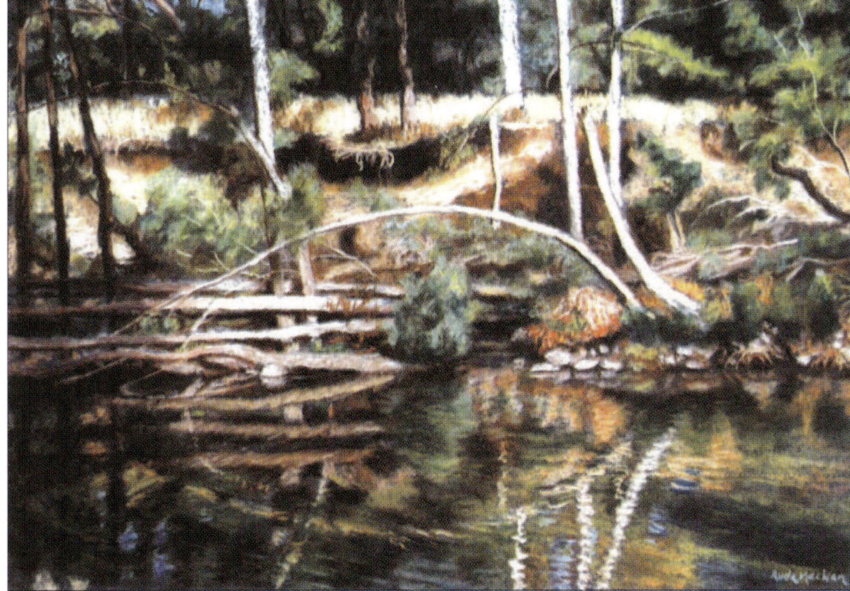

*Reflections at Carnarvon Creek* Pastel 45cm x 53cm Auda Maclean, Baralaba

## BARALABA
### *STEPHANIE BROADHURST, 1970s*

*I have been with Flying Arts since the late 1970s. As a teenager I was always sketching, mainly figures of women so I was thrilled when Flying Arts came to Baralaba. I particularly remember Flying Arts tutor Bev. Budgen with affection. She took us for a class at Kangalu Caves. These are Aboriginal cave art on Auda's property and Bev inspired us to paint using a cave theme. Thirty paintings from the outing were sent into the annual Flying Arts exhibition at Kelvin Grove. In those days we were ten hours by bus from Brisbane. Other Flying Arts tutors we have had over the years have been Brian Dean, Jean Macaskill, Ken Smith, Wendy Wright and Glennys Mann.*

*In 1984 my work was chosen by Brian Dean, Head of the Art Department at Kelvin Grove, Bill Robinson, Senior Lecturer in Art at Kedron Park Campus and Pat Hoffie, AFAS tutor and lecturer at the College of Art, Seven Hills, to participate in the collection of work to tour America with the Arts Council in 1985.*

*Called 'For the Love of it', the exhibition went to the Memphis in May Festival in Texas USA where all the artworks were sold. I received a cheque from the Arts Council for $150 for the sale of my work.*

*In 1995 my work was in the Regional Members' Exhibition Sense of Self at the Mackay Entertainment Centre which was put on by the Brisbane Shell Art Award.*

*I won a Flying Arts' bursary to the McGregor Summer School held at the University of Southern Queensland from January 4 – 15, 1999. What an experience. I thoroughly enjoyed my time and have come home with a lot more knowledge of my chosen areas, namely silk dyeing and freehand machine embroidery. After consultation with McGregor School Manager Margaret Clifford, I took Ken Smith's class. Even though I had worked with Ken through Flying Arts I had missed two days of his tour and felt he had a lot more to offer. Ken has updated many techniques in silk dyeing since I first started with him, and this proved to be most interesting.*

*Making good friends with the other students and sharing information about the best place to buy silks, dyes, etc. was very worthwhile. I completed one side of a silk-dyed and machine embroidered vest and being able to do this continuously for days was a great 'boost' to my learning process. I am much more confident now and have no fear of carrying on by myself. I will also be sharing my knowledge with other Baralaba textile artists.*

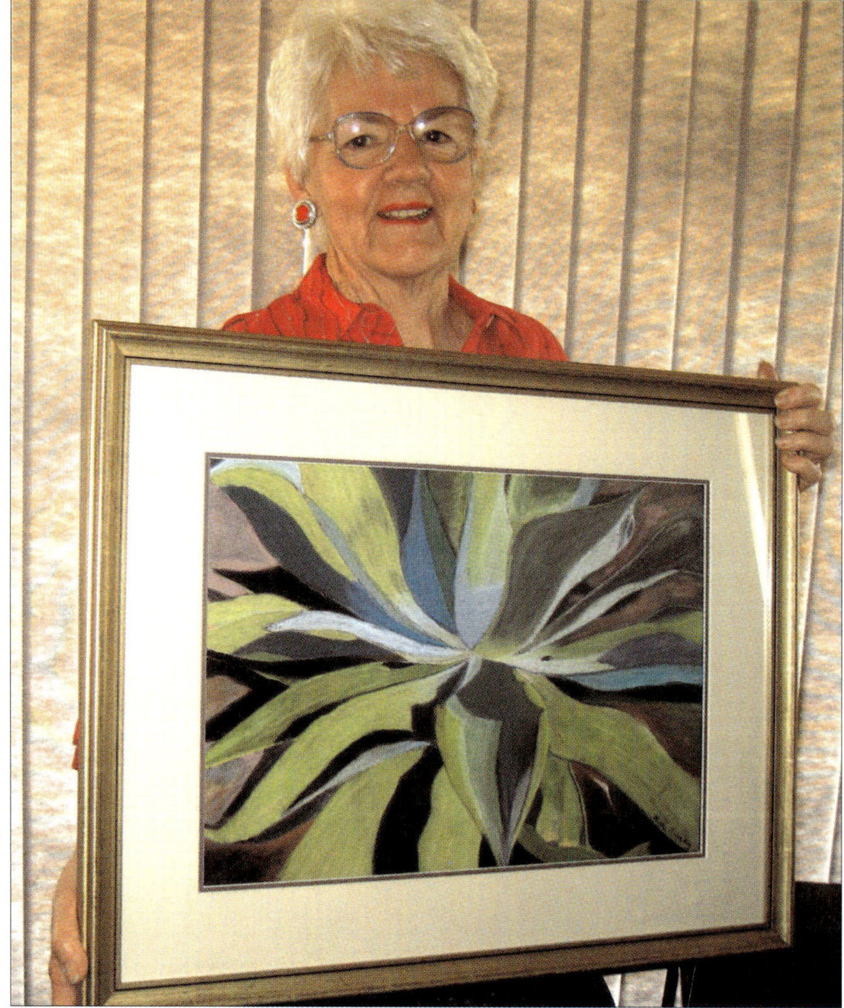

Stephanie holds *Agabe* a pastel 54cm x 68cm

## EMERALD

### *JULIE SHEPHERD, 1970s*

*I grew up in Rockhampton where I spent the first twenty years of my life. I had heard of the Flying Art school when growing up. An elderly woman around the corner from where we lived used to attend the Flying Art School in Rockhampton and went to Mervyn Moriarty's workshops, so I had heard the name and knew about Flying Arts but I really didn't do any art at school and it was not until I married in 1976 and went to live in Emerald that I began my first art course. Because I couldn't get a job as a registered nurse in Emerald I came back to Rockhampton to work. So I lived in Rockhampton, but on my days off I went back to Emerald.*

*That's when I first started doing pottery with TAFE in Rockhampton under Lesley Archer. Then, when I was able to get a job in Emerald working for Community Health I returned to Emerald to live full time.*

*In Emerald I joined the Emerald Pottery Group which, at that time, was just a small hobby pottery group. They had a workshop area underneath the National Fitness Centre and the Flying Arts School visited them regularly every few months. Their main tutor was Kevin Grealy. I believe that Kevin was one of the seminal teachers in my life although I didn't attend all his workshops because I was working full time. After the children came along I couldn't get to the workshops very often.*

*Kevin didn't come out to us every time. Sometimes there would be a different tutor each time. We had a variety of really wonderful tutors, people like Ian Palmer who came out once. Although I didn't get to his workshop I saw the results of his visit as the pottery group kept samples of the tutor's work and we knew what was made by each tutor. Gwyn Hansson Piggott came out also – another was Betty Crombie. Basically the people who came out with the Flying Art School were the who's who of the ceramic community. They always sent out the best possible tutors.*

*As well as Flying Arts the Emerald Pastoral College had holiday workshops during vacation time for their students. I think that was mostly in the winter and I remember attending one of those when Kevin was teaching. I also remember doing one with Dianne Peach. They ran them every year for quite a number of years.*

*In December 1988 we left Emerald and moved back to the Capricorn coast so we were there for twelve years.*

*I actually did a workshop with Jeff Shaw from Flying Arts after we moved back to the Capricorn coast. The Beach Potters, who were based in Yeppoon, used to have Flying Art School teachers up and I attended a couple of workshops there. One tutor was Jeff Shaw, another was a woman who used to work with him – Edith-Ann Murray. Jane Harthoorn was another who came.*

*The Rockhampton Pottery Group were fairly active too and they used to invite people up to teach as well. So I actually went to a lot of the weekend workshops they ran. They invited people like Brian Truman up from Melbourne and on one occasion Chester Neally came over from New Zealand. However, the person who really taught me the most about ceramics in my whole career was probably Kev. Grealy. He was very good.*

*I believe that the efforts of Flying Arts in bringing art to regional Queensland, even to Rockhampton, was really important. Contemporary art didn't reach Rockhampton until the Flying Arts brought it in. Flying Arts taught me to look at things differently and that helped me so much in my career as an artist.*

Julie is now a successful Brisbane sculptor and her work can be seen in several regional galleries.

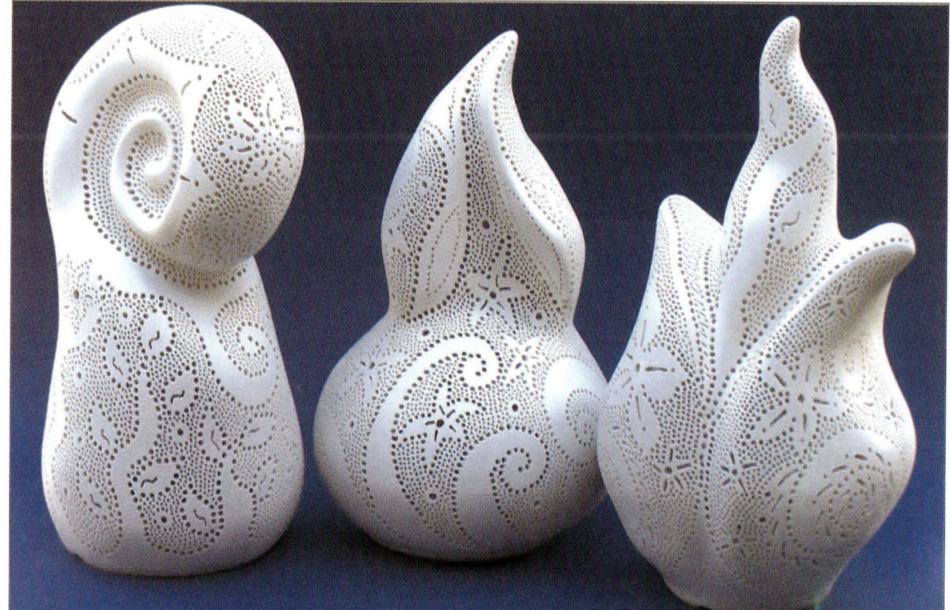

*Growths 2007* Slip cast pierced and polished Limoge Porcelain 30cm high Julie Shepherd, Emerald

## LONGREACH

### *RUTH FRANCIS, 1972-1980*

*I lived in Blackall before I went to Longreach. When I lived in Blackall the Arts Council, through Dr. Gertrude Langer, brought Mervyn Moriarty to Blackall to give us a lesson in Modern Art.*

*When Merv arrived he was very unhappy and grumpy and he apparently had crossed someone before our lesson because he was very anti the whole establishment and when he started out he said "I'm going to talk about modern art and by the end of this weekend you'll hate me." And we did, he worked on it.*

*So when I went to Longreach about a year later I became involved with the art group there straight away and they said to me "Oh, Mervyn Moriarty's coming out next week, are you going to come and join us?" I said, "Oh, no, I don't think I will." They said "Why not?" I said, "Because he's too grumpy for me" and one woman said "Oh, we must be talking about different people." She said "He's lovely", then she said "Why don't you come and give him a go?"*

*So I began with Eastaus then, and I didn't stop going to his classes ever again until 1980 when he suggested to me that I should bring my work to Brisbane and have an exhibition in the Gregory Terrace Gallery. Actually it happened then that I moved to Brisbane because my husband was transferred. So we came to Brisbane and were here for that exhibition.*

*In those days Longreach was a very parochial town, population of about 3000. A big pastoral centre with big pastoral pieces of land as well – huge. The people there had mostly sheep and some cattle and they were very hard working and found it difficult to get in to classes. It was a big deal to get into town for an art class. Especially when the men (it was mostly women who came to the art classes) didn't approve of all this 'arty stuff'. So the majority of men were not approving of what we were doing, they didn't like artists. They thought they were those strange people who were hippies and did amazingly risqué things.*

*Mervyn came four times a year and we would have a lesson with him for two days. He also brought us correspondence lessons which he would leave with us. Then when he went away he would say "do your homework" in the correspondence lesson. So we'd do it.*

*And then he would come back in a few months time and we'd take all our work to him (or most of our work because we would have picked out what we thought was best). So we said to him "this is our work". "Show me" he said, so we showed him and he looked and said "oh, yeh, now show me what you've got hidden over there". He knew. We would then bring out the stuff we thought was terrible and he said "now, this is good work, This is your best work" and we would be absolutely astounded. We couldn't understand what he was about but we didn't mind the praise so we kept on with it.*

*All of those western centres were absolutely starving for something like Eastaus. The women were like blotting paper wanting to soak up anything about art. It was just so amazing – he came at the right time for the people of the west.*

*He started off going to a few centres and gradually needed to go to more. I don't really know how many he went to – maybe ten?*

*On one trip he would go to ten and then on another trip in the southern part he would go to another ten, Then he went down into New South Wales I believe, too. We just lived from one class to the next so it was really an amazing time.*

*Mervyn, didn't take us to the river to paint. The river was about six miles out of Longreach to the north and this is a very flat area, it is the Thompson River and it is flat, flat, flat everywhere. The only place where there is any sort of indication of hills or anything is the channels in the river itself. I can remember taking John Rigby there once and he said "where can we go and paint where there are hills or something you can see." He couldn't come to terms with the subtle washed-out colours.*

*Our first lessons with Merv were in someone's home. Peg Perkins was one, we had it in her home one month and then the other one was Rae O'Rourke. Another person was Llyris Bird and then they would have it in my house so we took it in turns.*

*Then the local Arts Community got together and decided that they would have a centre somewhere and the Shire Chairman, Sir James Walker, suggested we have a little cottage beside his house. And so the potters came there and the Spinners and Weavers and the artists, and we all had to share that little cottage. That would have been about 1973 when that started.*

*However, it was about that time that we realised that what we had wasn't big enough or really suitable for a more organised arts group. By this stage we had a Longreach Arts and Crafts Council (I think that was what it was called) with a President and a Secretary and a team and Boo Hanrick was the name of the lady who really worked hard to get grants and things like that and she had the skill of lobbying for money and she could get it. She and Nancy Button.*

*Nancy Button was an amazing woman who had a vision of a future and she and Boo used to work together to get the money and the necessary place.*

*Then someone suggested that we should go to the old Ambulance centre in Longreach which was just not being used for anything at that time. This huge building with a cement floor. It had these little offices downstairs and a flat upstairs. But it hadn't been used for years and years and the verandah was breaking up, so we applied to the Education Department. First of all we applied to some government section, it might have been health, and they said "no, they had handed it over to the Education Department".*

*So we applied to them and they allowed us to use it. Then Boo Hanrick worked hard to get finance through the Historical Assn. in Brisbane and they granted money to have the building re-established so that it was safe to be there. The old broken verandah was pulled out and they put in a cement verandah right around the bottom section. Then eventually, by the time I left there, we had a painting group, a fabric painting group, a pottery group, jewellery making as in enamelling, leatherwork and there was a girl, Bonny Shore, who wanted to make basketry, so she went away and learned how to do it and came back to Longreach. She was the only person who did basketry but she did it beautifully.*

*Then Mervyn brought Bela Ivanyi. There were no other painters. The era I am talking about was up to 1980 before I came to Brisbane. It was the 1970s before the Flying Arts school was taken over by the Government.*

*About that time when I came to Brisbane Mervyn and Helen ran out of money. They applied to the government for funding but they said "no, you're not qualified to do this. We will only fund it if it is under the direction of Kelvin Grove." So Kelvin Grove then took over the Flying Art school and later they dismissed Mervyn.*

*Flying Arts from Kelvin Grove came in the 1980s and they used the new Arts building. But Kelvin Grove were not teaching those other crafts. In the late 1970s they were certainly teaching pottery and Rob Hinwood used to come to teach pottery. Before that there was Kevin Grealy.*

*I went to Mervyn's classes here in Brisbane for the two years between 1980 and 1982.*

*There is now a gallery at the Arts and Crafts Centre at Longreach. I ran it and Llyris Bird helped me and Nancy Button and Boo Hanrick were the ones in charge, but I actually physically ran the gallery there.*

*Back in Mervyn's time it was a wonderful time for art in Queensland and for women. Before that we didn't have anything except in Blackall when I went to art classes with Jan Shaw. She was a gifted teacher and her group produced some talented artists. We used to have our art classes on a Thursday. I would get up out of bed and I would fly around in the morning and have everything done and my husband would say: "I think it must be Thursday today!"*

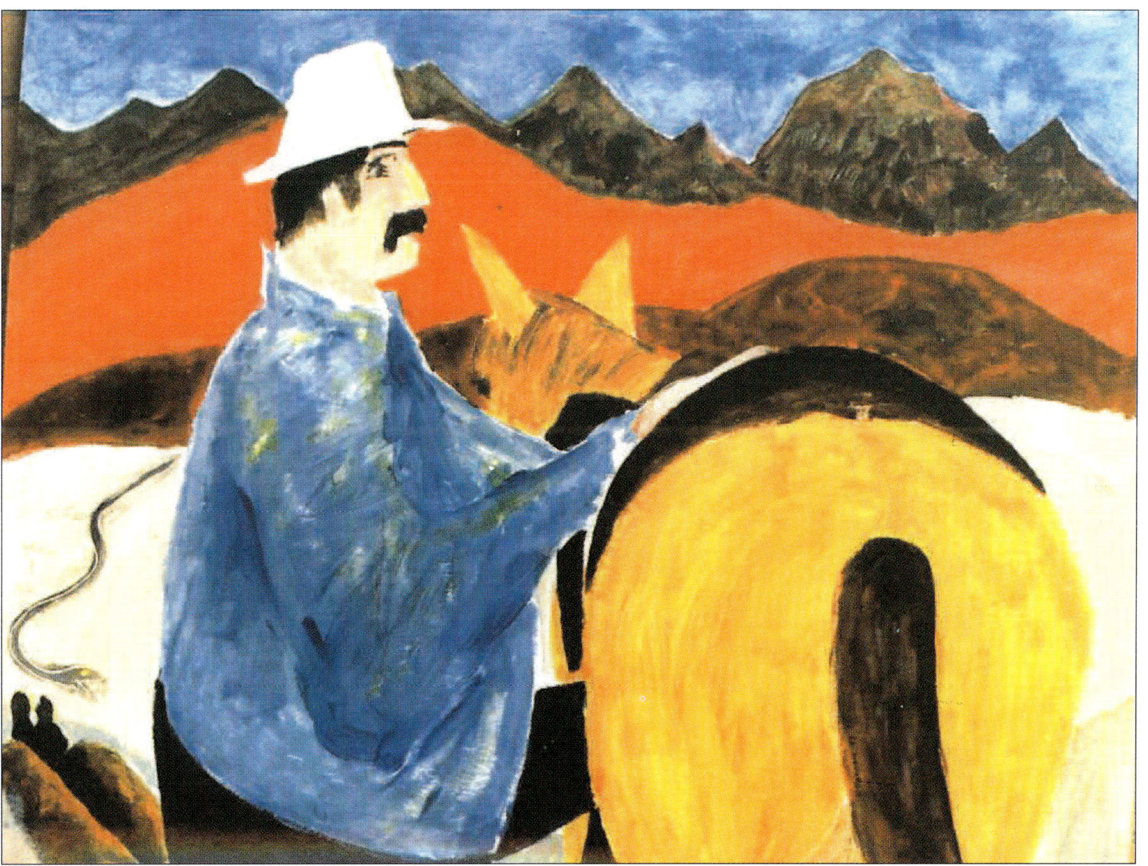

*Found* acrylic on card 80cm x 100cm Ruth Francis, Longreach

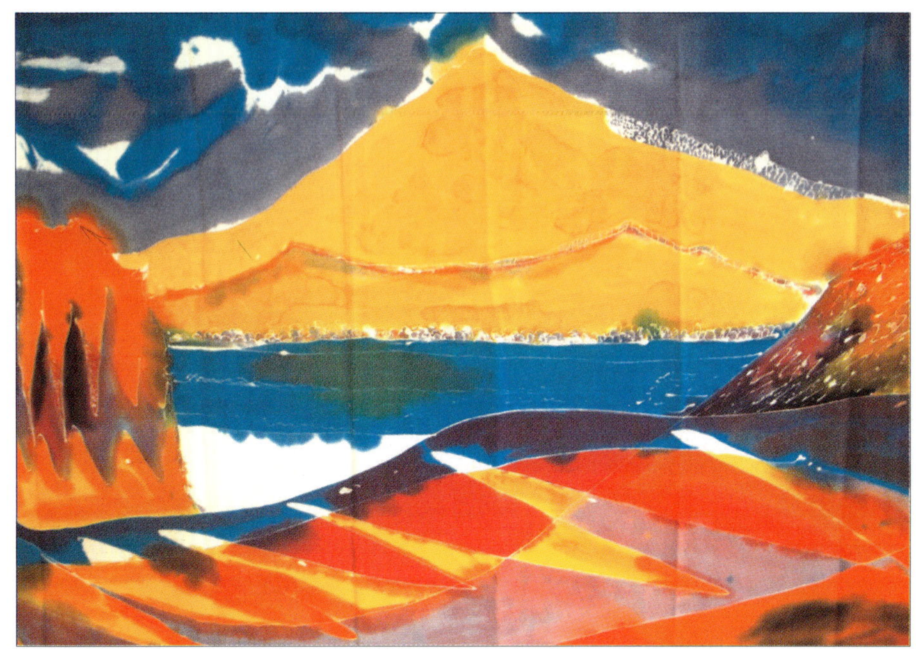

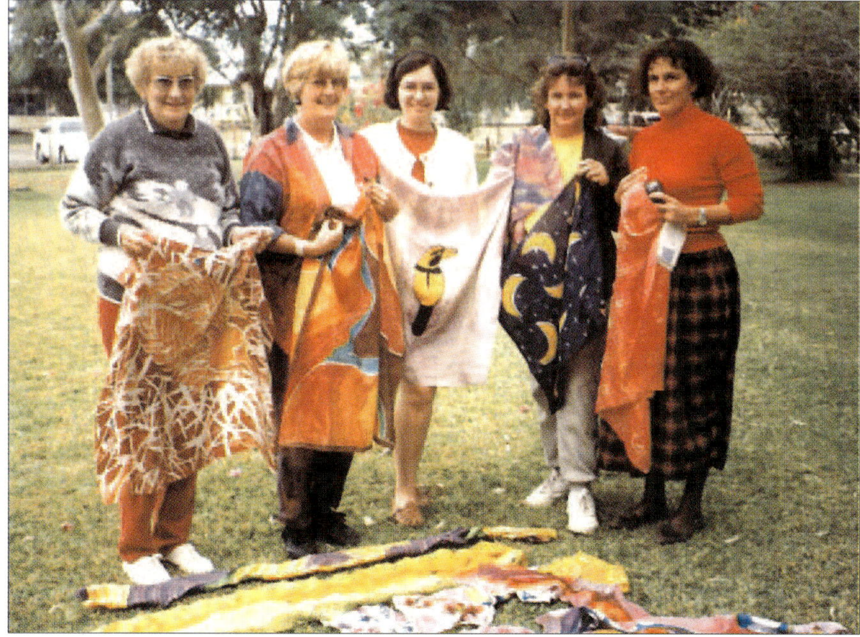

Ruth working with Silk Painting classes at Richmond and Julia Creek Courtesy Ruth Francis

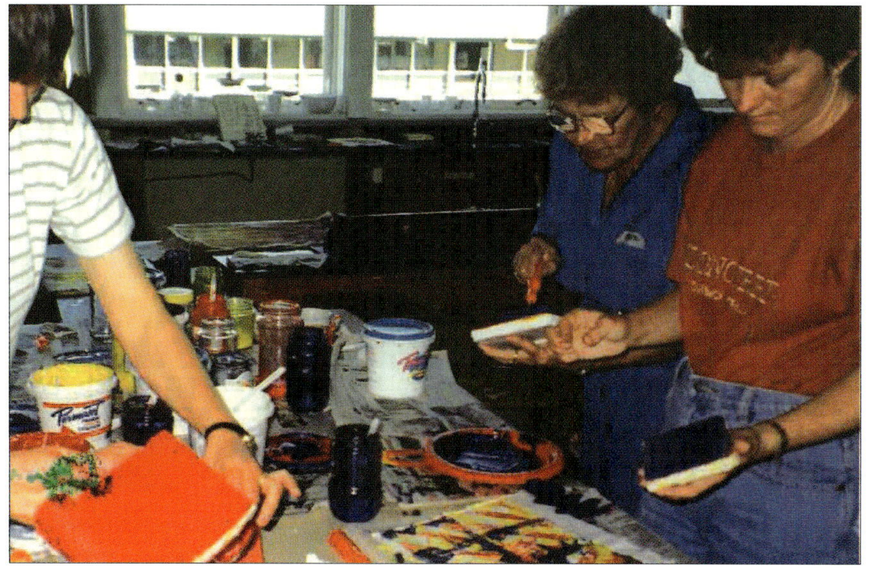

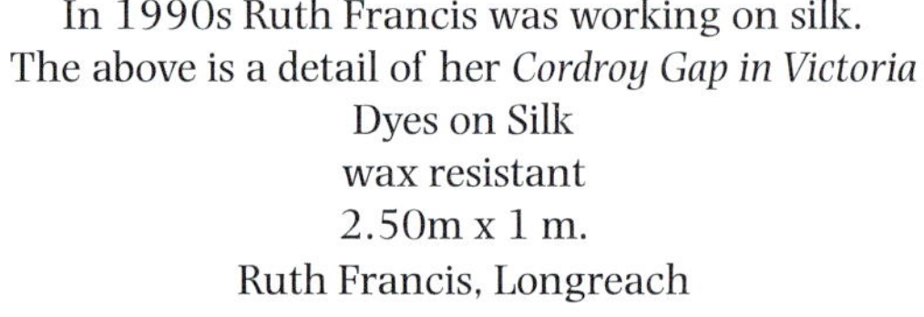

In 1990s Ruth Francis was working on silk.
The above is a detail of her *Cordroy Gap in Victoria*
Dyes on Silk
wax resistant
2.50m x 1 m.
Ruth Francis, Longreach

# EMERALD

## *MARIE BIGGINS, 1971*

*In 1970 I was teaching adult education classes in Emerald, Queensland, and one day I received a phone call from Mervyn Moriarty. He was contacting people involved in the visual arts from a list he had received from Arthur Creedy, the then Director for Cultural Activities in Queensland, with the aim of arranging public meetings to launch the beginnings of Eastaus (later known as The Australian Flying Arts School).*

*Those early days were heady and exciting ones, with visiting artists such as Clifton Pugh and Keith Looby travelling with Merv and Bela Ivanyi and a constant supply of slide lectures and chatty newsletters with students' work from the exercises in the lesson books.*

*So began my long association with this unique organisation of which I was a member for ten years, before going to Melbourne to complete a Bachelor of Fine Arts at the Victorian College of the Arts. In those days painting and printmaking were still my area of interest.*

*Then my arts practice evolved into sculpture and installation in the mid to late 1980s. At this time I also bought my first Macintosh computer and my interest in multimedia steadily grew over the following years.*

*I came from a rural background on a wheat and sheep farm in Western Australia where I spent my childhood, before going on to boarding school, teacher training, and later a posting in Esperance, Western Australia. After this I moved on to live on a property near Naracoorte in the south east of South Australia, and then on to Emerald in Queensland.*

*At present I live in Yeppoon and work from my studio on a small rural property overlooking the sea.*

*Since the mid 1980s I have been working in sculpture and installation, having had an initial training in painting and printmaking. Major solo exhibitions of my work to date have been at the Institute of Modern Art, Brisbane in 1990 and at Gallery 14 of the Queensland Art Gallery in 1992. Noosa Regional Gallery, Ipswich City Council Regional Gallery, Gladstone Art Gallery, 1993, Rockhampton Art Gallery 2003.*

*In 1994 I received a grant from Arts Queensland and travelled to Europe and the USA to research electronic arts. I worked in this area of interest for a number of years and have now returned to my first love of painting and drawing.*

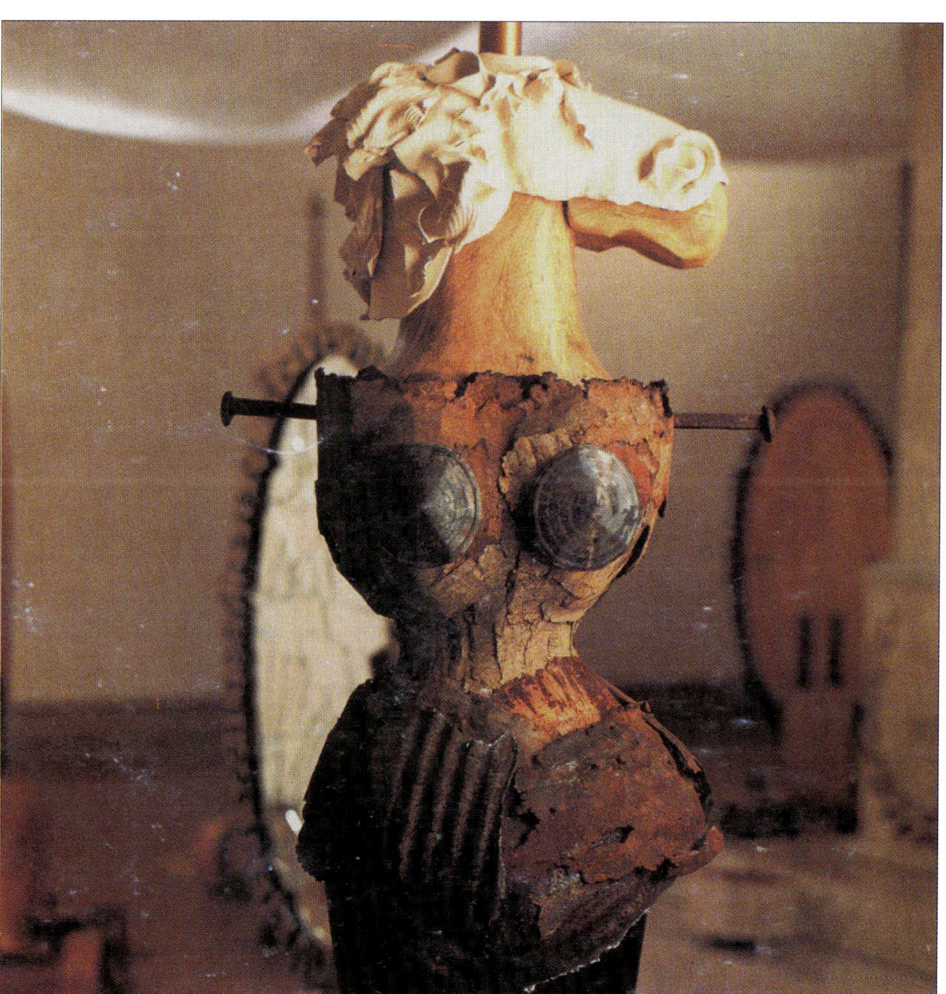

*Carousel*
Installation
at the Queensland
Art Gallery
1992

Marie Biggins,
Emerald

## HUGHENDEN

### *PATRICIA GEE, 1978*

*My husband was a bank manager and we were moving about. We'd lived in Brisbane and Townsville and then we were transferred out to Hughenden. I had four small children then. My next door neighbour was a mad potter and she thought I was a bit housebound so she dragged me off to do some pottery.*

*They had a really good set up in Hughenden. The council had given them this old shed, they had a couple of wheels, even a playpen for the kids, and everyone just helped everyone else. Of course once I started that was it.*

*They used to have visiting potters and of course Merv Moriarty used to come out and do the drawing and the painting. He was considered very way out at that time.*

*I actually went to a drawing class of Merv's in the early '80s when I moved to Brisbane. That was really good. I enjoyed his classes – they were different. But he wasn't my focus in the earlier days. Kevin Grealy was.*

*I think the first time I met Kevin must have been in Richmond one weekend, when he was doing the potters and Merv must have been doing the artists.*

*Then my husband and I were transferred to Weipa. When we got there, if I remember correctly, they'd just started to put a club together so several of us decided we'd try to get Flying Arts up because they hadn't been there previously. So for the next three years I worked with Flying Arts in Weipa.*

*Kevin was an excellent teacher, in fact I think he's probably one of the best teachers I've come across, very good at showing you how to do a thing. It's a real gift being able to impart that knowledge. It's one thing to have the knowledge, it's another to be able to impart it. Kevin was really good at that.*

*One of the problems our tutors have these days is that participants in workshops are at all different levels of skill. Was that the case in Weipa? I think so, but Kevin managed to cope with that. He was really excellent.*

*We used to have a good time because if they were staying for the weekend you'd have a function in the evening and there was a lot of camaraderie and partying on and so forth. It was always an occasion - something special.*

*I remember once someone gave Kevin a huge fish, a salmon I think, and he was anxious to get this fish home. I was taking him out to the airport for his flight back to Cairns, but as usual I was running late and he was sure he was going to miss his plane. He was a very worried man. We did make it, and they held the plane for us - nobody would do that nowadays – and he went off with his fish. He was a nervous wreck though, and I don't know that he ever forgave me.*

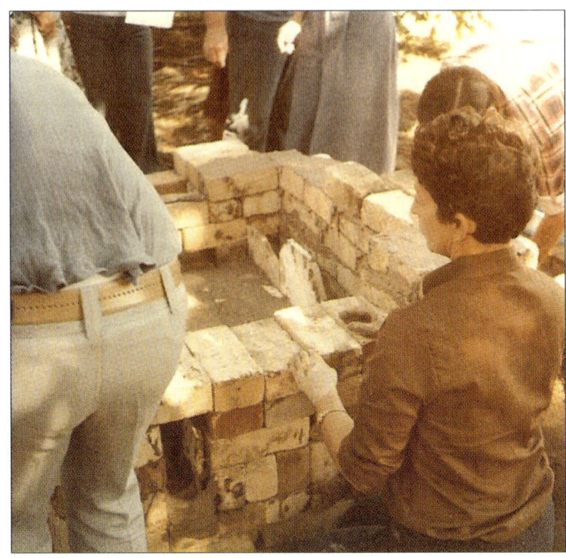

Flying Arts Workshops in Cairns
with Janet Mansfield
August 1979
Photos courtesy Patricia Gee

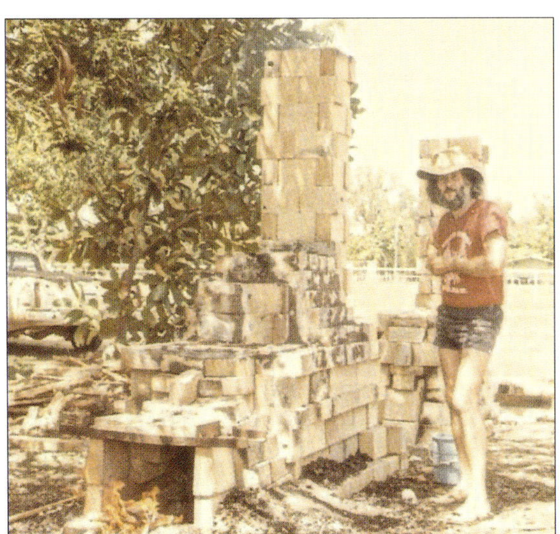

With Kev Grealy at a workshop in Weipa 1980

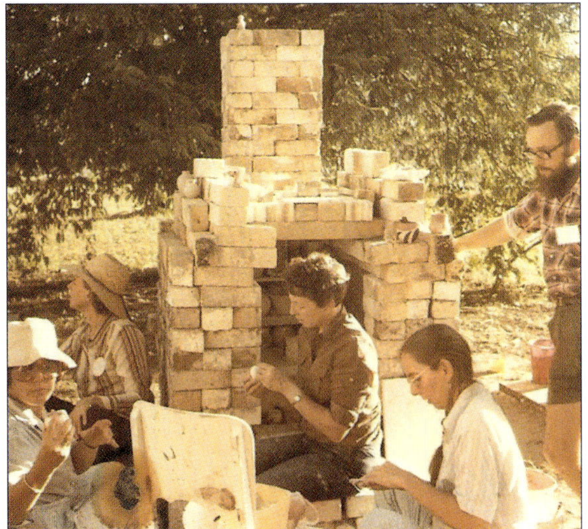

***Patricia Gee's cuttings from the Bauxite Bulletin describe how Kevin Grealy set up pottery in***

# WEIPA

***in the late 1970s***

Kevin Grealy, from the Australian Flying Arts School in Brisbane, visited Weipa last weekend to conduct a three day seminar for Weipa Potters.

Kevin, a Pottery advisor and teacher who travels widely to outback centres organized a program of practical and theoretical pottery instructions for about twenty local enthusiasts.

At the Friday class potters were shown glazing techniques as well as the preparation of glaze materials. The decoration of pots was also covered.

Saturday's group were involved in wheel work and Kevin demonstrated methods of throwing pots, bottles and platters correctly and effectively.

Individuals were then encouraged to try their skill under his guidance as he advised them on ways of self-improvement.

Sunday was devoted to salt firing and two kilns were built adjacent to the Potters Hut which was behind the Police Station next to the Cricket Oval.

One Kiln was used for firing unbisqued (no previous firing) materials. And the other for bisqued work (previously fired).

Kevin encouraged us to use local materials. Calcined bauxite was used for the kiln floors and red mud (slurry) was applied successfully to the pot bases to resist sticking to the kiln. Normally wax would have been used.

A number of pots were decorated with red mud and it was found to be most effective both as a colouring agent and as a glaze. The kilns were built from calcination bricks.

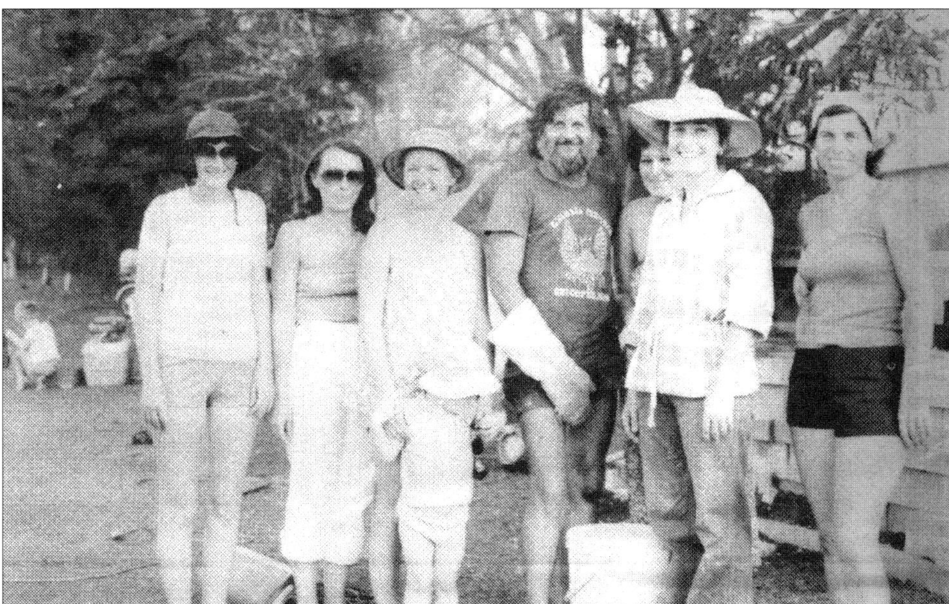

*Weipa Potters with Kevin Grealy*

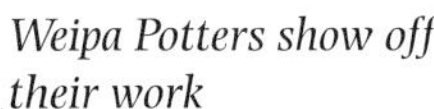

*Weipa Potters show off their work*

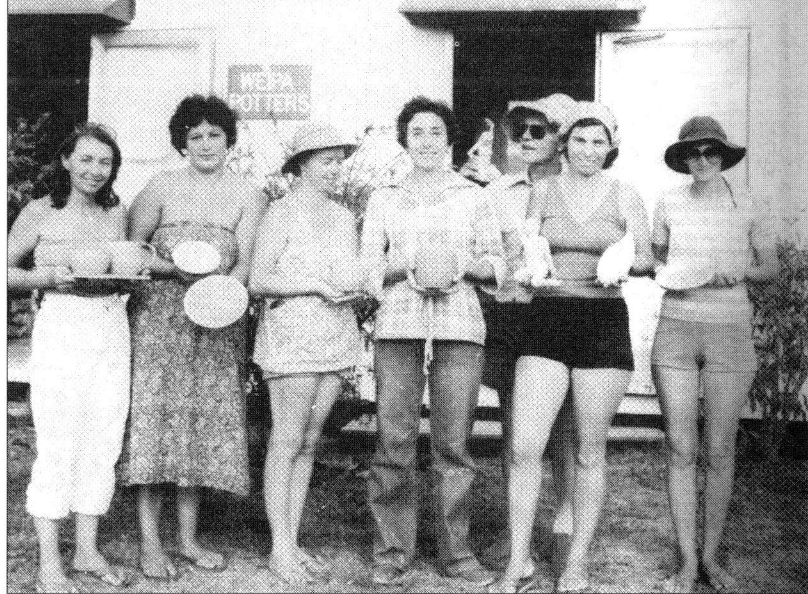

# Student Stories from the North

## MALANDA

### *SANDRA BURCHILL, 1995*

To walk into Sandra Burchill's home is like walking into a gallery. Sandra's talents are many and the work adorns the walls of her home. Not only the walls either, there are cupboards bursting their seams with bits and pieces of work.

*School provided me with the basics in 'conventional' painting and drawing but as I matured I always dabbled with different things 'weird, strange things'. In 1967 or 68 a visit to the Crafts Council exhibition in Townsville showed me that others did 'weird' things too.*

*I then became very interested in macrame and joined the Fibres and Fabrics group in Townsville. This made me more aware of textiles. The awareness of what others were doing, plus the quality tutors in textiles that we obtained from Flying Arts, influenced me to move into textiles. Also, large macrame pieces are costly and it is hard to find space to hang them. The macrame pieces I created were small tightly knotted shapes – shells and fossils and more recently – feathers.*

*As well, I turned to fabric and machine embroidery. My husband, Doug, had developed an interest in pottery which I enjoyed but found impractical with children around.*

*I am definitely a contemporary worker and open to new ideas all the time. My pieces cover areas such as dyeing, machine embroidery, fabric manipulation, patchwork, and silk paper work.*

*At one stage there was a 'love affair' with attic windows and then the Escher triangle patchwork styles.*

*An ongoing interest has been banners for the church, resulting in trips to other northern towns to help people there design and create their own banners.*

*I belong to a group called 'Artistic Licence' which has mounted a number of exhibitions in Atherton. I held a solo exhibition on the theme 'Sense of Community'.*

*There are regular entries to Townsville 'Fibres and Fabrics' Exhibitions.*

*For excitement, the outstanding achievement was winning the 1995 Shell Art Award with Flying Arts.*

## INNISFAIL

### *JOSEPHINE McTAGGART, 1971*

*I was born and educated in N.S.W.*
*Living in Australia, the unique beauty and quality of the landscape spurred me on to join up with the then fledgling Australian Flying Arts School, becoming one of the founding students of the school through the Innisfail group.*

*At this time my children were also beginning to explore their artistic inclinations, the girls learning the piano, and my son Steven developing an interest in dance. As an extension of my painting and art work with the Australian Flying Arts School, I volunteered to help behind the scenes, painting backdrops and doing backstage work.*

Following this small beginning in 1987, Josephine is now highly regarded as one of this State's leading freelance scenic artists. Over the previous six years she spent a collective eight months working with the Australian Opera Company. She worked on productions in a number of towns which included Caloundra, Moura, Innisfail, Sydney, Gladstone, Townsville and Nerang. She successfully achieved the status of being Queensland's only professional stage artist, as well as being one of this State's leading painters, having won prizes at art exhibitions from Gladstone to Rockhampton and Caloundra to Cloncurry. She believes that the further one travels west in Queensland, the more there is a demand for the arts.

Jo continues:

*The people in the bush seem to have a tremendous understanding of the meaning of life, and demonstrate a readiness to depict it through means of artistic expression. It is for these reasons that the Australian Flying Arts School has played such a vital role in Queensland - in fact it is what I consider to be one of the best things which has ever happened in this country.*

From *Farmers & Graziers* Magazine, December 1987.

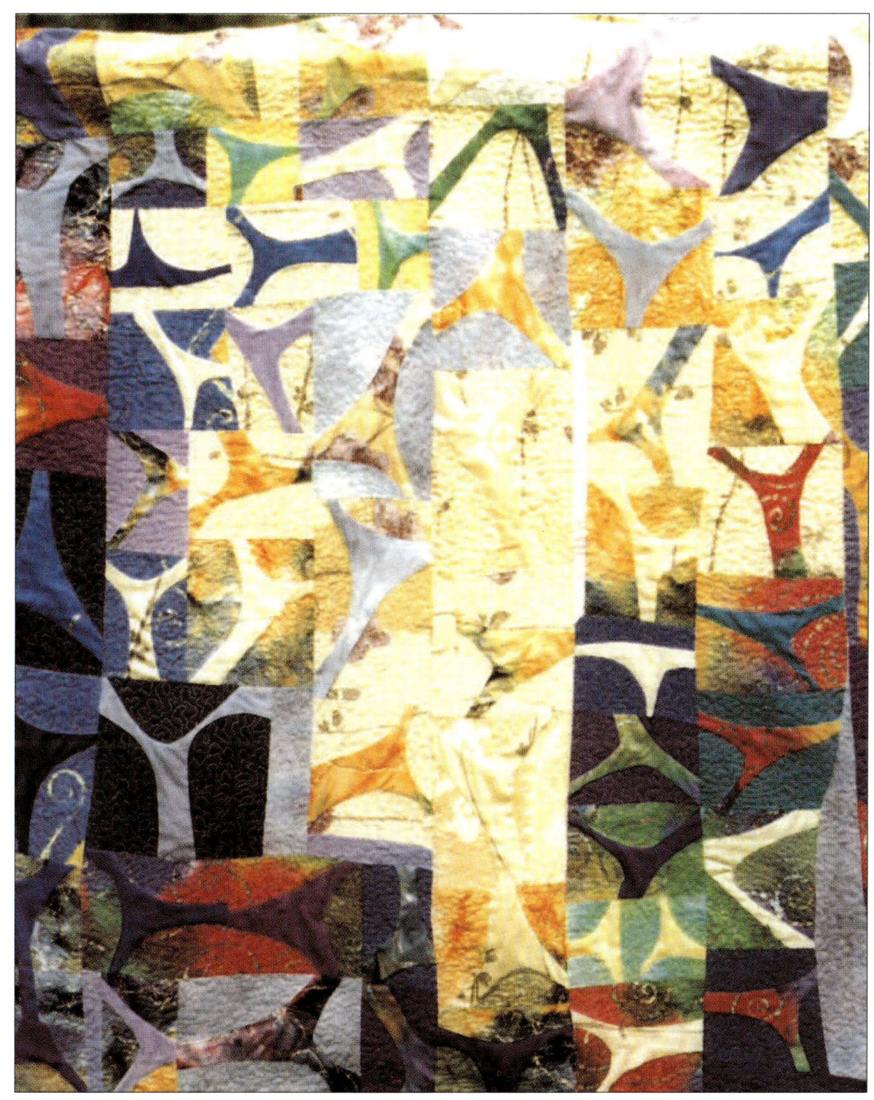

*Coming of the Light* Cotton machine pieced machine quilted
Sandra Burchill, Malanda

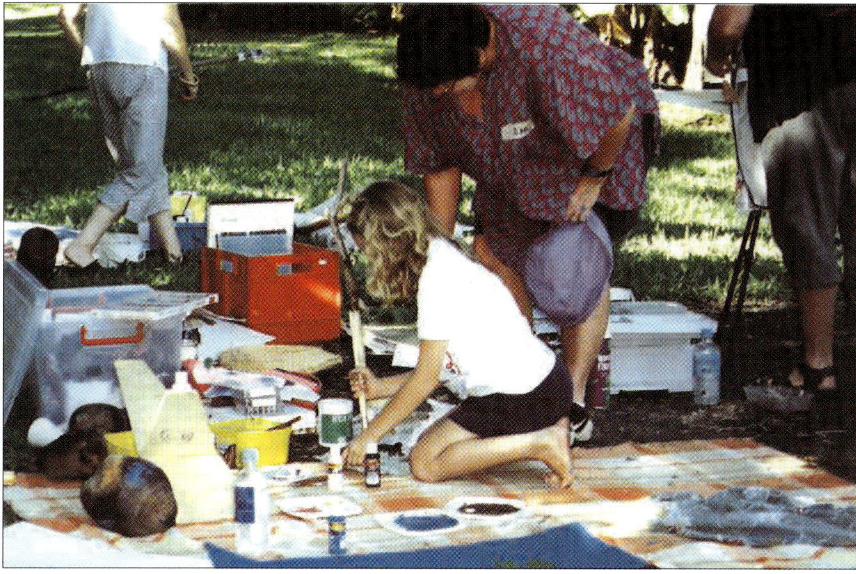

A Flying Arts workshop at Mackay, 2001 Courtesy Flying Arts archives

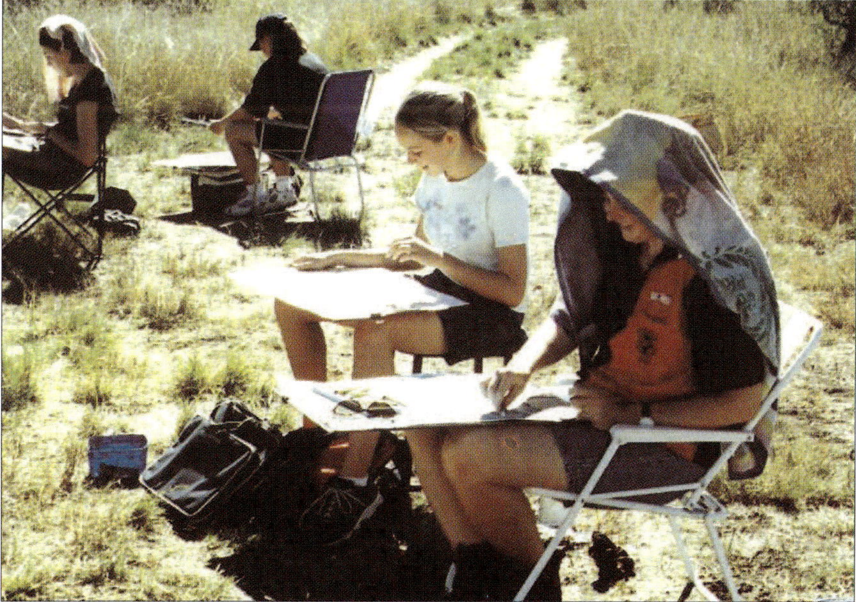

Bonney Bombach taking a workshop, Dysart State High School Courtesy Flying Arts archives.

# GORDONVALE

## *IVY ZAPPALA, 1970s*

Ivy's career in art is outstanding. Some extracts have been taken from Max Germaine's *Artists & Galleries Australia,*

Born in Gordonvale in north Queensland in 1933 Ivy is a semi traditional painter and portraitist.

She began her studies with the Australian Flying Art School through Mervyn Moriarty and Bela Ivanyi. She has received a number of awards including:

Mulgrave Shire Council Centenary Award 1976; Tully Open Award 1977; Herberton Shire Council Award 1978 (to hang in Parliament House Brisbane); Caltex Traditional Award, Innisfail 1978; Atherton Open 1980; Mulgrave Shire 1981; Wide Bay Open 1983; Shell Open Mareeba 1986; Mulgrave Shire Council Bicentennial Australia Day Award 1988; Certificate of Excellence – The International Art Competition – New York 1988.

Her work was selected for hanging in the Portia Geach Memorial Award 1978; The Blake Prize for Religious Art 1979, 1984, and in 1986 in the travelling Blake; City of Sydney Heritage Awards 1980 & 1987.

Her *Reconciliation* was acquired by the local member for Parliament House in 1998 and in 2002 her award winning painting *In Remembrance of Me* was presented to Mr Thomas Scheiffer, the American Ambassador to Australia, at the Cairns City Council as a gift by Ivy on behalf of the Bellenden Ker Rural Fire Brigade for the Fire Fighters of New York in memory of their bravery and endurance after the 2001 September 11 terrorist attack.

She exhibits her work and is represented in private collections in USA, Canada, NSW and Queensland.

Ivy Zappala's work is also represented in Mulgrave Settler's Museum, Brisbane Parliament House, the Museum of Villiers-Bretoneaux in France and at the Cairns Regional art gallery. Here is her story:

*We are sugarcane farmers in the Babinda District of Far North Queensland. In 1947 I left school at fourteen, worked at the Gordonvale Hospital, married my cane-cutter husband at seventeen and we have both worked hard ever since. Our only son was born in 1954 and joined our 'hard work brigade' when he was fifteen. When I was almost 40 I decided to do something I'd always dreamed of doing, becoming an artist.*

*There was an Adult Education class in Babinda conducted once a week by the late Mrs. Eula Jensen. I attended that for a few months and sold my first sketch of me chipping cane to another farmer's wife for $2.00. Then Bela Ivanyi appeared on the art scene in Cairns advertising for students in art. The study time suited me, so every Tuesday between 10am and 2pm I attended his class for nearly two years. He was a very good teacher. He taught us the basics and made us use our brains.*

*Bela then joined up with Mervyn and I followed and became a member of Flying Arts. Mervyn issued Certificates to his students after completion of his 24-lesson course. It was just wonderful. He'd fly in to Cairns or Innisfail and bring other famous artists we'd only read about with him. Sometimes his wife would model for us.*

*By developing Eastaus, his flying art school, he opened a door for country people to opportunities we would never have had otherwise. He deserves recognition for his service to Australian Art.*

*Mervyn was a gentle, kind person and where he'd say gently while criticising your work: "Time to get tough I think", Bela, on the other hand would say: "What the hell do you think you're doing!"*

*Mervyn would always say : "Be true to yourself!"*

*Bela said: "Imagine you just climbed up and looked out from the top of a big gum boot and you'd never seen the world before – PAINT THAT!"*

*So we had the best of both worlds and we admired and respected them both tremendously. They both had their students' learning at heart and they wanted us to succeed.*

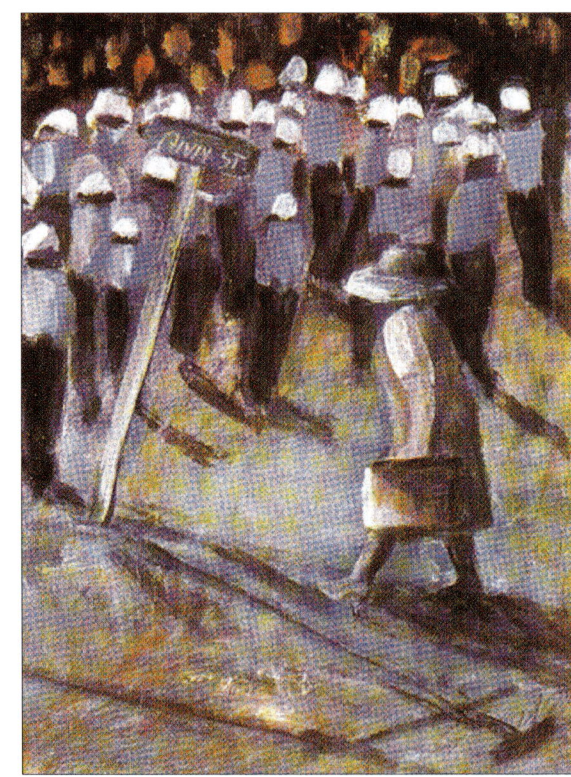

*Brisbane Street March in the Joh Era – 1970s*
Ivy Zappala, Gordonvale

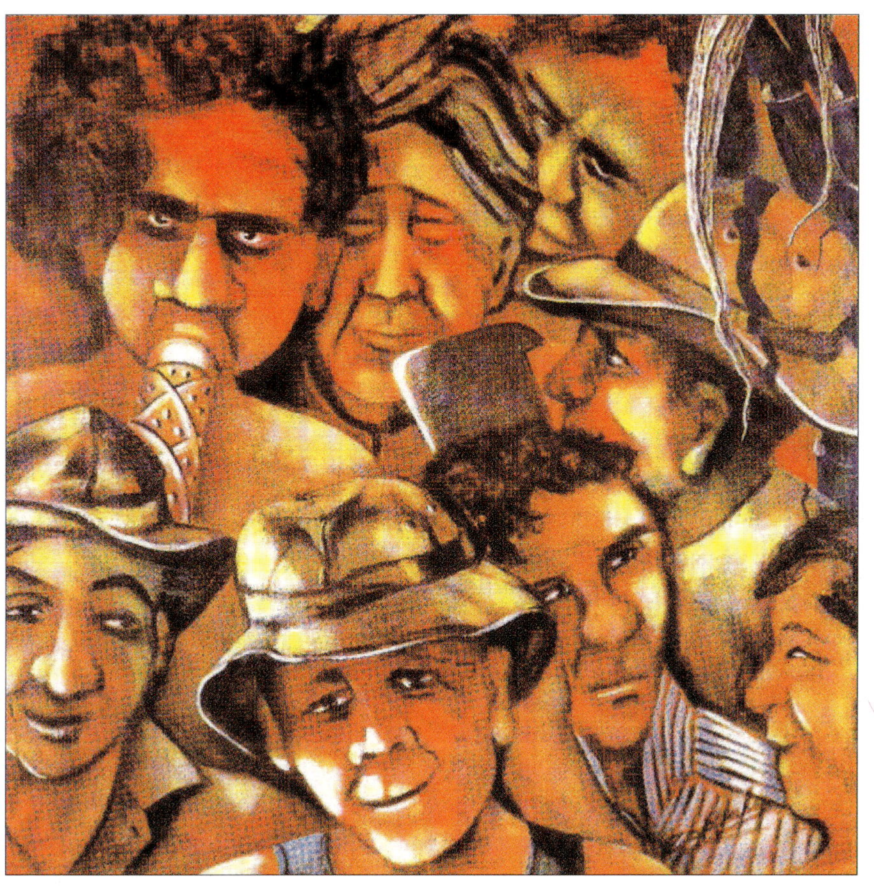

*The Fair Dinkum North – 1930s* Ivy Zappala, Gordonvale

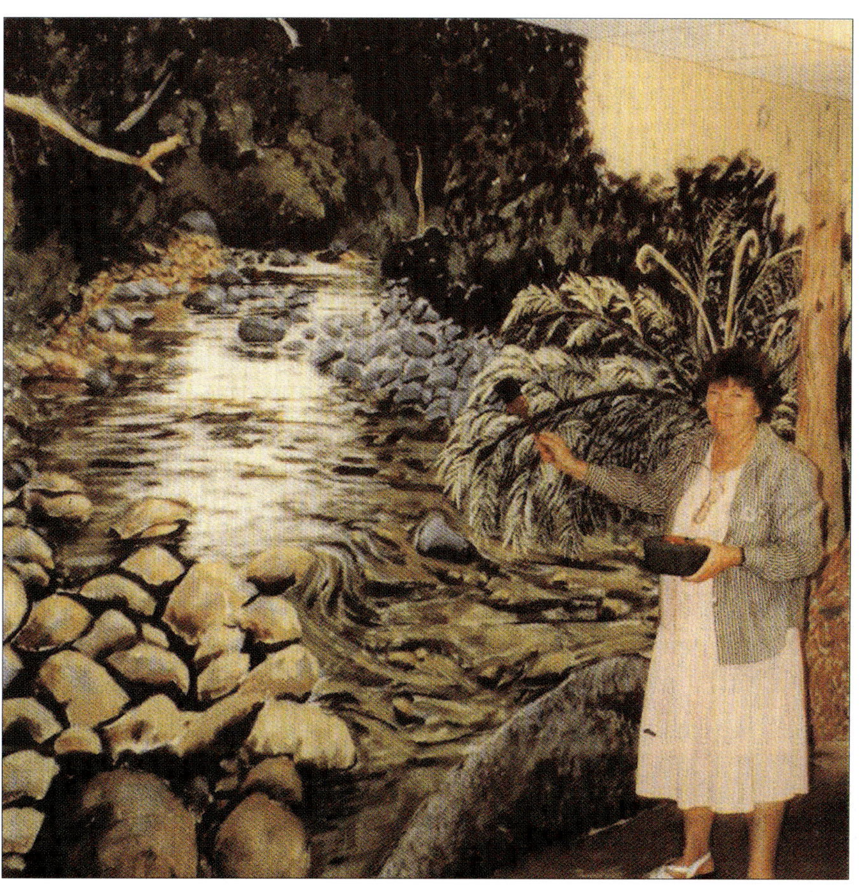

Ivy working on her *RAINFOREST MURAL* 300cm x 116cm
Acrylic/cement wall
Ivy Zappala, Gordonvale

Painted on the walls of the Mulgrave Settler's Museum, Gordonvale, North Queensland. It was dedicated to Ethel and Henry Hanson and their families. The museum was opened on 26th January, 1992. (Completion date 17th January 1992.)

# TOWNSVILLE

## *ANNEKE SILVER, 1972*

Born in Holland in 1937 Anneke Silver (neé Strik) recalls that her first fragments of memory related to her domestic surroundings: sunlight filtering through thin curtains, patterns on floor lino and tiny bright flowers in the garden. Brought up in a secure middle-class home in The Hague, her early childhood was disturbed only by the first sounds of impending war. Although her early school years were under German occupation, her worst memories from this time are of the last year of the war when the scarcity of food, lack of electricity and the terrible cold brought her to a sharp realisation that an urban society cut off from Nature was essentially futile. After the war she experienced a profound sense of liberation. The natural world that had been closed off by barbed wire and tank trenches was suddenly accessible.

*I was in Amsterdam when I was first introduced to the work of the CoBrA group, which stirred an interest in expressionist idioms. My training as an art teacher was strongly influenced by the Bauhaus philosophy of functionalism and the language of form. When I came to Brisbane in the late 1950s it seemed quaint and conservative in its social customs and intellectual climate compared to my experiences in Amsterdam.*

*I attended life classes and still-life painting with Melville Haysom and Arthur Evan Read at the Central Technical College in George Street and it was Haysom who taught me the craft of painting.*

*A job offer for my husband to assist in the survey of the Mt. Isa railway line was eagerly taken up and while in Mt. Isa I contributed to the revival of the Mt. Isa Art Group. I taught art classes and participated in group exhibitions with other local artists. These experiences were encouraging me to pursue a full-time career as an artist and teacher. For me the only question was how and where to make my start in my chosen career.*

*After spending almost a year living in Mt. Isa, we found themselves somewhat cut off and isolated and yearned to live near the coast once again. Townsville, the first northern coastal town we had visited on our way to survey the Mt. Isa railway line, seemed much more active and engaging than Brisbane.*

*A vacation school ran by Mervyn Moriarty was important in engendering an awareness of the relationships between the most diverse elements in the landscape.*

*I became a Flying Arts tutor in 1994 and was also a lecturer in Visual Arts at James Cook University, Townsville.*

*My main interest is painting but I also make prints, photographs and installations. I have been in 36 solo and over 40 group exhibitions in private and public galleries in Australia and overseas. My work is represented in major Australian collections such as the Queensland Art Gallery, Artbank, Qantas and Suncorp.*

In the 1970s Anneke received a grant of $2000 when the Prime Minister approved a scheme to support Australian artists on a $1 for $1 basis.

Anneke has a PhD and is an Adjunct Associate Professor at James Cook University's School of Creative Arts.

*Land into Sea.* Anneke Silver, Townsville
600cm x 120cm Mixed Media on canvas

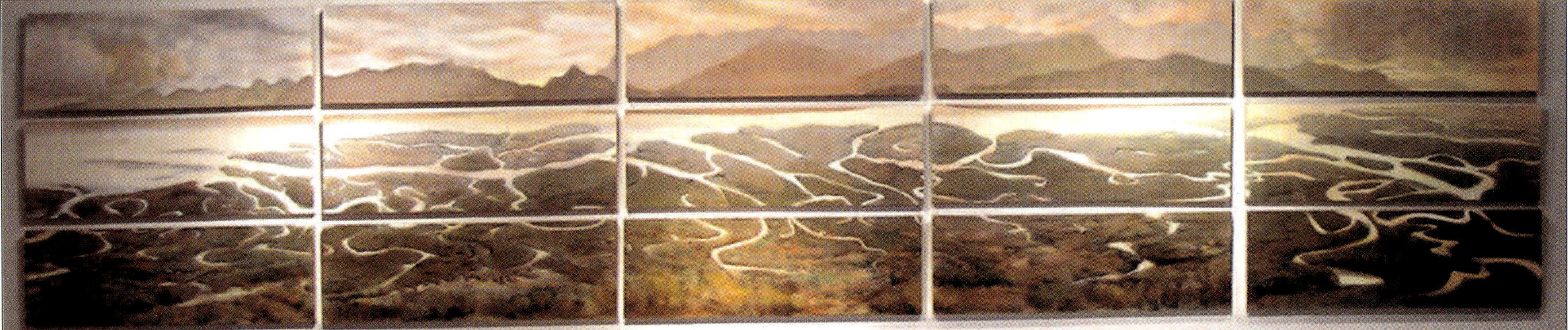

## *Anneke describes her experiences as a tutor with Flying Arts . . .*

*Boarding a small aircraft to Cooktown for a workshop recently it was nostalgically like Flying Arts years ago, when three tutors toured together in a tiny plane, departing from aero clubs or General Aviation, where rows of tiny planes were parked and tethered to the ground.*

*I have to say I love flying in small planes. I love the high speed on take off and the moment it leaves the ground. Always flying quite low, you get stunning views. And I know that Mervyn loved that aspect of it too, when he first conceived the idea of a Flying Art School.*

*This idea was spun around our kitchen table after a wonderful day on our yacht following his first workshop ever in the late 1960s, when Mervyn said that he'd like to just sail and give workshops, to which we replied "if you were to fly you can go everywhere!"*

*While flying to Cooktown I recalled an adventurous flight from Thursday Island as part of a Flying Arts tour in the middle 1990s.*

*It was a dark and stormy night, flying in complete blackness over the far tip of Cape York Peninsula. With only the tiny wing lights reflecting in dense cloud we seemed to tumble through fog and driving rain with the occasional flash of lightning.*

*Wendy was the Flying Arts pilot then and on that tour I was in the co-pilot seat. Oozing skill and confidence Wendy was great company.*

*During that fairly lively flight one of the tutors in the back seat asked anxiously if she really knew what she was doing, to which she responded that she was trained to fly Boeings and yes, she did know how to navigate in the dark, pointing to the tiny green radar screen blipping on the dash.*

*Finally, breaking through the cloud, Cooktown was a little string of lights reflected in the Endeavour River – but no landing strip loomed in the darkness beyond, which seemed strange.*

*Then all of a sudden as if by magic ... it sprung up. When I commented Wendy said that SHE had just switched the light on! What power... to switch on an entire airport—however tiny it might be.*

*And this recalls another evening flight on the same trip when we were to land in Richmond for a workshop in far Western Queensland. Coming in to land we saw two rows of houses along the highway, and a few hundred metres of street lighting. Again there were no airstrip lights to be seen, so I asked Wendy when she was going to switch them on, to which she replied: "I am trying to but they don't work!"*

*I then enquired if we were going to land on the road, to which she replied that it would be the third option. The first one was to radio Brisbane to get someone to switch the lights on manually while we waited, circling above.*

*From there we followed the whole little enactment. Headlights came on in one of the yards. Then they turned onto the main road, and after leaving the street lighting turned into the darkness beyond, casting a wedge of light onto a gate.*

*A little man (he was probably big, but from the air he looked small) hopped out, opened the gate, walked to a small shed and, hey presto, the double row of airstrip lights went on, and we could land safely. By the way, the second option would have been to fly on to the next township.*

*In Mount Isa – another active Flying Arts centre included in that trip – the traffic tower referred to her as 'The Wonderful Wendy' and pre-publicity for the workshops on local radio went along the lines of "The Wonderful Wendy has done it again...she's managed to land the Flying Arts team and avoid all the potholes in the airstrip. Yes!! she is the only pilot today who's made it; all the others are bogged".*

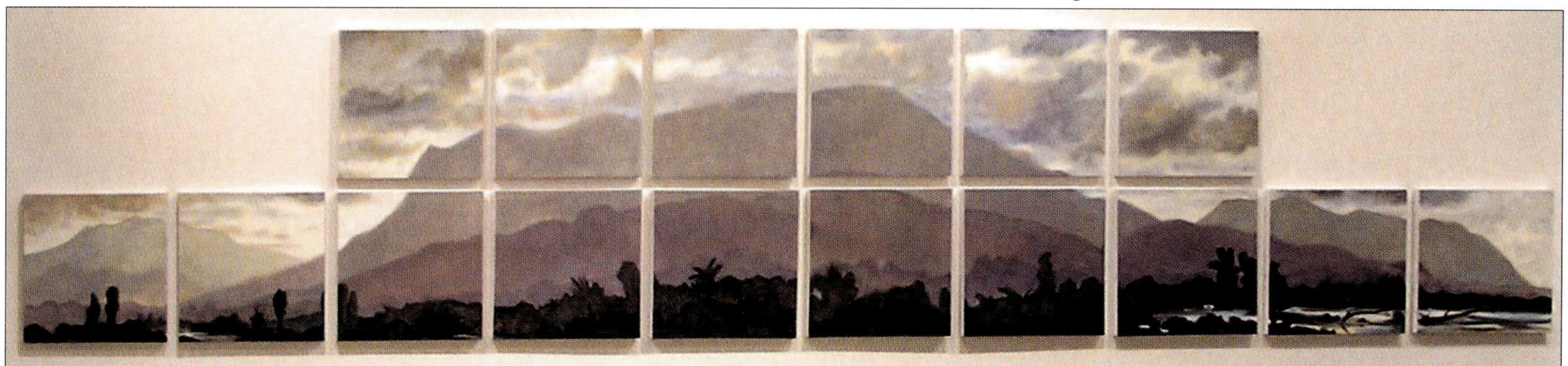

*Bartle Frere and Friends*
Anneke Silver, Townsville

600cm x 120cm
Mixed Media on canvas

# Student stories from the Mitchell Grass Country of the North West

## JULIA CREEK

### *GLADYS COONEY, 1971*

Gladys joined when Mervyn Moriarty first took his school to the bush in 1971. She had no ambitions to become a professional artist but she loved art and she loved the workshops and mixing with the people who went to them. Her great friend was Jo Forster, a well-known artist living on a property in the north.

In 1958, in her efforts to make things better for the women and children of Julia Creek, she became the first woman Councillor on the McKinlay Shire Council where she served until 1975. In 1992 she received an OAM for her contribution to the lives of people living in the north-west.

*My interest in art began at Teacher's Training College in Brisbane where, as a future school teacher, I was taught the basics of painting and drawing as part of my teaching qualifications. When I finished my training I was sent to Cunnamulla where I was in charge of an infants class at the local school. After the war I married and went to live at Julia Creek where I became good friends with Jo Forster. In the late 1960s Jo and I decided to start art classes for the children in our area.*

*In the early 1960s Dr Gertrude Langer had visited our town and over dinner we discussed opening an Arts Council Centre in both Julia Creek and Mt. Isa, so that was how I became the north-western representative for the Queensland Arts Council and had to travel to Brisbane for meetings.*

*I first met Mervyn when he conducted an Arts Council workshop at Mary Kathleen. The mine had closed down so the government allowed us to use the buildings for an Arts Council workshop. It was about 300 odd miles away from Julia Creek but we had a wonderful time.*

*As well as art they taught pottery, ballet and drama. They even supplied a chef so we all ate together at the old mess hall, taking our trays along to pick up our food. Some of the women had brought their children along so when they told Mervyn that the children wanted to paint too he set up an easel outside and gave them some paints and they painted a picture of Mervyn with his long red hair.*

*Through the Arts Council I attended a seminar held at the James Cook University in 1970 where I renewed my acquaintance with Mervyn and he told me he was thinking about starting a flying art school. I remember I thought it was a marvellous idea and encouraged him to bring his school out to Julia Creek. At that time I was also the local correspondent for the ABC at Longreach and through ABC Radio I asked all those who were interested to get in touch either with Jo Forster at Richmond or myself at Julia Creek to set up a local art workshop which would be conducted through Mervyn, so that is how it all began in North Western Queensland.*

*When Mervyn arrived in little Julia Creek with his wild red hair and his beard and sandals with Helen, his wife, in her Indian cotton dresses, I think many of those who lived there were shocked, but that soon changed when we began attending his three-monthly workshops and realised how exciting they were. Some of the women would travel for eighty miles to attend his workshops. We also loved the art books that Mervyn gave us, they taught us so much.*

*One of our group, a nun at the local convent, was a naive painter who was self-taught. Mervyn loved her work and was terrified that she would change her style. When he brought Clifton Pugh to us as a guest artist Clifton fell in love with her work and offered her lots of money for a painting. However she wasn't interested in money and so gave him the painting. It had been painted when she was stationed up in the Kimberleys and it featured a boab tree with some Aboriginals.*

*In those days we had our meetings in the local R.S.L. Hall. At the workshop we would show samples of our work and Mervyn would tell us how we could improve it.*

*I felt that he had brought culture to the region. We would look at this great, broad country of ours that we thought was featureless, there were so few trees, but he made us see the seasons. In the wet season the grass would be so beautiful and green but as winter came the green would disappear, yet as the grass turned to other colours we found they were just as beautiful, especially in the mirages which were dancing around us.*

*He taught us new ways of seeing our country and then painting it. At the Training College we had only learned to paint lady-like watercolours but Mervyn loved Indian music and we would sometimes paint to his music. One time our Richmond class went out to the bush to paint. We went to the Flinders River where it was more heavily timbered and settled at a creek which was dry at the time, although it would flood when the wet season came.*

*Mervyn played his music after giving each of us a big piece of white drawing paper and asked us to find our own place among the trees and quietly imagine what we would put onto the paper. I remember looking at some old Noogoora burr and as I looked the colours seemed to come to life and I thought 'this is a painting'; I became so absorbed in it as I began painting it – I wasn't just copying it, there was something more.*

*Sometimes when the classes were too small for Mervyn to come to Julia Creek I would travel down on the train to join the class at Richmond. One time the railway line was washed away by storms and I couldn't get home. Mervyn and Helen offered to fly me home to Julia Creek and on the way back I sat in the cockpit with him. Mervyn was a good flyer and was always very careful but this day it had just stopped raining when he took off and I could see the clouds of grasshoppers at the end of the runway and knew that the birds would be flying in to feed off them, I was terrified that we would hit them and ducked but Mervyn was able to miss them, although he told me afterwards that it was a close call.*

*After they dropped me off Mervyn and Helen continued on to their workshop at Mt. Isa.*

*I know dozens of people who became artists after he came out, he really brought out the creativity in us.*

Gladys has been living on the Gold Coast for some years and during that time she kept up her art. She has sold her paintings and several times has received "Highly Commended" for her work.

Some of her work has been exhibited at the Gold Coast Art Gallery at Bundall.

## JULIA CREEK
### *ANNE LORD, 1971*

Anne inherited her love of art from her grandmothers who were both creative, one had been a photographer, the other a painter. As a teenager growing up she had studied art briefly with Andrew Sibley and later with Betty Churcher during her high school years at Stuartholme College in Brisbane.

This is Anne's story:

*After returning home to the family property, 'Kilterry', I was able to study with the Australian Flying Art School for three years between 1971 and 1973 and attended the art workshops which were held at Julia Creek. I found Mervyn's books very important for the instructions and exercises between visits.*

*I first met Mervyn Moriarty when he flew into our centre as a dynamic person, an artist who was brimming with enthusiasm and creative energy, so I immediately became a student with the Australian Flying Art School, 'Eastaus' Flying Art School as it was known in those days.*

*Mervyn exuded creative thinking and after my high school training with Betty Churcher he was extremely important to my continuing interest in painting and later my going to Art School in Sydney.*

*It was he who told me that I should continue with my work and suggested I apply to the National Art School, so I followed his advice and attended that school during the subsequent changes it went through over the next few years.*

*His faith in my ability was important to me and it probably kept me going to art school when I was extremely homesick. Following his visits Mervyn had always left me eager to progress with my work and follow my dream to become a painter.*

*I remember that one of the early highlights was his visit with Clifton Pugh. I was nineteen and was very excited that they should be coming to 'Kilterry', our property, which lay on a very flat natural grassland with very few trees. At the time it was also fairly dry and hot.*

*I was anxious that Mervyn would be able to find the airstrip. It was part of a main road leading to the property and had occasional cattle trucks, the mailman's truck and local traffic using it to go into town. We needed to make sure Mervyn would be able to recognise this road as the airstrip, so we set up four big tractor tyres painted white to make the beginning and end of the airstrip, two at each end. He found the airstrip of course and he, his partner Helen, and Clifton Pugh were our guests at the main house for a couple of days.*

*In those days it was kept in a very gentile manner by my mother and formal dinners were always part of the evening with a lot of conversation.*

*I wanted to show them around the property so the next day I took them via a dirt road to a place I thought was interesting. It had a slight ridge which made it different from the surrounding land and the horizon was marked with scattered tree lines. I was used to walking out into the paddocks with a paint box of oils and canvas, but I think it was all a new experience for Mervyn and Clifton. I can imagine now that I look back on it that it must have seemed to them like landing in the middle of nowhere.*

*The next morning Clifton climbed our windmill tower to get a better view of the surrounding country. When he came down he produced a sketch that impressed my family very much and later he entered a little drawing into our guest book which thrilled my parents.*

*In the following years I practiced my art, supplying work for solo and group exhibitions and lecturing at Townsville TAFE and James Cook University.*

*In 1995 I was asked to go on tour as a Flying Arts tutor. It involved the Northern touring program: Julia Creek, Mount Isa, Charters Towers, Kuranda, Yarraba and Cooktown and one tour included New Guinea. It was fantastic, the experience enabled me to give back some of what I had gained from Flying Arts.*

*Since then I have also helped to curate the Flying Arts Inc. exhibition 'Transitions'.*

*In 2000 I was involved in helping produce a book through Lyrebird Press which featured a number of Flying Arts artists from the Northern region. This was followed by another solo exhibition at the Perc Tucker Regional Gallery in Townsville.*

*I continue with my lecturing position at the James Cook University and maintain my practice.*

*Mervyn's tuition has always stayed with me in approaching new work in any medium.*

Anne's work can be found in the collections for National Gallery Australia, Queensland Art Gallery, Parliament House, James Cook University, Perc Tucker Regional Gallery, BHP Collection, Artbank, Jupiters Casino, Hyatt Regency, Adelaide Hilton, Cairns, Warnambool Regional Art Gallery, National Library Aust., Allied Qld. Coalfields, and Remm Group Limited.

Anne is a lecturer at the School of Creative Arts James Cook University and a PhD candidate in 2007.

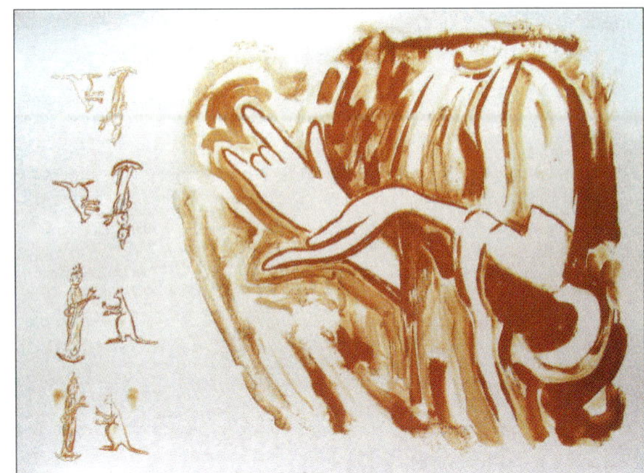

*Bodhisattva and kangaroo*
Anne Lord, Julia Creek
Umbrella Studio Contemporary Art
*Lithograph 56 cm x 76 cm. 2004*
*for an Installation* 'ABSENCE'

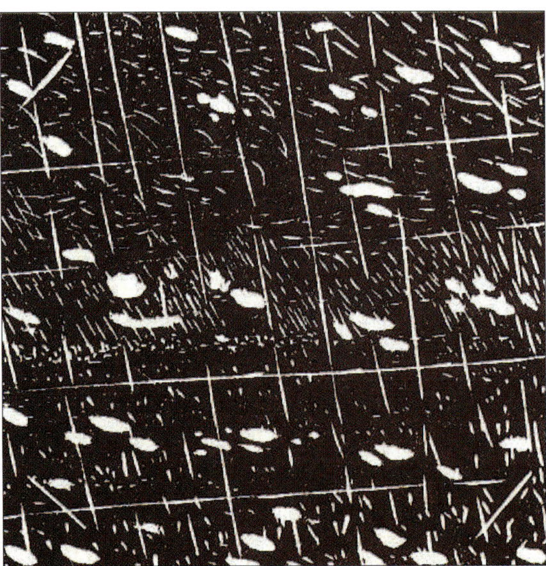

*Trapped 1989*
Anne Lord, Julia Creek
Wood Engraving on Arches paper 5.5cm x 5.3cm

*Impossible Bucket*
Anne Lord, Julia Creek
Humus and glue
*30cm x 25cm x 25cm*
*2005*

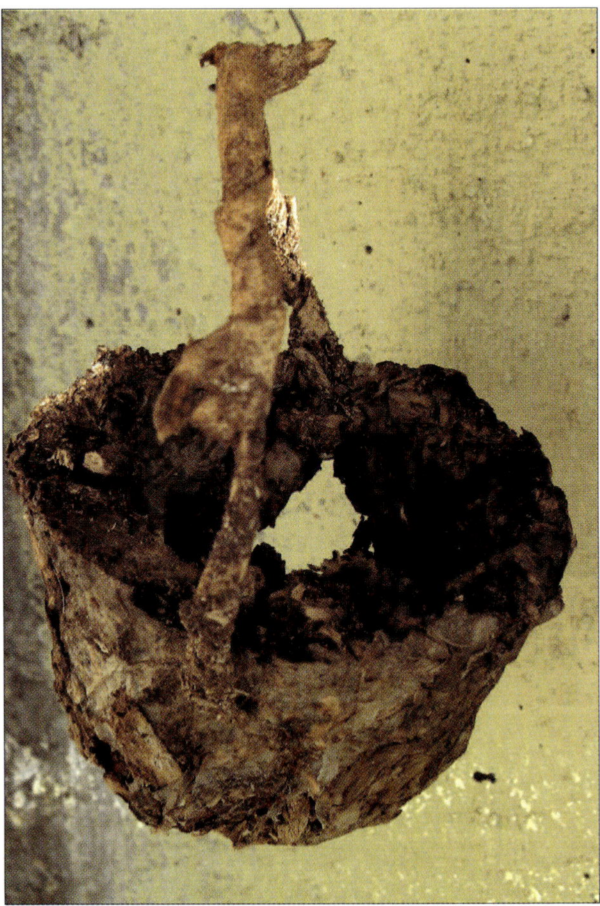

# MT. ISA

## *VINCE BRAY, 1970s*

Born in Mount Isa just before Christmas 1933 Vince is the eldest of seven children, four of whom still live in Mount Isa; Vince and brothers Mich and Tom all worked for Isa Mines. Sister Telia is married to Mount Isa Mine's Terry Casey.

He remembers his mother, Mrs. Ottillie Bray, was always sketching, just pencil and paper stuff, but they still remember it. She belonged to the Irwin family, who lived at Bushy Park Station before there was a Mount Isa. So the love of the bush which features in so much of Vince's work, is bred into him.

*My mother died in 1959. As the eldest child, I missed a lot of school to help look after the younger Brays, and in fact never got past grade five at the old St. Joseph's Convent.*

*Despite that I have read widely and have a fairly good knowledge, not only of art, but also of religion, music and literature.*

*After a stint working for the Mount Isa soft drink firm of Gardner and Jones, I spent a total of about eight years working for the Catholic Church at missions in the Northern Territory and Darwin.*

*Over the years I have been a truck driver, a welder, a builder and a fixer. Then I spent three years in Papua New Guinea based at Mount Hagen.*

*Returning to the Isa in 1968 I joined Mt Isa Mines, and, until my retirement, have been there ever since - as a trucker, a mucker, a safety man, and finally in 1980, my job as a Platman.*

*My love affair with painting began in 1972 when, bored because I had no real hobbies, tired of reading books, unwilling to become a slave to TV and sick of going over to the pubs looking for company I decided to learn to draw. My sister-in-law told me of the Flying Art School run by Mervyn Moriarty that visited the outback regularly to train country artists.*

*When I joined Mervyn's workshops he instilled in me the quest for knowledge; he not only showed me how and what, but gave me the desire to find out more.*

*I spent three years under Mervyn's tutelage and I owe nearly all of what I have since become to his mentorship.*

*I have had many solo exhibitions, won many prizes and I now have work in collections all over the world.*

*During my years in Mt. Isa I supported the development of contemporary art and artists in the region.*

Vince's work tends to be large and very brightly coloured. He calls it Expressionism. He is constrained to working in watercolours because most of his work was done in his room at Mt. Isa Mines' single accommodation. He tries to get out to the bush every weekend to paint from nature.

When Premier Wayne Goss officially opened the new mine on May 15 1990 his gift from MIM was a painting of the site, specially commissioned from Vincent Bray by the company.

*This story comes from Peter Beard, 'Starry Starry Night', 'Mimag'* October 1990.

Vince now has twelve etchings in the Print Collection of the National Gallery in Canberra depicting aspects of mining in Mt. Isa.

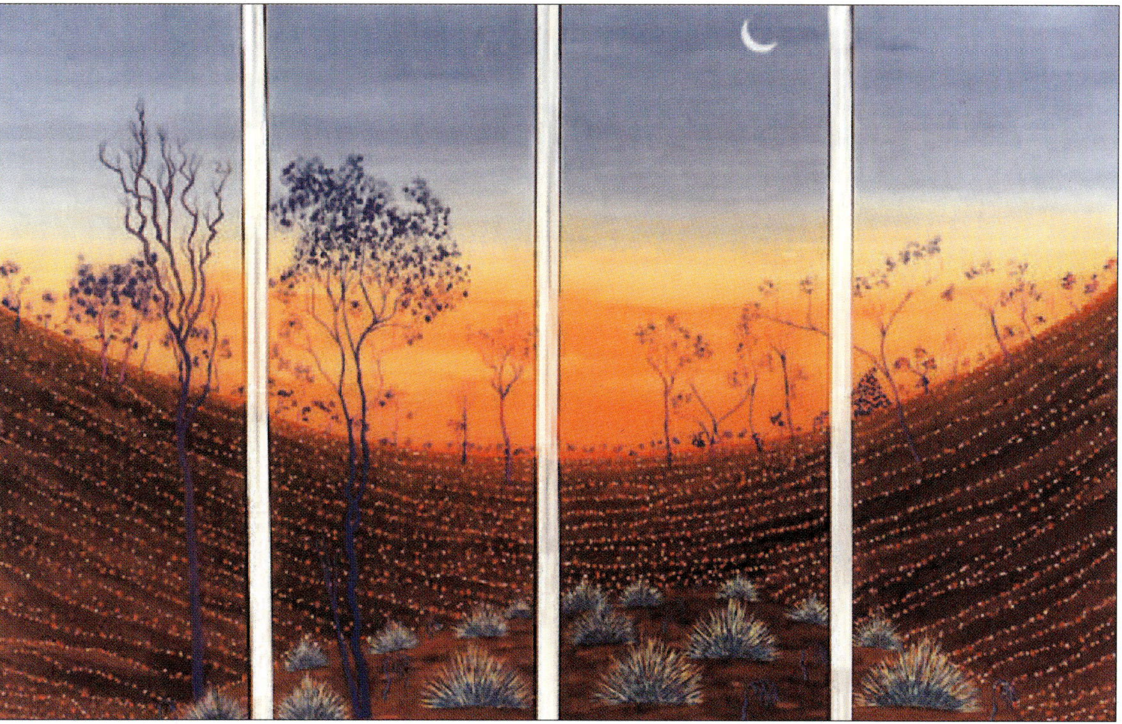

*Mt. Isa Sunset* Gouache on Silk 145cm x 230cm Vince Bray, Mt. Isa

# MT. ISA

## *CHRIS ELCOATE, 1990s*

Chris has been living in Palmwoods for the last twelve years. She is a visual artist and was an FA rep. for Mt. Isa in the mid 1990s . Her belief in F.A. has seen her continue as a rep. in her new area. . .

*I had had two years Fine Arts training with Rockhampton TAFE before leaving for Tennant Creek. Then I travelled 600km to attend workshops at Mt. Isa before moving there. (Only a strong craft Council was available in the Territory then to encourage and nurture artists).*

*Twice I won the Acquisitive Watercolour Award and in 2002 the Works on Paper Award. My watercolour training came through TAFE but my printmaking work was developed through Flying Arts. I am now living in Palmwoods and have been there for over twelve years.*

*My Flying Arts' life began when I was living in Tennant Creek. I daresay that if we had not moved to Mt Isa when we did, I am sure I would have had Flying Arts up and running in the Territory.*

*I was introduced through Jill O'Sullivan after meeting her at the USQ Summer School and I ventured over via the Barkly Highway (over 600 km) for a weekend workshop in Mt Isa. As there was only a very strong Craft Council in the Territory my arts practice had fallen by the wayside and this was my chance for a big revival.*

*I had attended two years of a Fine Arts Course through TAFE in Rockhampton prior to leaving for Tennant Creek and apart from craft I found myself in an art vacuum. Flying Arts saved my sanity.*

*The art group in Mt Isa was a very strong group and Flying Arts was well supported by them.*

*I have many fond memories of Flying Arts workshops, particularly one held at Shirley MacNamara's property west of Mt Isa when we all slept under the verandah or in the backs of utes.*

*The local dentist dragged his old iron bed out into the paddock and slept under the stars. I was the local Flying Arts rep at the time and had to deliver the tutor (Steven Royster) out to Shirleys.*

*However we were held up for fifteen minutes trying to get through one of the gates as her old horse wouldn't budge – it took a leftover Maccas burger to shift her.*

*We had an old press which we dragged out to Shirleys and we even made up donkey/kangaroo poo paper for printing.*

*Stoking up the old donkey for showertime was also a cherished memory – those were the days – red wine and a chat under the stars with like minded human beings is a very satisfying past-time worth bottling.*

*I find things not quite the same as before with not having to pick up the tutor from the light plane at the airport. In Palmwoods it is just a drive up to us, but I will never forget the old days.*

*Flying Arts have extended me to such a point where I feel confident I can hold my own in any gallery. They also gave a humble housewife the opportunity to be involved in a book of prints which is now held in Libraries around the Country. To be one of the chosen few was a reward in itself. I have also been given the opportunity to be involved in several tri-state travelling exhibitions which is great for my self esteem – which in the art world is quite a rollercoaster.*

*Flying Arts is run as a very efficient ship which passes through all parts of the desert stopping at any port possible to fill the artistic desires of people who need topping up with creativity.*

*They kept my passion going twice a year, with the bonus of a curated exhibition at the years end. This made my outback time a joy, it also made me energised to become involved in community happenings – artwise.*

*I believe in Flying Arts and I will always support them for what they've done for me and for my development as an artist.*

*I remember trekking out into the wide blue yonder with the 4WD packed to the hilt as Nance and I headed for Mt. Guide Station.*

*Linda volunteered to pick up Steven Royster, the tutor, and also Tom, our visiting guest artist from Papua New Guinea. They passed us just after the spectacular mound of perfectly shaped balancing rocks which take your breath away in the early morning and evening light.*

*Steven is quite talented in bringing out the creativity in artists at all levels. We had a diverse workshop in colour with tips on transferring your artwork with contact cement. It worked wonders on Shirley's images which looked superb transposed onto rock from her property. We all felt Steven had to be pampered by his North West groupies so that we could convince him to come again.*

*Our Brisbane Flying Arts' squad are a little more aware of our doings now, though I'm not sure they'll send another tutor out this way. AND IF ANYONE IS CURIOUS, WE DID DO SOME ART WORK!!!*

*Tom, our guest tutor, was a little non-plussed about us all, but I think being able to go down to the shed and actually complete two beautiful metal sculptures, which were so full of movement and a delight to look at, was a sense of fulfilment for him. I'm sure Tom would have loved to take 'the dump' from Mt. Guide Station home to PNG.*

*Tom Deko was an exhibitor at the Queensland Art Gallery Triennial Exhibition in 1996.*

*I have since won a bursary at the annual Flying Arts Brisbane Exhibition. The prize was a week's tuition with Textile Fibre Forum.*

*I chose a Masterclass with English artist Michael Brennand-Wood.*

*My work from the Masterclass was then part of an exhibition in Victoria, Hunter Valley NSW and Brisbane Gallery 139. It was also reproduced in the Textile Fibre Forum magazine.*

*In the last five years I have been the organizer of a cross-culture exhibition art exchange between Maroochy Shire's sister city Tatebayashi in Japan.*

*My eighteen years with Flying Arts gave me the confidence and ability to organize the workshops/exhibitions for the projects.*

*So, in a way volunteering for Flying Arts has enabled me to go to Japan – taking my art to a whole new level.*

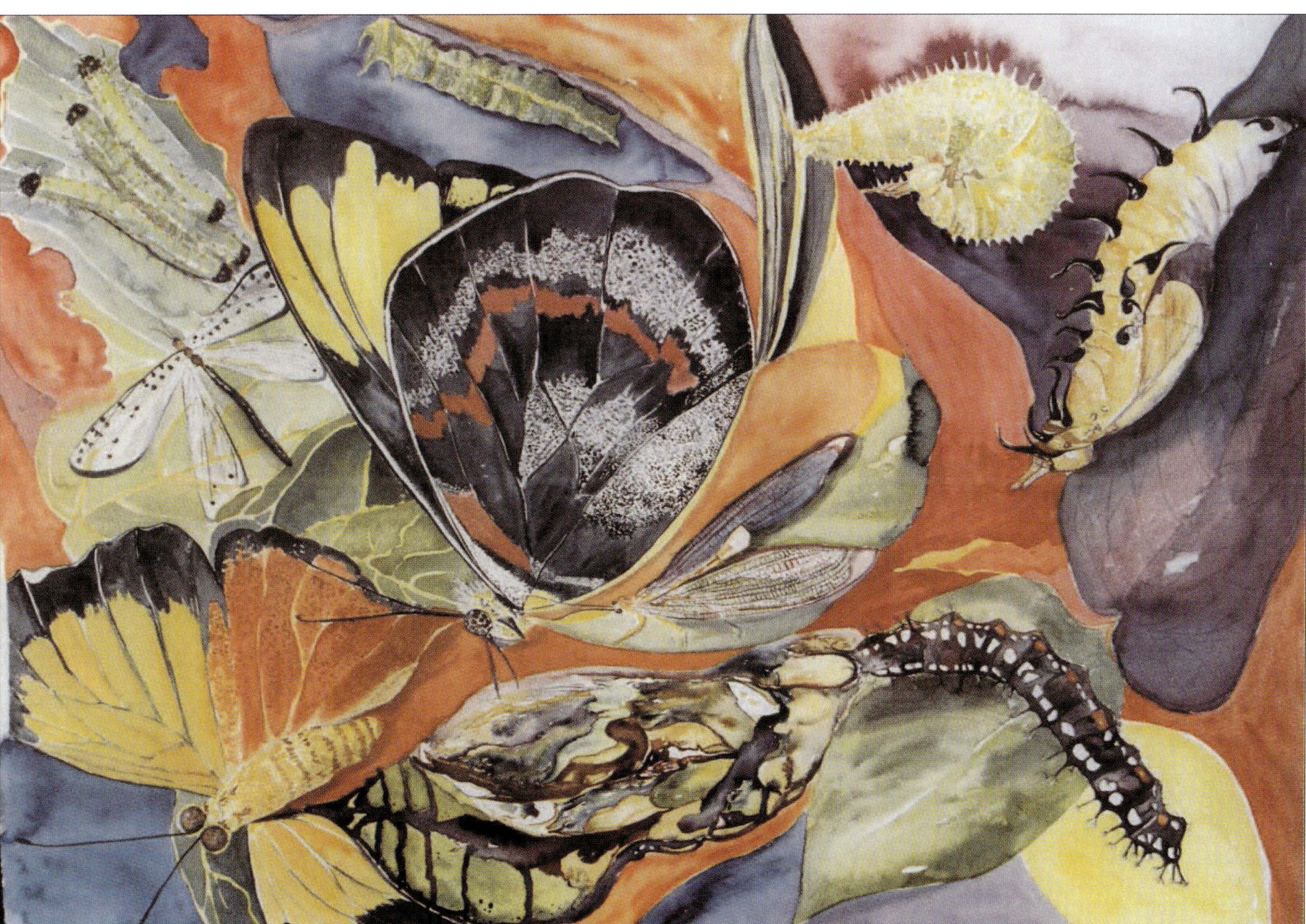

*All things Bright & Beautiful*
Watercolour
980cm x 820cm

Chris Elcoate ,
Mt. Isa
who is now living
at Palmwoods

# RICHMOND

## *JOSEPHINE FORSTER, 1971*

Jo was born in Brisbane. She is a semi-abstract painter using mixed media. She was a nurse who first trained in art in Brisbane and then worked at the Richmond District Hospital for a year when she was young. She left the hospital to take a trip overseas before coming back to marry and live at 'Trivaltore'. This is her story:

*The only way to learn art when living at Trivaltore was by Stott's Correspondence courses and work on the property was demanding, As with most country women, I had more work than I could cope with in a day.*

*I began my studies in Brisbane with Melville Haysom at the Central Technical College. Then I moved into creative art with Andrew Sibley and Roy Churcher. When Flying Arts came to the west I worked with Mervyn Moriarty and Bela Ivanyi at Richmond through the Australian Flying Arts School workshops.*

*Later I became a Board member of the Qld. Arts Council from 1973-1976; a Committee member of the Qld. Federation of Art & Craft Societies; a member of the CAS Brisbane until 1973 when it disbanded; and from 1975 I was a member of the IMA in Brisbane.*

*I found my AFAS experience invaluable. My first solo exhibition was at the AFAS gallery in 1977. Since then I have exhibited with others at numerous exhibitions throughout regional Queensland, Brisbane and Sydney and I am represented in private collections in Australia and overseas.*

From *Artists & Galleries Australia*, Max Germaine, 1984.

Jo joined Flying Arts in 1971, She was in the first workshops held by Mervyn Moriarty. Since then she has worked tirelessly in her isolated community, teaching and developing art opportunities. At the same time she has developed her art practice extensively, becoming a highly regarded professional artist from the North-west. She gained her Masters of Creative Arts through James Cook University some years ago, and has had many solo and group exhibitions, as well as gaining some 80 odd prizes for her works over the years. Her works are held in many collections around the country.

An anecdote from Jo written in 1995 demonstrates the difficulties facing students who attend the Flying Arts workshops:

*The roads at the moment are 4WD passable. The Flinders River is under its bridge, but the Saxby is high and running. This is part of the "wet" season here. Normally you can't move at all, except by helicopter in an emergency. We have to get enough stores to last for about twelve weeks. This is the story for Feb/March/April or earlier. Even your workshop here for April 4 is a bit early - we can be still drying out then, if the Monsoon comes. This is when we get all or most of our rain - if it doesn't come we're in BIG TROUBLE. This is why I may not be able to get to your Regional Arts Writing Forum.*

*Josephine Forster*

Jo Forster's studio at Richmond 1996.

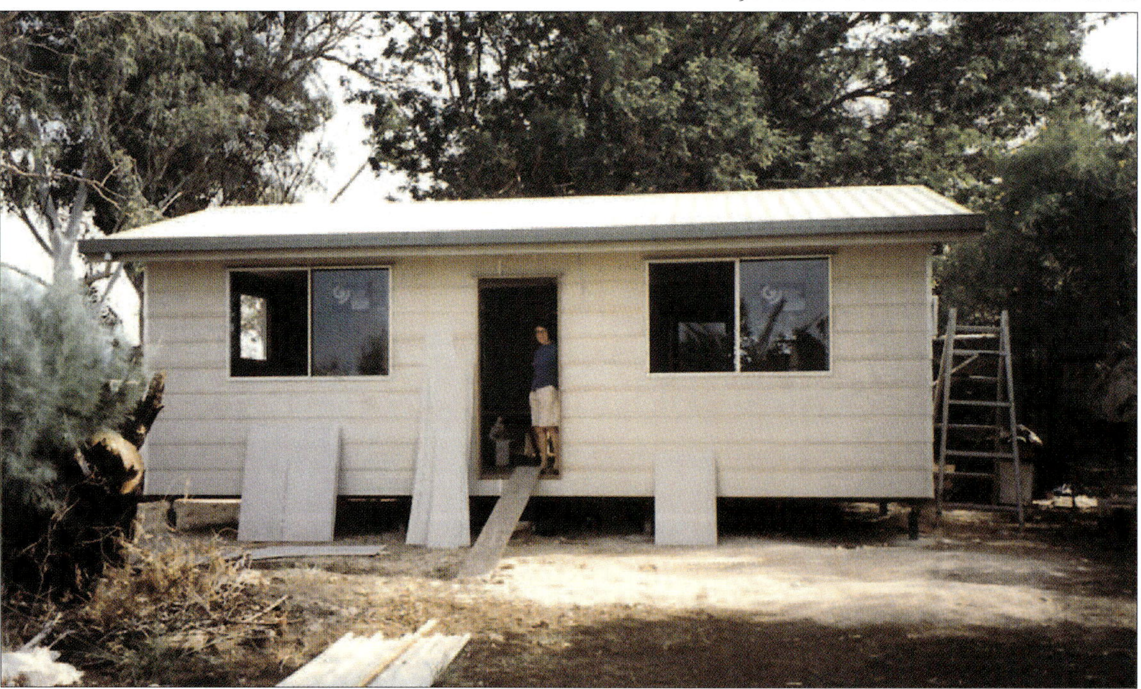

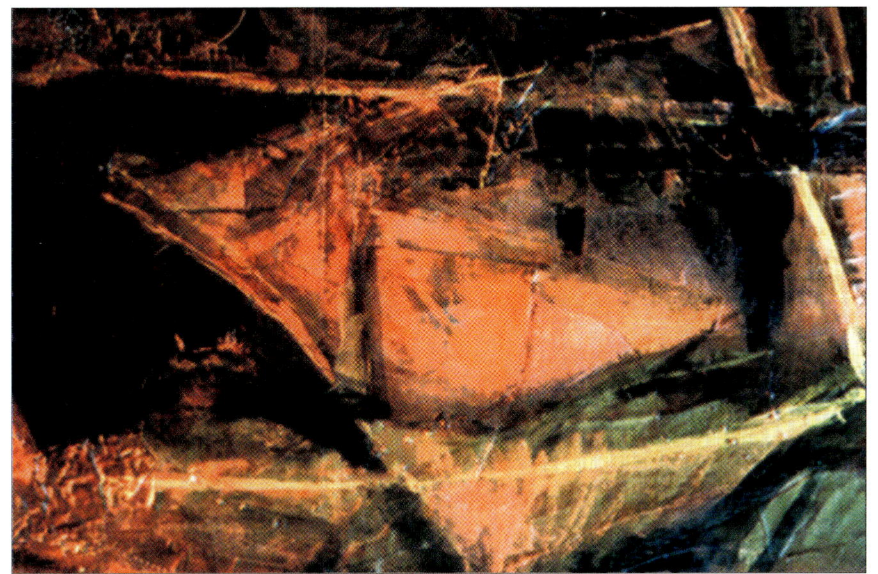

*Untitled* Jo Forster, Richmond

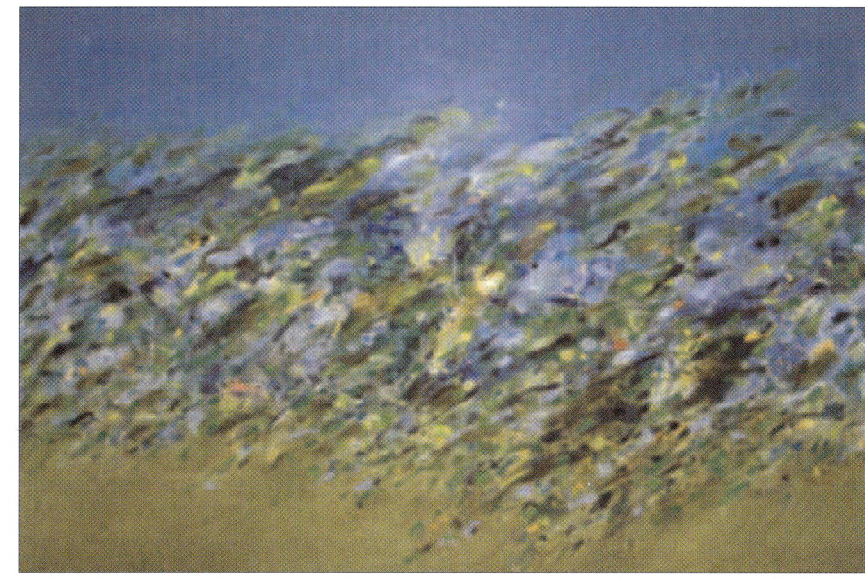

*Budgerigars in Flight* Oil and acrylic on board 90cm x 120cm Jo Forster, Richmond

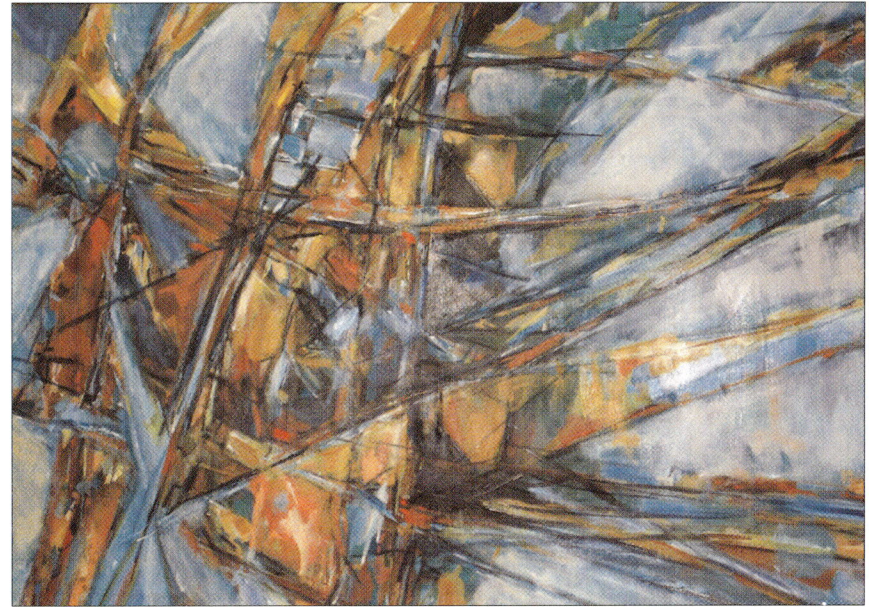

*Ammonite Painting 3* Jo Forster, Richmond

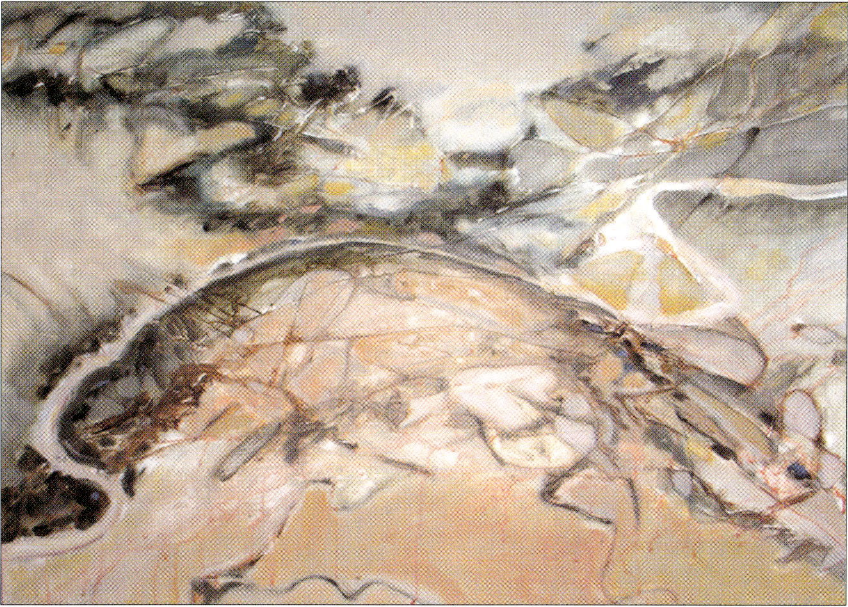

*Flinders River Aerial* Oil and ink on board 71.5cm x 87cm Jo Forster, Richmond

# Student Stories from Northern New South Wales

## INVERELL

### *PEG UEBERGANG, 1978*

Peg was living in Moree from 1966 but remembers that in the early 1970s there were art classes at Goondiwindi. She first met Mervyn Moriarty when he was tutoring at a Binna Burra workshop.

*We had an art group in Moree and they would get tutors in. This was before Flying Arts, but when Mervyn brought Flying Arts to Inverell I attended his classes there.*

*The art classes were held at the primary school at Inverell, it was an adult class, and around 25 attended. I felt Flying Arts were helpful because they asked students to do their own thing and let their own ideas flow.*

*I remember Mervyn and Roy Churcher and someone for pottery so it was probably after 1978 when I started going to the Flying Arts classes. When Flying Arts were coming it was really something - something to look forward to.*

*Mervyn was great with colour. It was all about getting the colour to glow in the paintings and he was a big help in that direction – putting semi permanent colours over a wash.*

*Flying Arts was a great benefit to my future as an artist. The freedom of expression taught by the school was invaluable. The Moree group had given me tremendous support, but Flying Arts was more in accord with what I wanted to do.*

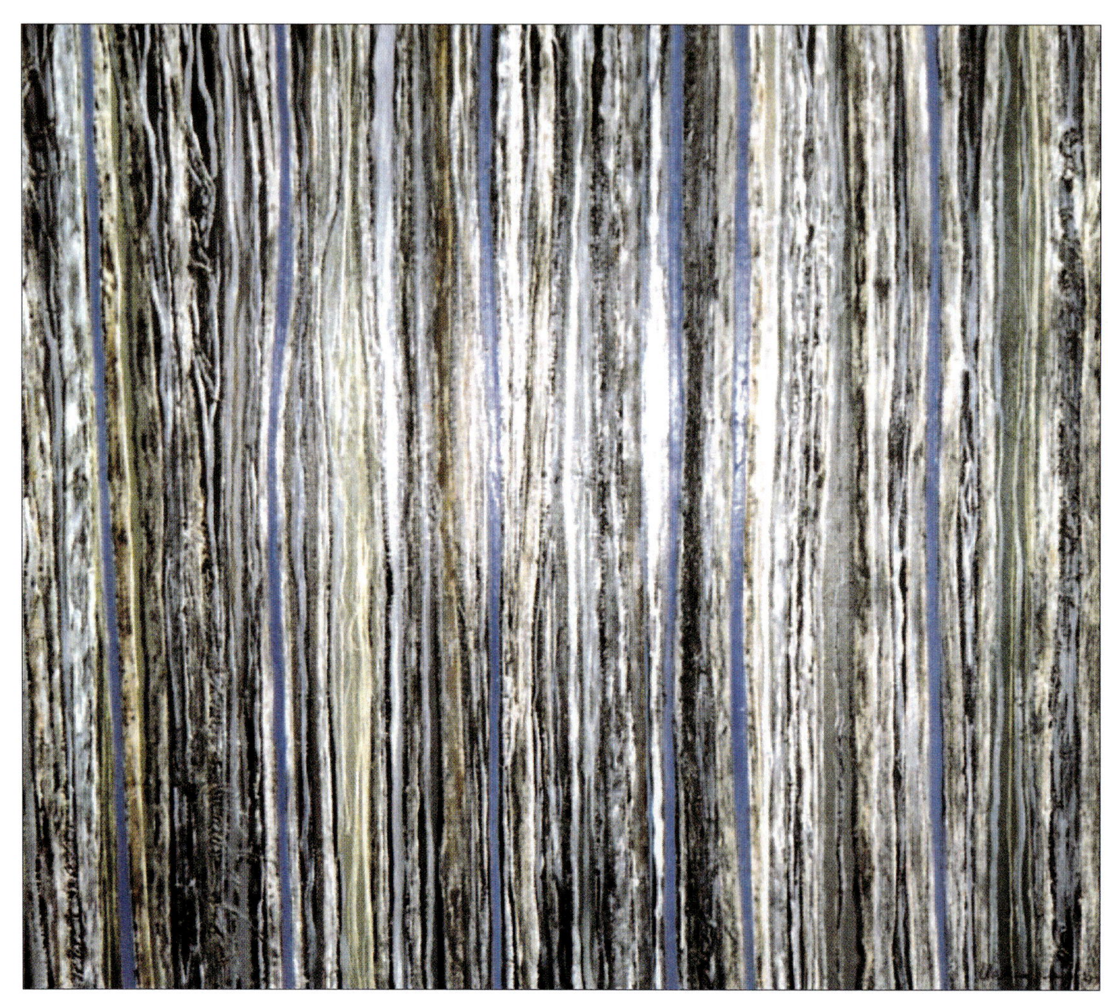

*Saplings by the Sea* Collage mixed media acrylic on canvas 100cm x 115cm Peg Uerbergang, Inverell

# Index of People

# General Index

**Galleries**



**Localities**

**Organisations**

## SELECT BIBLIOGRAPHY


**Bradbury, Keith, and Glenn Cooke.** *Thorns & Petals: 100 years of the Royal Queensland Art Society,* Royal Queensland Art Society, Brisbane, 1988.

**Burke, Joseph**. *The Postwar Years in Australian Art: some lessons for the future,* The Sir William Dobell Art Foundation, Sydney, 1982.

**Campbell, John.** *Arts Education: Report by the Senate Environment, Recreation, Communications and the Arts References Committee,* Commonwealth of Australia, Canberra, 1995.

**Churcher, Betty.** *Molvig: The Lost Antipodean,* Penguin Books, Melbourne, 1984.

**Clarke, Eddie.** *Technical & Further Education in Queensland: a History 1860-1990,* Department of Education, Queensland, Brisbane, 1992.

**Collins, Judith, John Welchman, David Chandler, David A. Anfam.** *Techniques of Modern Artists,* New Burlington Books, London, 1987.

**Cooke, Glenn.** *A Time Remembered: Art in Brisbane 1950-1975,* Queensland Art Gallery, Brisbane, 1995.

**Crumlin, Rosemary.** *The Blake Prize: passion as well as art,* National Library of Australia, Canberra, 2003.

**Dalton, Pen.** *The Gendering of Art Education,* Open University, Buckingham, 2001.

**De Bono, Edward.** *Lateral Thinking: Creativity Step by Step,* Harper & Row, New York, 1990.

**Donovan, Peter**. *So, You Want to Write History?* Donovan & Associates, Blackwood, SA, 1992.

**Fitzgerald, Ross.** *History of Queensland: From 1915 to the Early 1980s,* Queensland University, 1984.

**Franklin, Margaret-Ann, Leonie M. Short, and Elizabeth K. Teather** (eds.). *Country Women at the Crossroads: Perspectives on the lives of rural Australian women in the 1990s.,* University of New England Press, Armidale, 1994.

**Fridemanis, Helen**. *Artists and Aspects of the Contemporary Art Society,* Queensland Branch, Boolarong Publications, Brisbane, 1991.

**Gorry, Shane D.** *Queensland: A State for the Arts, Report of the Arts Committee, Queensland Government,* Brisbane, 1991.

**Hanrick, Phillipa Louise.** *Policy or People – where should the focus be? Arts West: A case study of a rural community arts organization in Queensland,* Griffith University, Brisbane, 1997.

**Helmer, June.** *George Bell: The Art of Influence,* Greenhouse Publications, Melbourne, 1985.

**Elizabeth Hogan,** *'Making Women Visible: Reflections on Working with Women in Agricultural in Victoria',* M. Franklin, L. Short, E. Teather (eds.) *Country Women at the Crossroads: Perspectives on the lives of rural Australian women in the 1990s,* University of New England Press, 1994.

**Hogan, Janet.** *In Memory of Dr. Gertrude Langer, O.B.E. 1908-84,* Queensland Art Gallery, Brisbane, 1985.

**Hughes, Robert.** *The Art of Australia,* Penguin Books Ltd., Melbourne, 1970.

**James, Kerry,** ed. *Work, Leisure & Choice: Women in Rural Australia,* UQ, Brisbane, 1989.

**Johnston, W. Ross.** *The Call of the Land: A History of Queensland to the Present Day,* The Jacaranda Press, Brisbane, 1982.

**Logan, Greg. & Eddie Clarke.** *State Education in Queensland: a Brief History,* Department of Education, Queensland, Brisbane, 1984.

**McCaughey, Patrick.** *Jon Molvig Expressionist.* Newcastle Region Art Gallery, Newcastle, 20002.

**Parr, Lenton.** *Creating: The Victorian College of the Arts,* Macmillan Publishers, Melbourne, 2000.

**Pechey, Susan and Paul Thomas.** *Telling Tales: An oral history of Kelvin Grove College 1942-1990,* Queensland University of Technology, Kelvin Grove Campus, 1992.

**Phipps, Jennifer.** *I had a dream: Australian Art in the 1960s,* National Gallery of Victoria, 1997.

**Queensland Art Gallery.** *We Have Arrived,* Queensland Art Gallery, Brisbane, 1991.

**Ross, Malcolm.** *The Aesthetic Impulse,* Pergamon Press Oxford, 1984.

**Rumley, Katrina**. *Jon Molvig Expressionist,* Newcastle Regional Art Gallery, Newcastle, 2003.

**Serle, Geoffrey.** *The Creative Spirit in Australia: A Cultural History,*William Heinemann Australia, Melbourne, 1987.

**Smith, Bernard**, ed. *Education Through Art in Australia,* University of Melbourne, Melbourne, 1958.

**Smith, Bernard, with Terry Smith.** *Australian Painting 1788-1990,* Oxford University Press, Melbourne, 1991.

**Snowman, Daniel.** *The Hitler Émigrés: The Cultural Impact on Britain of Refugees from Nazism,* Chatto & Windus, London, 2002.

**'The Rural Women and ICT's Research Team'.** *The New Pioneers,* The Communications Centre, QUT, 1999.

**Thomas, Kay.** 'Women's Health and Welfare in Rural and Remote Queensland', *Country Women at the Crossroads: Perspectives on the lives of rural Australian Women in the 1990s,* University of New England Press, Armidale, 1994.

**Thomas, Laurie.** *The most noble art of them all,* Queensland University, Brisbane, 1976.

**Timms, Peter.** 'Reactivating the Senses: Takeshi Yasuda', *Art Monthly,* July 1993.

**Warner, Lesley.** 'Educational Needs and Opportunities for Rural Women: The Queensland Experience', Margaret-Ann Franklin, Leonie M. Short and Elizabeth K. Teather, eds., *Country Women at the Crossroads,* University of New England, Armidale, 1994.